Long-Distance Hiking

New Jersey weeds.

Long-Distance Hiking

LESSONS FROM THE APPALACHIAN TRAIL

Roland Mueser

RAGGED MOUNTAIN PRESS
CAMDEN, MAINE

International Marine/
Ragged Mountain Press

A Division of The **McGraw·Hill** Companies

10

Copyright © 1998 Ragged Mountain Press

Library of Congress Cataloging-in-Publication Data
Mueser, Roland.
        Long-distance hiking : lessons from the Appalachian Trail /
Roland Mueser.
              p.   cm.
        Includes bibliographical references and index.
        ISBN 0-07-044458-7 (alk. paper)
        1. Hiking—Appalachian Trail—Guidebooks.   2.
Appalachian Trail—Guidebooks.   I. Title.
        GV199.42.A68M84 1997
        796.51'0974—dc21   97-21278
                                                                                    CIP

Questions regarding the content of this book should be addressed to:

Ragged Mountain Press
P.O. Box 220
Camden, ME 04843

or

Roland Mueser
7 Crystal Road
Mountain Lakes, NJ 07046

Questions regarding the ordering of this book should be addressed to:

McGraw-Hill, Inc.
Customer Service Department
P.O. Box 547
Blacklick, OH 43004
Retail customers: 1-800-262-4729
Bookstores: 1-800-722-4726

A portion of the profits from the sale of each Ragged Mountain Press book
is donated to an environmental cause.

This book is printed on 60-pound Renew Opaque Vellum, an acid-free paper which contains 50 percent recycled waste paper (preconsumer) and 10 percent postconsumer waste paper.

Interior photos by Roland Mueser
Printed by Quebecor Printing, Fairfield, PA
Design by Carol Gillette
Production by Publishers' Design and Production Services, Inc.
Edited by Jane Crosen, Kathryn Mallien

DEDICATION

To my wife Sonja, who made it all possible.

Crossing bogs is a mess!

CONTENTS

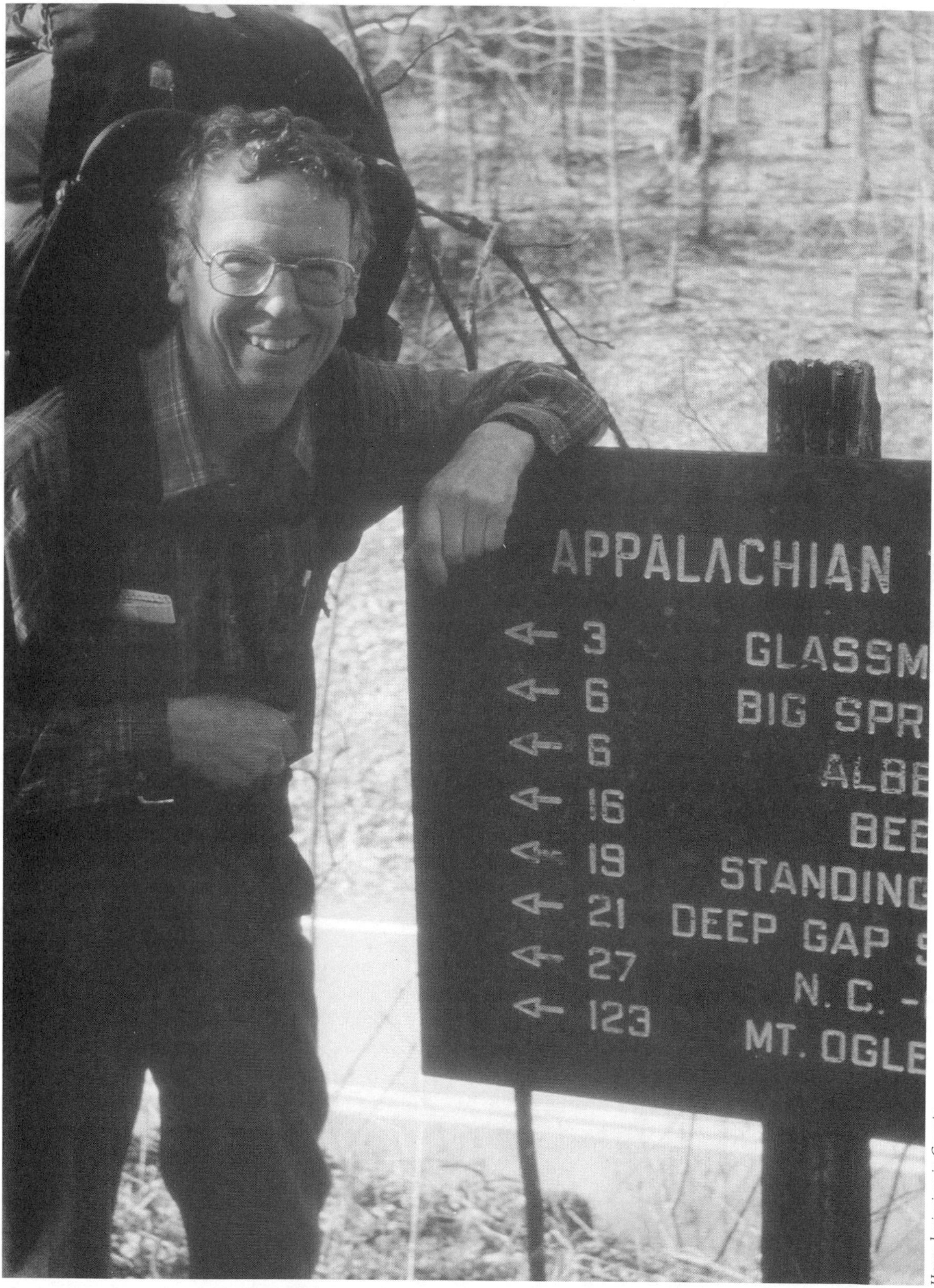

Happy beginnings in Georgia

ACKNOWLEDGMENTS

The hundreds of hikers interviewed for this book became my friends. In a real sense they are the authors, and I am deeply grateful to them for spending time and sharing their lives. Their names and comments on their hikes appear in Appendix 3. I hope they will enjoy seeing some of their keen observations and valuable insights in print. And I trust they will excuse any errors of omission, which are inevitably due to the author.

Every hiker on the AT owes a debt to those who maintain the trail and provide services. Thank you all. In addition, many hikers meet kindly souls who stop their cars, take them into town, and even provide food, shelter, and help as needed. Local people, tourists, angels, and other hikers add to the experience sometimes described as "trail magic."

Thanks go to dozens of friends and relatives who contributed to the making of this book. I first met Cindy Ross and Todd Gladfelter in 1989; since that time I have leaned heavily on their expertise as authors and backpackers. Larry Luxenberg began writing a book on historical AT trips several years after I started, and he finished it long ago. His street smarts and sage advice have been invaluable on the long road to publishing. Thanks go also to members of the Woods and Lakes Hiking Club, with whom I have spent many a night along the trail. George Schindler, often my companion in the woods, made my initial manuscript readable. Gordon Glover, hiking buddy and president of the Maine Natural Resources Council, never lost faith. Other believers include Tom Carr, Annette Hanna, Joan Ostrow, and Steven Pottash. Lynda Baydin is both my lawyer and my hiking companion; her husband Dr. Jeff Baydin both patched me up and hiked with me on the trail to make sure I could continue.

Lorraine Matta, Peggy Bulfer, and the friendly staff at the Mountain Lakes Public Library found references and books galore. The staff at Appalachian Trail Headquarters made me welcome at all times. And most of all, just knowing Jean Cashin, "the mother of the thru-hikers," would have made my hike worthwhile. Dr. Barbara Mueser brought order to my reference notes, and Henry and Tom Popp were always available when I needed encouragement. Dr. Donald Wilson provided important insights and in particular brought to my attention the similarity between the classical religious pilgrimage and American long-distance hiking. And finally I wish to thank the folks at Ragged Mountain Press, particularly Acquisitions Editor Jeffery Serena, who first telephoned with the magic words informing me that they would publish the book, and Managing Editor Kate Mallien, for carrying out the painstaking editing chore and shepherding the work through the maze that leads to publication. In addition, many persons at McGraw-Hill, unknown to me personally, have contributed their expertise to making this book something I am proud of.

My three backpacking sons provided active help in writing this book. Ted, now an expert mountaineer, in the 1970s was the first person to urge me to do the whole trail—and he never let me forget it. Kim, a psychologist and prolific author, advised me at every corner and probably has influenced me more than any other person. As a psychologist he knew what was most important to keeping a thru-hiker going, and he cooked and shipped brownies along the entire AT. Peter and his wife brought the sociologist's view to the experience, and they joined me on the trail, bringing a never-to-be-forgotten dinner to celebrate my 66th birthday.

Finally, my wife Sonja stayed at home, supported her wandering spouse, took care of house and garden, and, when required, fixed the plumbing. It was she who, after hearing me talk about it for ten years, told me to pick a date and start. She waved goodbye in Georgia as I started up the trail in the rain.

The trail in New Jersey

The promise of the Appalachian Trail

THE THRU-HIKING TRADITION

Walking the Appalachian Mountains all the way from the deep South to the range's northern terminus is an unusual and exciting adventure. But it wasn't until 1948 that Earl Shaffer completed the first thru-hike on a trail just a little over 10 years old. Before the twentieth century and the construction of the Appalachian Trail, few ventured in these mountains. As noted by Laura and Guy Waterman in their book *Forest and Crag*, those who took to the woods did so largely for business reasons. They were "mountain men" (trappers and hunters), military men, surveyors, or lumbermen. Before them and prior to about 1700, the deep woods and eastern mountains were totally unexplored by European settlers. Only

T he woods are lovely, dark and deep,

But I have promises to keep,

And miles to go before I sleep. . . .

—Robert Frost

Indians lived in and frequented the lowlands along the western Atlantic shores, but as the Watermans note, "for the Indians these mountain tops had no practical uses." Even in the absence of written records, we know them as sensible and knowledgeable folk, intent on their own traditional concerns, and one cannot imagine a circumstance that would have tempted them to undertake an uninterrupted journey up the Appalachians.

Several hundred years before there was a trail, however, at least one group of reluctant adventurers followed the Appalachians, walking the whole distance from south to north. According to Rutherford Platt in *Adventure in the Wilderness*, after a disastrous battle with a Spanish squadron in the Gulf of Mexico in 1568, a group of British seamen tackled the long trek as an alternative to starvation or worse. David Ingram and 22 others struck out northward to avoid being captured by the Spanish. Only Ingram and his mates Browne and Twide survived; they were spotted by a French captain a year later on the coast of Nova Scotia and rescued.

Ingram's route was probably not along the rugged crest of the mountains, which is followed by the modern Appalachian Trail. The English seamen, however, had no established path, no food caches, and no maps, and so would certainly qualify for some kind of an end-to-end certificate.

THE CONCEPT OF THRU-HIKING

Long-distance hiking was not on Appalachian Trail founder Benton MacKaye's mind when he proposed the trail in a 1921 article in the *Journal of the American Institute of Architects*. MacKaye was thinking about a refuge from metropolitan life—about carefully located camping communes removed from the centers of urban stress. In describing his concept in a 1922 followup, he wrote, "And now I come straight to the point of the philosophy of through trails. It is to organize a Barbarian Invasion. It is a counter movement to the Metropolitan Invasion." MacKaye's objective was to have this outdoor environment as a widely available back-door escape from the "humdrum of the regulation world." The paper, delivered before the New England Trail Conference in 1927, was called "Outdoor Culture—The Philosophy of Through Trails." However, by *through* MacKaye meant the trail, not the hiker. Nowhere is there any mention of "thru-hiking" as we now use the term: an uninterrupted journey of the trail completed within one year. Indeed, while Earl Shaffer was en route on the first such thru-hike in 1948, an article by editor Jean Stephenson appeared in the *Appalachian Trailway News* explaining why such a trip was almost impossible. When Shaffer finished, the initial reaction of Appalachian Trail Conference officials, including chairman Myron Avery, was disbelief.

MacKaye was critical of thru-hikers attempting the AT transit in record time. Writing in praise of O.d. Coyote's leisurely thru-hiking style (which O.d. calls "slackpacking"), MacKaye's literary executor, Harley P. Holden, wrote in the November/December 1994 *Appalachian Trailway News*: "Benton MacKaye would very much approve. During the last 12 to 15 years of Benton's long life, I visited with him frequently on weekends when at my home in Shirley Center. In late summer and fall, hikers who had completed the Trail would stop by to visit with the 'father' of the Appalachian Trail. Benton would become quite acerbic if any hiker mentioned that he had hiked the trail in record time." Holden has suggested that O.d. be awarded the "Benton MacKaye prize" for publicizing an almost ignored style of hiking.

In the early days the usual picture was that the Appalachian Trail was a place to escape from city life for a few days or a week, away "from the rush and strain of modern life into the great peace and solace of the wilderness and high places," as described in the August 1928 *Saturday Evening Post* article "The Appalachian Trail." Hiking was done in sections, and this was how Myron Avery himself eventually completed the AT in 1936. But some people were already responding to the invitation of an almost endless path extending an insurmountable distance. For example, R.R. Ozmer, a 30-year-old former forest ranger, wrote about his proposed AT thru-hike in an article in *Camping and Woodcraft* in 1929. He planned to go from Georgia to Maine carrying a 40-pound pack, cacheing food supplies, and covering 20 miles per day. His parting words were: ". . . the challenge . . . the only way my conscience might be eased is by making the trip. I had heard the call of the wilderness ways and nought could postpone the start." On May 1, 1929, he made his start. But Ozmer's words were more clarion than the depth of his commitment. Shortly thereafter he ignominiously abandoned his trip because of a "severe wrench in the back."

Other planned thru-hikes were announced with ringing words, but did not come to pass or were forsaken after the first leg of the trip. There was excitement and wide interest at the time in contemplating this grand adventure, but for almost 20 years the failure rate was 100 percent. So it is small wonder that knowledgeable hiking leaders considered it an impossibility. In the years preceding Shaffer's 1948 thru-hike, five men and one woman actually did hike the whole AT, but by sections and over a number of years; Myron Avery was the first successful section hiker. But once thru-hiking had been proven feasible, interest became focused on doing it all in one grand expedition. Over the next several decades, about half of those to complete the AT did so in a thru-hike.

Except for repeaters who have done the trail a number of times and those who are hiking under auspices of some special organization, modern hikers are chary about announcements that they are going to thru-hike; many are aware that the odds are against being able to finish. For those who do finish, the trip is often crowned by newspaper stories, celebrations, and sometimes going on the lecture circuit. Although in the 12 years between Avery's completion and Shaffer's pioneering thru-hike there were only five others who did the whole distance, the number increased gradually over the years, as seen in Table 1.1.

The really explosive growth in AT completions was in the 1970s. In that decade there was a tenfold increase in thru-hikers, and there were dire predictions of overwhelming crowds in the future. However, since that time

TABLE 1-1.
COMPLETED APPALACHIAN TRAIL HIKES (INCLUDING BOTH SECTION HIKING AND THRU-HIKES)

YEARS	NUMBER OF HIKES	COMPLETIONS PER YEAR
1936 TO 1948 (12 YEARS)	8	0.6
1949 TO 1958 (10 YEARS)	10	1.0
1959 TO 1968 (10 YEARS)	25	2.5
1969 TO 1978 (10 YEARS)	553	55.0
1979 TO 1988 (10 YEARS)	1,270	127.0
1989 TO 1993 (5 YEARS)	930	186.0

there have been cycles of increases and decreases, with much slower overall growth. Not until 1990 did the number of finishers reach the 200 mark for the first time. Brian King, Director of Public Affairs for the Appalachian Trail Conference, whose headquarters sits astride the trail at Harpers Ferry, West Virginia, believes that the completion rate in recent years has been rising. He noted in 1993 that between 190 and 200 people were completing the trail each year from among 1,200 starters—about 16 percent. In an October 3, 1993 Associated Press article by Jerry Harkavy, King commented, "It used to be closer to 10 percent, and now it's moving up."

The 1995 Appalachian Long Distance Hiker Club's membership directory reveals that in a sampling of 416 end-to-end backpackers over the last 25 years, about two-thirds of the finishers were thru-hikers, completing the trek in one year. Data from 211 finishers in 1988 and 1990 indicated that a slightly higher number, 73 percent, were thru-hikers. Most of the section hikers completed the trail in a few years, but some took 25 years or even longer. Carol Magill, who finished in 1988, may be the record holder, having taken 61 years to complete her trip. Over this period about 40 percent of the thru-hikers traveled with a companion; the rest hiked alone, at least during the day. Section hikers were more likely to have a companion. Almost 60 percent traveled with one or more partners.

WHY THIS BOOK?

My own plan was to hike the AT after retirement. I therefore had many years to dream, plan, and read earlier ac-

counts of the trip. Most of the books about the AT are journals kept by the hikers. There are over 30 separate volumes by thru-hikers, section hikers, and even a number describing unfinished hikes. The Bibliography (page 174) lists some of the most interesting books. In my own reading I fell upon James R. Hare's 1975 two-volume classic, *Hiking the Appalachian Trail,* which includes accounts from 46 men's and women's AT journals for the period 1936 through 1972. These provide extraordinary insight into the adventure, despite being a bit outdated and long out of print.

Probably the most widely read AT journal is Edward Garvey's *Appalachian Hiker,* originally published in 1971. Garvey, who thru-hiked in 1970, set the standard for conscientious daily reporting and detailed coverage of the experience. Not counting the various trail guides issued by the Appalachian Trail Conference, his is the only AT book I ever saw tucked into the pack of an AT thru-hiker.

Like many others, I used Garvey as my model in planning my thru-hike in 1989. Garvey is not only a gifted writer, but also was a powerful and experienced backpacker. In 1970, at 57 years of age, Garvey was in superb physical condition and quite capable of outhiking friends and relatives who joined him for short intervals along the way. I used Garvey's statistics as my guide. Before starting, I laid out where I would stop each night. This planning turned out to be a waste of time; I reluctantly discovered that I could not keep up with my model.

It was, however, this experience that prompted me to write this book. The dozens of thru-hike books recount the personal experiences of the hikers. But here was an adventure in which individuals found their own way of coping, where the "people experience" was sometimes reported as the most remarkable part of the adventure, and yet where more than half the hikers, including many women, preferred to walk alone. Some hikers had walked thousands of miles before starting; others had never spent a night in the woods. It was certainly not obvious what was typical and what should be the basis for planning your own hike.

To add zest and purpose to my thru-hike, I decided to try to sample the diverse population of long-distance hikers. I hoped to gather a wide enough variety of experiences so that a reader could say, "So this is what people in general did." Such information would be better than planning the trip based on only one or two individual experiences. For example, if you talk to a backpacker who is carrying a staff, he or she will enthusiastically tell you its unique ad-

Overlooking the Smokies

vantages and certainly be able to convince you that you must use one, or even two. Ask the hiker who is not carrying a staff, and he or she will give you convincing reasons as to why it is merely a nuisance.

The thru-hikers in the sample reported strikingly similar patterns in their selection of packs, tents, stoves, shorts, and raingear. Most averaged close to 15 miles per hiking day. Macaroni and cheese was declared the favorite trail dinner and ice cream the most longed-after refreshment when in the wilderness. Conversely, in some areas there are marked differences (and long-distance hikers were very different from one another): Although most hikers took one day off from hiking per week for reprovisioning, rest, and getting clean, one thru-hiker in the survey took off only three days in his entire trip. Another vacationed on a trip abroad for six weeks. Furthermore, many successful thru-hikers had little or no hiking experience, but about half had been planning for 10 years and one had backpacked over 10,000 miles. And while most found that sex and thru-hiking do not mix, several couples enthusiastically undertook trail honeymoons. Finally, although married couples carry through a long commitment and usually stick together, most other hikers end up being alone for much of the hiking day and for extended periods.

So, on April 8, 1989, after a hike up muddy and snow-covered roads, I squeezed into the last bunk space of Springer Mountain shelter at the start in Georgia and joined two dozen other hopeful thru-hikers. And the next day I collected my first name and address—the first of 190 men and women from whom I eventually received 136 detailed accounts of their trips in answer to my questionnaire. I was hoping to thru-hike and decided to seek out those hikers making a real effort to go the whole distance. In the end, the defining description of those hikers in the survey was that they were long-distance backpackers, on the trail from several weeks to six months. Two-thirds were successful thru-hikers, but all respondents were old-timers by the time they got off the AT, even those who did not go the whole 2,100 miles.

It took six months to put the questionnaire together, a year to contact people and collect their answers, and another year to analyze the data. The main questionnaire included 265 questions and was followed up by several short ones investigating interesting corners of hiking lore that had not been explored. The survey, a brief nontechnical discussion of the statistics, and a list of the participants are included in Appendices 1, 2, and 3.

The book is an attempt to answer the question of what is typical, what characteristics of long-distance hikers are similar, and how varied and individualistic these hikers are. Since the material is a collection of 136 experiences over a period as long as six months, a lot could and did happen. Boots wore out. Pack straps came off. Stoves clogged, and friendships blossomed and waned. Although the chances of getting sick, turning an ankle, or falling in a stream may be small on a weekend hike, the probabilities build up as the months go by, to the point where some events are almost expected. The practical experience gained may agree with or contradict trail lore and conventional wisdom. There tends to be a consensus in such areas as pack weight, miles per day, or cooking hot food for dinner—but not in all matters. Such dictums as "Never hike alone," "Always purify your water," and "Be physically fit before starting" are often ignored.

While this book's setting is the Appalachian Trail, most of these long-distance hikers had either hiked other long trails or were planning to do so. And although location is important, it is the protracted separation from our usual world that seems to set these hikers apart. Thus, the patterns noted here are due to the length and nature of the commitment rather than being unique to AT hikers.

Although my own prejudices must invariably sneak in, I have tried to base conclusions and recommendations on the survey, rather than my own experience. May you enjoy coming along with this group of interesting backpackers, and may reading about them inspire you to try it yourself!

The trail in northern New Jersey

WHY THRU-HIKE?

In general, "Why?" is *not* a question thru-hikers are asked. People inquire mostly about practical matters having to do with coping and survival; such questions come up so often that they are an inside joke on the trail. Indeed, an enterprising 1989 thru-hiker, Carol Moore, has created "The Official AT Answer Shirt," a T-shirt with the following answers printed on its front:

1. *15–20 miles a day*
2. *yes, I've seen bears*
3. *mac & cheese*
4. *50 lbs or so*
5. *in a tent*
6. *4–6 months*
7. *over 2,000 miles*
8. *yes, I walked here*

The ultimate challenge. I hiked to give myself time away from the confines of society in which I found myself. Time to think about what I was doing and where I was going in life.

—Adam Ticknor,
long-distance hiker

Note that an answer to the question "Why?" is not included in the list. As for the hikers in our sample, their favorite frequently asked questions are covered in Chapter 18.

A hiker may quietly ponder the whys and wherefores of the trail, but the problems of food, water, shelter, and the trail crowd out such philosophical concerns. In my own six months on the trail, no one ever asked me why I was there, and I lacked the introspection to go much further than say to myself, "Because I want to."

Nevertheless, it is an interesting question, even if hikers do not have a clear answer. In the book *End to End on the A.T.—The Long Haul,* Craig Haire focused on several factors that hold especially true for the AT adventure. "Most of us have grown up in a culture steeped in the traditions of our pioneer past, romantic stories of the conquering of the American wilderness. But now our wilderness is already overconquered, and there are very few adventures left to satisfy our romantic spirit. The vast majority of us will never climb Mount Everest, row across the Atlantic, or cross the continent in a balloon. Such undertakings are beyond our reach, financially and physically, and the associated hazards may be more than we wish to risk. But hiking the AT is a relatively safe undertaking which most people are capable of completing—yet the sheer magnitude of the feat and the effort required are formidable enough to satisfy our deepest longings to soar above the mundane."

Myron Avery believed that traveling the trail filled a fundamental need. According to James Hare's *Hiking the Appalachian Trail,* so did Harold Allen, a member of the Potomac Appalachian Trail Club who is credited with probably the most widely quoted trail description: "Remote for detachment, narrow for chosen company, winding for leisure, lonely for contemplation, it beckons not merely north and south but upward to the body, mind, and soul of man."

Asking the thru-hiker "Why?" is not enough. If you seek to find out why he or she is on the trail, look for answers to questions such as: "When did you first think of hiking the whole AT? How did you actually pick a date for starting? While hiking, did you seriously think of quitting early? What was the happiest experience you can remember? Your worst? Looking back now, what was the greatest thing you got out of your hike?" These were all questions asked in my survey of long-distance hikers.

In reviewing what hikers say in response, it becomes apparent that there are two categories of answers: basic, underlying motives that reflect the very personality of the hiker; and reasons-of-the-moment. The basic motives are always there. The other reasons are made up of a host of incidents in our everyday lives that often trigger the decision to go. The most common reason is a break in lifestyle, which we'll look at more closely in "The Decision to Go," below. In a Spring 1989 article in *American Hiker,* Phil Hall wrote: "It all started when my girlfriend broke up with me at the end of January last year. She was tired of waiting for me to decide if I was ready for marriage." But this was presumably only the final motivating incident; underneath there would seem to be a more fundamental reason for the journey.

THREE FUNDAMENTAL MOTIVES OF LONG-DISTANCE HIKERS

In reading the responses to the above questions, three deep-seated, underlying motives emerged. Hikers typically identify one of these as their single, main reason for hiking:

Challenge and Adventure. This is the thrill of experiencing something new, of doing something totally different, and perhaps being noticed and admired for the achievement. Responses indicate that about 60 percent of the hikers are reacting to such feelings.

Love of the Outdoors. In reading what thru-hikers say about their feelings, I was surprised to find how often the word "love" appeared together with "outdoors," "hiking," or "nature." These people belong to a select group of career hikers who would like to spend 12 months a year on the trail. They truly love trail and wilderness. If we attempt to classify any motive as a pure one, this would seem to be it. These lovers of the hiking scene made up over 20 percent of those in the survey.

Escape and Simplicity. About one in five of the hikers is not so much attracted by the challenge or beauty of the trail as they are repelled by what life is offering them at home. These backpackers seek a change in their environment and often stress simplifying their lives.

Men and women are divided in about the same proportions into the above categories. Like so many of the statistics about thru-hikers, the similarities between the sexes far outweigh the differences (more on this in Chapter 18).

In 1967, Vincent Bolduc sent out 1,200 questionnaires to all the members of the Green Mountain (Vermont) Club, in a survey designed to provide insight into the motivation of the wilderness backpacker. In his 1973 paper "Backpacking: A Pilot Study of Hikers," Bolduc wrote of the 849 responses: "Backpacking seems to be a reaction to segmentalization and interdependence, a reaction to modern life in precisely the same way that romanticism was in response to the industrial revolution."

It is interesting to compare the reasons given for hiking in Bolduc's survey and those I collected. Certain trends are clear, even though the terminology is sometimes different and the categories not necessarily precise. They compare as shown in Table 2-1.

CHALLENGE AND ADVENTURE

The lure of the adventure is not hard to identify. Consider the hiker who writes: "It was to prove to myself and maybe others that I can do something huge against odds, that very few can do. My problem is, I enjoyed it so much that I can't seem to get it behind me. The truth is, the glory is in the doing, not in the finishing."

TABLE 2-1.
WHY THEY HIKE LONG-DISTANCE

Long-Distance Hiker Category	Green Mtn. Club Category	Percent of Responses	
		LDHC	GMC
Challenge and adventure	Physical and self-esteem	60%	32%
Love of the outdoors	Aesthetic, emotional, and spiritual	20%	37%
Escape and simplicity	Escape and simplicity	17%	14%
Sociability	Sociability	3%	11%
—	Other	—	6%

As shown in the table, the challenge—or, as some hikers put it, the lure and curiosity of a great adventure—accounts for more than half of the long-distance hikers surveyed. Successfully meeting the challenge is rewarded by a rare sense of accomplishment. A hiker writes: "It is the best adventure I ever had in my whole life. All up the trail, I couldn't imagine that some folks would want to make the hike again. But the feeling at the end—my last steps—made me understand it as an irreplaceable high."

Again and again, certain themes appear in the questionnaires: "Perhaps I needed to prove something to myself." "A sense of accomplishment—although it's all so much like a dream—and I still cannot realize that I actually did it." "In the end I realized it wasn't only the achievement of having hiked the whole trail, but the process of living in the moment." "I did something special that only willpower and self-strength can achieve. I have what it takes to hike 2,000 miles. As the Lion in the Wizard of Oz would say, 'I have courage.'"

Some circumstances have the ring of a challenge about them: "I got divorced from a man who told me I couldn't hike a week on the AT because of my knees, when I suggested we take a weeklong vacation to hike." "I told everyone back home I was going to do it." Trail consensus is that the more people you tell, the harder it is to quit; this is particularly true if you have been given a big going-away party.

Although the experience is intensely personal, few hikers can resist the temptation of basking in the sunshine of public acclaim. Stardom is a heady nectar, usually reserved for a few successful politicians, artists, entertainers, and professional athletes. Occasionally someone will be thrust into the limelight when he or she discovers a gold mine or wins 10 million dollars in a lottery. A few, like Lindbergh, Hillary, or Amundsen, make it by extraordinary feats. But for most of us, there is not even a moment of fleeting fame in a long lifetime—unless you do something unusual.

Thru-hiking the AT is unusual. The local inhabitants, the tourists, dayhikers, old and new friends ask questions and wonder. For a brief period the thru-hiker tastes the attention and admiration usually reserved for the famous.

I can remember a hot night in Virginia, walking alone, sweaty, and tired. The *Philosopher's Guide*—that indispensable volume of gossip and hostelry information (see Chapter 17)—indicated the availability of a bed-and-breakfast just a mile off the trail. It was too tempting, and I detoured to the lovely, trim, Victorian B&B. I was the only overnight guest, but although the rooms were empty, the posh restaurant was booming. We were on the outskirts of Washington, D.C., and dozens of elegantly dressed men and women, some in evening clothes, were having dinner there. I showered and put on my cleanest pair of shorts (I was not carrying any long pants at the time), and the restaurant hostess seated me discreetly. As I drank my whiskey sour and enjoyed the steak and salad, the guests at neighboring tables started asking questions. The men spoke in a mixture of envy and awe, the women with admiration. I talked through dessert and several cups of coffee, basking in the attention of my audience. It is doubtful whether anyone has dreams of fame and glory when they seek to thru-hike. But even such a limited taste is sweet.

I was reminded of Nick Danziger's travels through Asia following the old Silk Road. Danziger was a young man in his mid-20s with a flair for picking up new languages, unquenchable curiosity, and an ability to be comfortable in any society. He traveled overland from Turkey all the way to China in the mid-1980s. Doing something adventurous and unusual changed his life from a sometime art student, wanderer, and loner to that of a celebrity. In his 1987 book *Danziger's Travels: Beyond Forbidden Frontiers,* he describes how, deep in the Chinese desert of Taklamakan, uncertain of where he might eat or sleep, he is met as he steps off a bus in Keriya. He is led to the local Communist headquarters: "I stood in the hallway of the bunker-like building

Meadows in Virginia

whilst my escort went into one of the rooms that led off it. Then there was a sudden flurry of activity not unlike the kind of scene you find in old farces, with doors opening and shutting and people scurrying in and out of them like mice. This was followed by a short period of total calm. Then the door opened and [my host] beckoned me in. All the county leaders had assembled there in a long line. They greeted me warmly as I passed from one to the other, shaking hands. My visit was clearly a great event for them and they had thought of everything to make my stay pleasant. They had reserved the best room at the guesthouse for me."

This is what Carol Collins meant when she said, "I'll have to admit, the attention that I got (and there was a lot) contributed a lot to my drive."

A few thru-hikers said they had never thought of long-distance hiking and had never hiked before attempting to do the whole trail. But they were the exception. The typical thru-hiker had been mulling over the idea for about 10 years, and not a few traced plans back to their teens and childhood. One 62-year-old had been planning since the 1930s.

I remember an evening when, hiking in southern Maine with my sons in the 1970s, we met two thru-hikers at Full Goose shelter. They arrived separately but knew each other. I was appalled by the ragged, dirty clothing and their gaunt appearance. In those days, when out for a weekend, we ate well—hamburgers or even lamb chops, frozen vegetables, soup, coffee, and cake. And although we carried a stove, we did much of our cooking over the fire in skillets, pots, and kettles. The two thru-hikers lit up their stoves, and with barely a word between them each mixed up a big mess of glop in a little pot, heated it, and then ate the contents right out of the pot. They were not unfriendly, though hardly garrulous. But they were in the final phase of the great adventure, and it was compelling, even sublime to observe them. Was it something a sane and normal hiker might consider doing? For me it posed a provocative question that traveled the back roads of my mind for the next two decades.

LOVE OF THE OUTDOORS

Although the majority of hikers are responding to a challenge, what about that strange minority (about 20 percent) who are out there just because they love it? When you meet them on the trail, they seem to have a dreamy quality. At an overlook on a clear day we all stop, admire the blue haze, the little farms, and the rolling mountains. But how long can you sit and admire? There are miles to travel and shelters to reach, so the rest of us move on after an ex-

change of pleasantries and few minutes' rest. But we leave some hikers behind, drinking it in and living it in a manner beyond our comprehension.

My son Ted clearly is motivated to hike by a "love of the outdoors." Whether climbing Mount McKinley or getting married in a Seattle park, he is attracted to mountains, wilderness, and woods. Such "love the outdoors" hikers view reaching the top of the mountain differently than those who are seeking adventure and challenge. Whereas getting to the top is the *raison d'être* for most of those out in the mountains, Ted may turn around and head down, leaving the summit for another day. His tendency to react more to the sights than to the challenge showed up early: When Ted was about 10 years old and his brothers a little older, we were on a fall weekend hike in the White Mountains. It had been a beautiful day, but it was dusk and we were hurrying to make the shelter before dark. Suddenly I realized Ted was missing. "Go on ahead," I said, "and I'll go back." About half a mile back the trail turned sharply at an outlook and there he was, sitting on a rock watching the sunset.

Discussing these "Why?" categories with Ted's psychologist brother Kim, I commented on the nature lovers: "You won't believe it, but these people often work only long enough the save the money to go out hiking again. They are an atypical lot." But Kim disagreed, saying: "Dad, you should pay more attention to them. They are the only true thru-hikers on the trail. All the rest of you have some ulterior motive: You want to do it because others can't, or to prove something, or to get away from something. Not these lovers of nature."

It has been suggested that this love of the outdoors may have a genetic origin. The term coined by Dr. Edward O. Wilson in 1984 for the condition was *biophilia*, and in the November 30, 1993, *New York Times* William K. Steven discussed the phenomenon: "'Can humans be truly human and truly fulfilled in a world of glass and concrete set apart from nature, surrounded by cultural artifacts and pursuits, enclosed in electronic cocoons where much of reality comes from the television screen and the computer display?' Not in a million years, according to this hypothesis. Wilson holds that eons of evolution, during which humans constantly and intimately interacted with nature, have imbued *Homo sapiens* with a deep, genetically based emotional need to affiliate with the rest of the living world. Meeting this need, according to the *biophilia* hypothesis, may be as important to human well-being as forming close personal relationships."

The motivations of these hikers who love the outdoors are clearly different from those of hikers seeking challenge, adventure, or an escape. They write: "Between hikes I live for the next one." "I love to hike and be in the outdoors." "Love the wilderness." "Quitting just wasn't in my head. I love it out there, and if my body and God would let me, I'd do it my whole life." "I don't like to work, but it is a necessary evil. Hiking is the best time of my life."

Hiker Helen Gray wrote: "In telling others why one hikes, I always feel as though there is no way to establish understanding for them, so I have tried relating a difficult, positive experience from their lives to my hiking. Still feeling the explanation is inadequate, I usually follow with something from Henry David Thoreau, about walking for the joy of walking, not to arrive at a destination."

Catherine Eich, a thru-hiker in 1987, is one of those backpackers with an overwhelming love of the outdoors. Indeed, on finishing her hike atop Mount Katahdin she immediately turned around and backpacked the 262-mile Long Trail in Vermont. On a hike in June 1977 she wrote:

Thru Hiker

I rise with the sun in the morning
And hope that the rain will not hide his warm light.
But sunshine or storm uncomplaining
I keep to my trail 'til the coming of night.

Two miles or twenty, no difference.
My body can't say what the distance might be,
But pray with some sleep's assistance
The ache that now plagues me just might let me be.

I know not the power that possesses
My mind and my spirit in such a strange way,
But "Onward" the path ever beckons me
"Just one more mile" or "Just one more day."

The vistas, the valleys, the mountains
I know in my heart that they won't be the same
When one mile high on Katahdin
The title "Thru-Hiker" I finally can claim.

ESCAPE AND SIMPLICITY

About one in every five thru-hikers is primarily motivated by a desire to get away, to leave something behind them. Of course, they enjoy the adventure and beauty of their experience, but they still reflect a fundamental need to get away from a situation and life they can no longer endure: the complex, competitive, noisy world. They want to make life simple, get back to basics.

For example, they comment: "The feeling of being free to walk all that way on my own schedule, sampling such a myriad of experiences." "Hiking long distances is like living in another world." "To have time to myself, away from the mainstream, so I could think about many different things in my life, career, goals and my marriage—reevaluate my priorities." "I really wanted to get away by myself and away from civilization to really think about things—also to get away from all the bad news and negativity." "To break out of a rut, I needed to get out and live, and needed to take time rather than being taken by time." "It had come to a personal crisis—had to be away from all those silly businesses, cars, houses, and careers. Hate to say it, but I am back working."

These feelings from late in the 20th century are most certainly not unique. Philosopher and outdoorsman George Schindler notes that more than 2,000 years ago, Petrarch was reputedly the first person to climb a mountain just for the fun of it. The peak was Mt. Ventoux in Greece.

The three hiker motivations—challenge, love of outdoors, and escape—are mirrored in earlier tales of the mountains. In *Forest and Crag*, their monumental history of hiking in the Northeast, Laura and Guy Waterman trace the prevailing moods that seem to govern the reasons for hiking. They note that until 1830 the mountains were generally regarded as "daunting terrible"—and people stayed away from them. From 1830 to 1870 the generations were less interested in climbing mountains than in "simply being among them"—like the hikers who visit the mountain because of an intrinsic love of the outdoors.

The Watermans describe the next era, 1910 to 1950, as "Mountains as escape from urban society," the philosophy preached by Appalachian Trail founder Benton MacKaye in the 1920s. After 1950, they write, hikers looked to "mountains as a place for recreation": "The 1965–1975 generation might aspire to live all the time in touch with nature; the 1980s group was more at home in boardrooms and at conference tables, but a sizable number of them also wanted the mountains regularly in their lives, to them the backcountry was a readily available natural gymnasium in which to find vigorous physical tests, a cleansing of the spirit, and the deliberate pursuit of challenge."

In my survey the focus is on one specific kind of hike. Since thru-hiking the AT is intrinsically somewhat more of an adventure than a Sunday afternoon stroll in the woods, it is not surprising that challenge is the predominant reason for our thru-hikers to be out there. But it is also true, as the Watermans point out, that it is fashionable now to run a marathon, sail your own boat to Bermuda, and test your mettle. So, these thru-hikers appear to fit into the mood of the times as they tackle a task that is more than just a nominal challenge.

THE DECISION TO GO

The need for a challenge, the love of the outdoors, and the desire for getting away reflect deeply held personal feelings, but they fall short of the rationale that finally puts the thru-hikers on the trail. Many start in accordance with a long-held plan. But it is commonly noted by hikers themselves that their start was due to some kind of a break in lifestyle. Such a break usually happened at work or at home.

At work they might have been fired or eased out; or they were bored, frustrated, and quit. Maybe they were between jobs. One young woman, Bonnie Goulard, had been laid off from a state job and had taken her employers to court. When I met her in New England, she was still awaiting the court's decision. I learned later that she had won, been rehired, and had reluctantly returned to Florida to pick up the pieces of that old life. There were several people who had been refused leaves-of-absence to go off hiking—the refusal propelling them to quit immediately and take off. So much for the boss.

Events at home also stimulated hikers to take to the trail. The breaking up of a long partnership or marriage would result in the need to take time out to think it all over "and get my act together." A young woman from the West was out alone recovering from the untimely death of her boyfriend. She carried some of his hiking equipment as she followed the trail through North Carolina.

Some hikers took advantage of life's natural breaks. These included graduating from school, finishing military duty, or entering retirement. A naval officer in Maine had given up a military pension by retiring after 17 years of service. It was not worth it to him to spend three more years doing what he did not wish to do; he was leaving for graduate school and an academic life.

Although a break in lifestyle is the most common trigger, many other factors contribute to the decision to thru-hike. Most important is the encouragement of family and friends. I remember Norman Tubbs, a fast-moving older hiker who had to give up with knee trouble while still in Georgia. He had left home with all intentions of a long absence, and here he was back again. But at home Norm's wife provided nursing, succor, encouragement, and the 800-mile ride back to get on the trail where he had left it. Just a few days later, south of Beach Gap, North Carolina, Norman caught up with me as I sat sprawled across the trail eating lunch.

Finally, there are the books, articles, and TV shows about the AT, which have been growing in number every year. One commonly noted inspiration is *Mountain Adventure* by Ron Fisher, published by the National Geographic Society, containing a plethora of unbelievably beautiful pictures by photographer Sam Abell.

Some hikers trace their interest to days with the Boy Scouts, some after meeting thru-hikers, and several mention the magic of seeing the white blazes. Regardless of the mix of memories and reasons, they bring over 1,000 aspirants to Georgia each spring.

THE PILGRIMAGE

There is an outward similarity between the thru-hike and the tradition of religious pilgrimages, such as those in the Near East to Jerusalem and Mecca, and in the Far East across to India and Tibet. Through the centuries, long-distance walks have been undertaken by pilgrims the world over—Christians and Muslims, Buddhists and Hindus, and the faithful of countless other religions.

One of the most famous pilgrimages today is to follow a route from central Europe across the Pyrenees to Santiago de Compostela in Spain. Although the religious origins are confused and contradictory (there is no real evidence that the Apostle St. James is buried there), thousands of pilgrims follow the erected signs of the scallop shell over roads and paths 1,000 miles or more. They follow one of four traditional routes, carrying Society of St. James passbooks, which are stamped and authenticated along the way. These pilgrims stay in hostels that are usually much larger, and seemingly much less attractive, than any on the AT. But like AT thru-hikers, they have a final, climactic goal: The great Cathedral of Santiago is Mt. Katahdin for the pilgrims of St. James.

There are the obvious similarities in the two journeys. For example, there is the very act of personally walking a great distance, and the shared experience of reaching a goal relying only on oneself. On the Santiago trek there are great crowds, numbering more than 10,000 per year.

But many, if not most, of those on the way to Santiago are not classical pilgrims. Although the criteria of spiritual experience and escape are more common among the pilgrims than for AT thru-hikers, the trip, despite its religious basis, seems to be characterized by enjoying good company, meeting the opposite sex, and having a cheap, fun holiday. And the simple physical challenge, which attracts so many to the AT, is absent. Some pilgrims ride on vehicles or on horseback, some pedal bikes, and many are in van-supported groups.

THE ULYSSES FACTOR AND GENES

A few years ago, Karen Robbins called my attention to a theory proposed by J.R.L. Anderson in the book *The Ulysses Factor: The Exploring Instinct in Man.* Anderson wondered why a person might choose to sail around the world or cross the Antarctic by dog sled, and decided that such journeys cannot be adequately explained as merely a search for fame and fortune. To explain this urge, or thirst for adventure, Anderson reaches back 2,800 years to Homer's *Odyssey*, the story of the adventures of Odysseus, or Ulysses, in the decade following the fall of Troy. "In the story, Ulysses angers the sea-god Poseidon, who sends a gale to wreck his ship and besets him with troubles on his journey home. He is, however, befriended by the goddess Athena, who in the end persuades Zeus, the most powerful of gods in the Greek Pantheon, to permit him a safe homecoming. *The Odyssey* is one of the best adventure stories ever written; it is also a case study by a writer of the keenest psychological insight of man powerfully affected by the Ulysses Factor."

Anderson points out that as with Ulysses, the adventures of modern men and women undergoing long trials, often undertaken alone, are not pointless, but result in a personal achievement, can be communicated, and are often interesting and exciting. He states that the Ulysses Factor includes attributes valuable for the biological survival of the human species, such as courage, imagination, self-discipline, and endurance. "Neither gold nor fame will do. They may be won by a successful endeavor, but they do not explain this particular kind of endeavor. The anthropological approach remains: there is some factor in man, some form of special adaptation, which prompts a few individuals to exploits which, however purposeless they may seem, are of value to the survival of the race."

On the other hand, the Ulysses Factor may only be a term describing the actions of some individuals who have inherited a specific genetic trait. On January 2, 1996, in a *San Francisco Chronicle* article by Natalie Angier, it was reported that the first gene scientists found linked to an ordinary human personality trait was a gene involved in the search for new things. "Two teams of researchers have reported detecting a partial genetic explanation for a personality trait called 'novelty seeking.' Research on animals, as well as extensive studies of human twins of both the identical and fraternal variety, indicate that about half of novelty-seeking behavior is attributable to genes. . . ."

The thru-hiker usually sees himself or herself as a little different than others on the trail. It may be the Ulysses Factor or genes or something else, but the evidence of something is there. At any account, Ulysses himself would be very much at home attending a meeting of the Appalachian Long Distance Hiker Association.

A PERSONAL CHALLENGE

In my case, I made the decision to go suddenly on November 15, 1987, as my wife and I walked up the Tourne, a small New Jersey mountain. On the way down she said, "If you're ever going to hike the AT, you'd better pick a date to do it." I had wondered about being away so long. I had dreaded indulging myself while she stayed at home earning our livelihood, keeping the home fires burning, and fixing the plumbing. It seemed like a fool's dream, so I selected April Fools' Day, 1989; I almost made it, starting on April 7, 1989.

I left home reluctantly rather than joyfully, so escape was certainly not my objective. I love the outdoors and we live in the countryside, but I find looking at trees and scenery a bore, so I don't qualify as a spiritually impelled thru-hiker. No, it is clear that I wanted to hike the Appalachian Trail because it looked like the adventure of my lifetime. It was a personal experience, an extended challenge that lured me from bed and home. I never considered why.

Tristan Jones was an adventurer all his life, traveling—often alone—in the most inhospitable areas of the world. He suffered extreme hardships in the Arctic, on the oceans, and in some of the worst jungles of the world. His answer to "Why?" borrowed from Tennyson's "Ulysses": "We were made to do this—not to sit in a mental or spiritual cave. Man's destiny is to strive, to seek, and to find, and not to yield."

Good company is often the best part of a meal.

WHO HIKES WITH WHOM

I never found the companion that was so companionable as solitude.

—Henry David Thoreau

The best people alive.

—Laurie Mack, 1989 thru-hiker, reflecting on her AT companions

One of the delightful things about the AT is that it is open to such a wide range of people. Male and female, rich and poor, old and young, thru-hikers come from a broad spectrum of backgrounds and professions.

Although in the population of long-distance hikers men still heavily outnumber women, there are more women now than in earlier years. Approximately 20 percent of successful thru-hikers are women; my sample of 136 contains 26 percent women. (For more about the experiences of women on the trail, see Chapter 18.) Generally, the shorter the hike, the

higher the percentage of women; they make up almost half of AT dayhikers.

Most long-distance hikers are young people. In my sample, about 70 percent were less than 35 years old; the average hiker was 29. Young people are most likely to have those three qualities essential for a thru-hike: time, adaptability, and the desire for adventure. And they can take a break from school, military service, or a job before becoming deeply involved in family and work. When it comes to short hikes, there are many youngsters on the AT, in youth groups and with families. Teenagers are common on the AT on weekends. However, among the thru-hikers in this sample there was no one younger than 20.

Despite the potential for midlife-crisis escapees, there were particularly few thru-hikers between 35 and 45—the years of growing responsibilities. To the outside world the thru-hike can appear self indulgent. Society tends to think that is okay for the young—the hike is a major experience before settling down, and younger hikers may have the time and energy (though usually they are short of money). Older hikers have time and money, but often not enough energy. Middle-aged persons, however, due to the demands of job and family, usually don't have the time—and there are few from this group on the AT.

From the standpoint of available time and money, you would expect retirement to provide the perfect window in the calendar of our lives for the thru-hiking adventure: almost unlimited time, fewer family responsibilities, and, usually, retirement savings to pay the modest costs. Considering this, the number of retirees is small. In my sample there were only a dozen hikers over 60, the oldest being 68. As I sat exhausted on a log with a retired postmaster after a 12-mile day, he said, "The thru-hiking is great, but it is really a game for the young." Older people suffer one significant disadvantage: They have difficulty putting in enough miles over the hills—day in, day out, for months on end—to complete the rugged trail in one year. From the last snows in Georgia to the bitter cold in Maine, there are only about six months available to do a complete thru-hike—but there are alternative approaches, as described in the next chapter.

As for work and career of the thru-hikers surveyed in the sample, the elite included professionals and managers but few businessmen, teachers, or representatives of the financial world. The largest portion were working people such as carpenters, technicians, mechanics, computer operators, government employees, and doers of odd jobs. A good many described their previous jobs as "just working," which reflects little inspiration from the work itself and probably made the prospect of six months of getting away from it all doubly enticing. Many were students, and a considerable portion were just finishing or had finished a term of service in the military.

Table 3-1 summarizes what hikers were doing before and after their experience on the AT.

The biggest surprise is not a surprise—the shift in interest to working in the outdoors and environment. Before the hike, only one hiker out of 136 had been working in a job involving the environment; but after months of following the Appalachian Trail, some 18 individuals said they had changed or were going to change jobs to work in ecology and the environment. They wrote: "I now see myself as able and motivated to help protect other areas in their natural state." "I plan a career change and am starting classes in park management." "I am going back to school to major in environmental science."

In general, there are also a few who completely change their lives and become career hikers. These people work

TABLE 3-1.
WORK, BEFORE AND AFTER THE THRU-HIKE

TYPE OF WORK	BEFORE	AFTER
MANAGERS, PROFESSIONALS, SCHOOL, SERVICES, TECHNICIANS, CRAFTS, ETC.	66%	57%
"JUST WORKING"—ODD JOBS, TEMPORARY, UNEMPLOYED	18%	19%
RETIRED	9%	9%
MILITARY	6%	0
OUTDOOR, ENVIRONMENTAL	1%	15%

only to save money for the next hike: They program computers, repair cars, or wait on tables long enough to save the nest egg for the next adventure in the wilderness. Their work year is usually six to nine months, after which they are back on the trail—sometimes the AT, but also the Pacific Crest Trail or some other challenge for those preferring life in the woods.

TRAIL RELATIONSHIPS
The majority of Appalachian Trail thru-hikers go it alone. Most of the others hike with a single partner of the opposite sex. But the experience is fluid, and it is a long trip with many happy—and some disastrous—relationships.

Although many thru-hikers cite wonderful experiences interacting with others along the way, it is still primarily a solitary experience. The idea of having friends along is appealing, and the Appalachian Trailway News always carries notices of hikers seeking companions. And there is companionship on the trail—at night, when hikers congregate in the shelters, campgrounds, and hostels, and compare experiences. But next morning they usually take off singly or in pairs down the trail. (This is in contrast to the weekend backpacker, for whom the trip is a visit with friends—and no environment is more conducive to a warm, friendly interchange than walking though the woods for a few days.) The ultimate good fortune is to find someone along the trail who enjoys hiking just the same way as you, and to join together for a few days or weeks. A long-term commitment of some five or six months, however, is quite a different matter.

Long-distance hikers' comments about relationships are revealing. Many spoke of the wonderful experience in sharing. But an even greater number described the difficulties in staying together—their worst moments being not physical hardships and rain, but arguments and disagreements. The observer gets an impression that this long involvement brings out both the best and the worst of life together. One young man traveling with a female companion from his hometown told me they had gone on several very successful long hikes together but never saw each other when not backpacking. But more commonly, trail partnerships simply did not survive.

Trail partnerships present a strenuous intimacy. As noted by many hikers, not even in a marriage are partners expected to spend 24 hours a day with each other for months at a time. Sharing your life with another person— eating, sleeping, and walking all day long, six or seven days a week, through two or three seasons—is a togetherness experience unmatched in most lives. Furthermore, the idiosyncrasies of each hiker are multiplied by every mile and every day. Because of this, the long traverse can be stressful, despite the best of intentions. In this survey, the hike brought a stormy end to several close relationships and planned marriages.

On the other hand, for some staying together was more than a trail experience. Within the first years after their hike, four trail couples in my sample got married.

The most successful partnerships are those of the long-married couples, who have achieved an ability to compromise and have forged a bond of tolerance strong enough to survive the hundreds of daily interactions of a long hike. They seem to adjust better to the togetherness than newly formed partnerships do, and they suffer few breakups.

In my survey there were only two threesomes staying together, and no larger groups. However, a number of well-organized groups have hiked the AT. Warren Doyle, until recently Director of the Appalachian Trail Institute, has hiked the AT alone a number of times and has put together highly successful group trips for about 20 participants. Meticulously organized with support functions, such trips provide an intensive group experience under the guidance of a true professional. However, lacking such experienced leadership, any group larger than three seems to contain an almost explosive diversity, too much to stay together for 2,000 miles.

THE HIKER PERSONALITY AND O.W. LACY

A thru-hike on the Appalachian Trail is, for almost every person, a complete change in lifestyle. The physical challenge and exposure to nature and weather, the simplicity of the food, the limited social life, and the interruption of almost half a year of normal activities combine to make it a truly unique event. Studying who would make such a decision leads to the obvious question, "Is there a certain kind of personality that characterizes the thru-hiker?"

Psychologist O.W. Lacy undertook to answer the question. From 1970 to 1980 Dr. Lacy, at the time professor of psychology at Franklin and Marshall College and Dean of Students, hiked the AT end-to-end. He decided to explore hiker personalities using the Myers-Briggs Type Indicator test (MBTI). Based on theories of Swiss psychiatrist Carl Jung and developed by the mother-daughter team of Katherine Briggs and Isabel Briggs Myers, the MBTI is the world's most frequently used personality test. Lacy personally undertook the extraordinary task of gathering MBTI test results from hundreds of AT hikers, including men and women thru-hikers and hikers who had completed less than the whole 2,000 miles. As of 1994, Lacy's total sample was approaching 1,000. Psychologist Lacy, known as "Red Owl" on the trail, is unquestionably the authority on AT hiker personality. His work is too extensive for even a sketchy review, but we can note a few of his most interesting findings.

Lacy's most striking finding concerns the hiker's tendency toward extroversion or introversion. Extroverted individuals are oriented to the outer world of people and action; introverted individuals to a greater extent live in an inner world of ideas and concepts. Lacy estimates that the general U.S. population represents 25 percent introversion, 75 percent extroversion; however, his study of backpackers (as of 1992) revealed that the extroversion/introversion balance of 2,000-mile hikers was the reverse.

Table 3-2 indicates that introverted people were more than three times more common on the trail than in the general population. This would seem to point to a selection process as to who drops out and who stays on to become a 2,000-mile hiker. It is not difficult to hypothesize an explanation: Almost two-thirds of all long-distance hikers reported that they hiked alone on the trail; and the other one-third, although traveling with one or more companions, were often separated from them during the hiking day. Thus, long-distance hikers in general are unaccompanied during much of the trip. Extroverts, primarily oriented to the outside world and to people, think twice about immersing themselves in an environment mostly devoid of other humans. Some hikers do complain of loneliness; perhaps these are the 23 to 31 percent minority extroverts.

The Myers-Briggs Type Indicator is much broader than just extroversion-introversion. It consists of four personality tests, but only the extroversion-introversion scale revealed any significant difference between hikers and the general population.

TABLE 3-2.
MEASUREMENT OF EXTROVERSION FOR 2,000-MILE HIKERS

	MEN		WOMEN	
	NUMBER	%	NUMBER	%
EXTROVERTED IN U.S. POPULATION (ESTIMATED)	—	75*	—	75*
EXTROVERTED AMONG 2,000-MILE HIKERS	298	31	111	23
EXTROVERTED AMONG LONG-DISTANCE HIKERS NOT GOING THE WHOLE DISTANCE	94	36	104	46

*As of March 1997, Lacy was still adding to his data bank. He noted that hiker trends had remained unchanged over the last 20 years. However, recent U.S. general population data indicate only about 50% (instead of 75%) extroversion. Even so, there still was a preponderance of introverts among long-distance hikers.

ALONE TOGETHER

Table 3-3 gives the breakdown for who traveled alone and those who had partners.

These figures reflect the final rating given by the hiker after completion of his or her travels. The statistics imply a more stable situation than is actually the case. For example, follow-up questions indicate that about half the time, the original partnership breaks up. But then, new partners sometimes join on the trail. Thus, some "alone hikers" end up with partners, some partners find new partners, and some who started with companions end up hiking alone.

A survey published in *American Hiker* in 1990 by Susan Puretz reported similar results. Sixty percent of the long-distance hikers were solo. But she also commented that many followed a hiking pattern where they were "officially alone but never really alone."

The definition of "hiking alone" is blurred. Some pairs stay together the whole day—that is, they stay within talking distance of each other all the time. This is most common among married couples. It is also the way most people who are out for only a few hours, or perhaps the weekend, usually hike; it permits a relaxed socializing among friends. But this is not typical for long-distance hikers. When hiking day in, day out for weeks or months, it is common for partners to rejoin nightly but hike separately all day. Sometimes they even separate for several days, rejoining down the trail. The record "alone" is a hiker who traveled only two hours with one person the first day

TABLE 3-3.
WHO HIKES WITH WHOM

	MEN	WOMEN	TOTAL
HIKED ALONE	76% 17 MARRIED 50 SINGLE	41% 1 MARRIED 13 SINGLE	66%
HIKED WITH OPPOSITE SEX	12% 5 MARRIED 6 SINGLE	50% 5 MARRIED 12 SINGLE	23%
HIKED WITH SAME SEX	12%	9%	11%

of the trip and then with no one all the way to Maine. On the other hand, in Maine, as hikers converge on Katahdin in early October, groups of old trail friends will form during the last few days and climb that last big mountain together.

SOCIETY VERSUS SOLITUDE

"Seek partner(s) for thru-hike beginning mid-March 1996 from Georgia, average 12–15 miles per day." This ad was placed in the November/December 1995 issue of the *Appalachian Trailway News* by Kelly Douglas of Barrington, Illinois. Kelly's ad was only one of six in that issue seeking hiking partners, and every issue contains such invitations. This would seem to be a logical step when contemplating a six-month sojourn in the wilderness—good company and a sharing of weight and uncertainties, what could be nicer?

When I planned my own thru-hike I, too, cast about for a partner to share the unknown. I was also aware of the experience of my friend Gordon Glover, an experienced backpacker and a convivial companion on the trail. One fall, when the urge to spend a few days in the White Mountains struck, none of his friends could make it. So Gordon shouldered his pack and took off for five days, all alone. But Gordon is the farthest thing from a loner. As a newspaper reporter, speechwriter, and member of boards, councils, and parties, Gordon loves people. It took only one night in the deserted forest for him to ask himself the question, "What am I doing here?" Next morning he headed back down the mountain and rejoined the peopled world. My own background as a scientist was not as intensely people-oriented as Gordon's. Indeed, as a profession, scientists have a reputation of being able to hide in the corner of the laboratory night and day without the need of any human communication. Even so, I was not sure about being alone in the woods for long periods. I had hiked a great deal, but always with friends. However,

Bog crossing in New Jersey

I sensed that this was intrinsically a challenge to be undertaken alone.

It turns out that among long-distance hikers, about 20 percent specifically seek solitude. At the other extreme, about 40 percent make an effort to hike along in close contact with friends and plan to be all together, if possible, for the night.

How much "alone" is really alone and what is it to be "together"? The 136 hikers in the survey were asked, "When hiking with friends, were you close enough to converse?" They answered:

USUALLY	27%
SOMETIMES	53%
RARELY/NEVER	20%

A better test is to ask, "How often did you meet with friends for the night?" They reported:

USUALLY	50%
SOMETIMES	32%
RARELY/NEVER	18%

From this overall picture, about half the hikers maintained contact on a day-to-day basis, but while actually hiking fewer stayed together. And again, clearly about one in five are solitary hikers.

In James Hare's *Hiking the Appalachian Trail,* Raymond Baker summarized the problem as viewed by such hikers: "In case of an accident, a buddy would come in handy. But when you consider that no two persons are so much alike that they would want to hike the same amount every day, get started at the same time in the morning, eat the same meals and be of like disposition, it becomes quite a problem. Also, we decided, it would be almost impossible to find someone having the time and inclination to hike the whole trail at the same time you wanted to hike it. We came to the conclusion that if you figure on doing the whole trail you are better off alone."

Wendy Harris thru-hiked alone in 1988. She did so as a conscious decision to strike out by herself on the trail that spring. She reported in the March/April 1993 issue of *Appalachian Trailway News:* "I felt compelled, and I don't think my choices were foolhardy. I knew what I was doing. My moments of solitude on the Trail were not as frequent as I wish they had been, but they were powerful and memorable. Those who are alarmed by solitude in general find the idea of the lone hiker in the woods downright scary. If the solo hiker is a woman, the idea becomes positively radical. After all, the rugged outdoorswoman is a relatively modern phenomenon. . . .

"Without the distraction of conversation, I've discovered, the fabric of life has a different texture. You become free to examine the world around you with a concentration which is difficult to sustain with the least oppressive company. Alone on the AT, I witnessed things that I had never seen before. Green baby walking sticks strolled across my thigh. The wind swirled clouds above the trees, and I felt the chill of rain on the way. Rhododendrons bloomed voluptuously into pink and red and green, a scented corridor of flowers rising over my head."

Only a few hikers rate their solitude as highly as Bill O'Brian, but for some it was the very essence of a long thru-hike. His thoughts appeared in Hare's *Hiking the Appalachian Trail:* "As I was resting near the top of Springer Mountain I heard several young men's voices. Soon four backpackers appeared and I joined them in hiking to the summit. We took pictures of each other and of the summit sign, and signed the register at about 3:00 P.M. on March 29. It started to rain. We hiked along in the rain toward the first shelter a mile and a half on the way to Mt. Katahdin. That mile and a half was the longest hike I would make with another hiker on the entire 2,000 miles. Much of the solitude was by chance, yet when I could have had company I chose not to because I found it better to be totally absorbed in what I was doing and not to be distracted by other hikers' conversation, or by their faster or slower paces. The decision to hike the trail alone had been carefully arrived at, and I am sure that much of the enjoyment of my trip was because I had nobody to worry about but myself, nobody to please but myself, and nobody to gripe at but myself."

Most backpackers ended up hiking alone, but got together at eating and sleeping times. As Bob Schroeder noted: "All the people I met had different paces. So, day-hiking was alone. . . . And nights at the shelter meant company to talk to while you could relax and enjoy it. Although in Waynesboro, Virginia, I went to a motel room and hid for two-and-a-half days." In 1986 Hugh Thomason sent out a questionnaire to advertisers who, like Kelly Douglas, had sought a partner by posting a notice in the *Appalachian Trailway News.* Thomason reported in the March/April *Appalachian Trailway News* that of 17 respondents who found partners and met with them, eleven pairs split and six stuck together, but only three actually completed the whole hike together. As noted by one of the respondents in Thomason's survey: "Any long distance hike is a very special and difficult journey. It takes a special relationship to be able to make such a journey with another person. . . . I don't know that it is reasonable to expect such

Table 3-4.

LONG-DISTANCE HIKER PREFERENCE: HIKE ALONE OR WITH COMPANY

THE PEOPLE ARE THE THING; I MADE EVERY EFFORT NOT TO BE ALONE BOTH [AT] NIGHT AND WHILE HIKING	2%
I REALLY ENJOYED THE PEOPLE AND ONLY RARELY WOULD TAKE ANY TIME AWAY FROM MY FRIENDS	16%
I WANTED TO HAVE COMPANY AT NIGHT AND OFF THE TRAIL BUT ENJOYED HIKING ALONE MUCH OF THE TIME	43%
THE PEOPLE WERE FINE BUT I WAS GLAD FOR THE PEACE AND SOLITUDE OF BEING ALONE WHILE HIKING AND OVERNIGHT	32%
THE PRIMARY THING WAS TO ENJOY THE TRAIL AND WILDERNESS BY MYSELF, AND I WOULD OFTEN PLAN TO HIKE ALONE SO AS TO BE IN BLISSFUL SOLITUDE	7%
I REALLY TRIED TO AVOID BEING WITH PEOPLE—THIS WAS MY CHANCE TO BE ALONE WITH NATURE	0

a relationship with a person met through an advertisement. . . ." As summed up by another of the respondents: "It is difficult to find through the mail, or even on the trail, a partner who can stay with you for the entire distance of a thru-hike, because a divergence of goals can appear somewhere along the way, and lacking a commitment based on marriage or long friendship, each person goes his own way."

Dave Horsfall's hike is like many: "I started off with Joyce, but on our climb up Springer we hitched up with Gene Michale (dropped out after 11 days) and Greg Lohmueller. The four of us stuck together at night, but during the day we hiked at our own pace. If our pace matched, we hiked together; if not, we hiked alone. This continued for Greg and me until Hanover, New Hampshire, where he took a couple of days off and I pushed on. I held to this behavior with other people as well, like Paul Meleski, Bill Gunderson, and Taylor Walker. We were agreeable on distances, and if we were in synch we'd hike the day together, if not I'd see them at the night's shelter. I actually spent the most time alone in Maine. I was alone (no other thru-hikers) two out of the three weeks at the end of my trip."

For some short-distance hikers, the need for forests and mountains and human companionship are blended together in hiking and mountaineering clubs, the activities often being predominantly social. In contrast, the population of long-distance hikers is skewed in the direction of those fond of solitude and who tolerate, or even look forward to, being alone. In a separate questionnaire, 67 long-distance hikers reported on how they felt about the general circumstances of having company while on their hike. The results, ranging from most social to most solitary, are summarized in Table 3-4.

Thus, although there were no true hermits among the group, over 80 percent specifically noted they sought to be alone at least part of the time. The long-distance hiker is not like most of the general population, nor the membership of hiking clubs. Friends made on the trail turn out to be a wonderful surprise, but it is solitude, simplicity, and wilderness that lures them to undertake the long-distance adventure.

As I hiked alone hour after hour, I found the engulfing solitude pleasing, restful, and refreshing. It was the ultimate freedom to sit down when you felt like it, talk to the birds, deer, rocks, and trees, compliment the builders of good paths and rage at those who had located unreasonably steep or muddy trails. All this was mine without effort, without a second thought. Most of all, there was the freedom to go as slowly as I wished without holding anyone up. I could leave ridiculously early in the morning or hang around and not hike at all—and never have to explain, compromise, or be persuaded. I was a little ashamed of my antisocial attitude when, as I approached a shelter one evening, I found myself hoping that no one was there. Yet I can remember coming over a mountain crest on a rainy, dreary afternoon and practically embracing the approaching human being, my first contact after a couple of days of lonely walking.

Dinner out of the pot

OLDER HIKERS

If you are not yet 60, have some hiking experience, and exercise regularly, this chapter is not for you. You can start tomorrow on the AT with a good chance of finishing the whole length, if it means enough to you to take the time and make the effort. If you are over 60 but are one of those extraordinarily athletic men or women who win master's division races in 10,000-meter runs or compete in marathons and confound younger competitors, you also should skip these pages. What follows is for the rest of the older population who are not athletes and still would like to hike the AT.

This generalization is due not to the character of the AT but rather to the grueling nature of long-distance hiking. Whether you are on the Continental Divide Trail, the Pacific Crest Trail, or some other trek, if the duration of the hike exceeds several months, the wear and tear on older

> *Some work of noble note, may yet be done.*
>
> —Alfred, Lord Tennyson, "Ulysses"

hikers often is too much. About half of the hikers under 50 in the sample reported that fatigue makes going long stretches of the AT tough. However, for backpackers over 50, this fraction increases to four-fifths.

However, specific hiking experience is not necessary. A successful AT thru-hike is a reasonable objective even for those not physically "fit"—particularly if they are realistic and know what to expect. What are the chances for a senior citizen, not an athlete, to successfully hike the whole trail? Some sports—skiing and gymnastics, for example—look deceptively easy but take years of practice and effort to perfect. Not so, backpacking or even preparation for an AT thru-hike. Although training and experience will increase the chances of success, every year people complete the AT who previously had hardly been in the woods, carried a pack, or walked around the block to get some groceries.

TIMING: STRETCHING THE SEASON

The facts are that the average age for thru hiking is about 30, a typical pack weighs 45 pounds, and the average length of the backpacking day is 10 hours. For older hikers, these requirements appear somewhat daunting. But seniors have an advantage if they choose to use it, worth more than youth and strength: time. Upon retirement, most older people suddenly are granted a bonanza of free time such as they have never dreamed of before. The time necessary for the great adventure can be obtained at the cost of a few uncut lawns, unvisited relatives, an unpainted back porch, and unwatched TV. The senior citizen can depart from his or her environs for months, even years, and not be seriously missed.

Another advantage is freedom from financial constraints: While young people must save and forgo earning while they walk, the retiree with social security or a small pension can live like a king on the trail. Indeed, many older hikers find that it costs less to walk the trail than to stay at home. (Costs of the trip are covered in Chapter 17 under "A Dollar a Mile.")

AN EARLY START

Counting one day per week off the trail for obtaining food, cleaning up, and resting, plus a few days extra for off-trail visits, you will need to average about 13 miles per hike day to finish the AT in six months. The younger hiker will find that he or she can easily average this, once in hiking condition—usually after six weeks on the trail. Hikers 50 to 60 years old will, on the average, do just about 13 miles per day without the trip becoming a trial. But hikers 60 to 70 will usually only be able to comfortably average 10 to 11 miles per day. Those doing a little better can finish in seven months; but those who are close to 70, or on the slow side, may find it takes up to eight months.

Is it practical to take as long as eight months to hike the whole AT? Yes, but it requires an early start, beginning as early as March 1 in Georgia, notwithstanding the possibilities of a wet snow or late-winter cold snap. In case of severe weather, the hiker can hole up in a shelter for a day or two and wait until the worst is over. At this time of the year even a heavy snow melts quickly, and although the trail may be sloppy, the hike can proceed.

Starting early is usually safer than hiking late in the season. After November 1, the Maine mountains can become bitterly cold, and carrying much more winter gear and food makes the late-season trip an alternative only for those experienced in winter backpacking.

O.d. Coyote, the original proponent of the leisurely hiking style that he has tagged "slackpacking," did a slow thru-hike of 263 days (about eight months), starting on February 29, 1980. His slow transit was certainly not dictated by age; O.d. was about 40 years old, a peak age for high capabilities on the trail. Stretching the season at both ends, O.d. did have to hole up for some zero-degree weather in Georgia during his first few days, and he had to put up with light snow and temperatures dropping to about 20 degrees in Maine at the end of his trip. Although hardly as easy as midsummer hiking, O.d.'s experience demonstrates that it is possible to stretch the season.

O.d.'s primary problem was a Baxter Park ranger who adamantly refused to allow him to enter the officially closed Baxter State Park. O.d. did so anyhow, climbing Mount Katahdin on November 17, 1980. October 15 is the closing date for Baxter State Park and is considered a cut-off date for thru-hiking in Maine. In fact, there are many good fall climbing days after mid-October, when the gear and experience for winter climbing are not required. But Baxter State Park rangers have a record of guarding their park against intrusions after the closing date. Winter camping is allowed only by special arrangement, and permission is not readily granted.

THE FLIP-FLOP

A number of hikers have taken advantage of the flip-flop approach, an attractive alternative for late starters and those who want to take it easier than pushing for 13 miles per hiking day. Assuming a start at Springer Mountain, the hiker heads north to a point as early in the trip as Harpers Ferry, or as late the White Mountains. He or she then finds transportation to Baxter State Park, climbs Mount Katahdin in fair weather well before the park closes, and heads south to the point where he or she left the trail.

There are two real disadvantages to doing it this way: First, you must leave your well-worn friends, some of whom you have been meeting and communicating with for months; you are breaking away. Second, you are deprived of the climatic and traditional ending with its climb up magnificent Katahdin. Upwards of 90 percent of the hikers do it the traditional way, and the picture of the hiker hugging a companion (or leaning on the sign on Baxter Peak) is *de rigueur*.

One of the main advantages of a flip-flop is that if a late start or slow progress results in having to hike in October through early December, the late months in the year will be much more comfortable in the mid-Atlantic states and southern New England than in Maine and New Hampshire. The mountains aren't so high and winter weather is less severe. Furthermore, the trails are not as steep, and elevation changes average only about 200 feet per mile. This compares with more than twice as much change in elevation per mile in northern New England.

As for friends, you actually *will* meet your old buddies, probably more of them than if you were going in the same direction. But you are now on a reverse course, and except when you are sharing a campground or shelter, the chance of socializing will be briefer.

With some arranging in advance, you can still finish your hike on a mountaintop or in an especially meaningful place. It could be Mount Washington, the highest peak in the Northeast and the mountain that was initially to be the AT's northern terminus. Mount Washington has the additional advantage of being accessible for non-hikers, so friends and relatives can be right there to celebrate the hike's completion. Much farther to the south, Harpers Ferry is another natural finish where non-hiking friends can wait in a beautiful spot and the ever-warm staff at Appalachian Trail Headquarters can join the congratulations.

Crossing the White Mountains late in the year sounds rather dangerous to many hikers more accustomed to the milder winters in the South and the usually sheltered mountaintops. However, on a basis of more than a dozen hikes in the months of October through early December, my experience is that this is the nicest of all times to be in the Whites. The weather is nearly perfect for hiking, and both trails and shelters are relatively uncrowded. If there is snow, it is almost invariably light enough so that you can still walk the trails fairly easily and conditions do not require special winter hiking gear. Although temperatures at night can be below freezing, days may be so warm as to invite hiking in shorts. Most of the AMC huts are closed then, but Carter and Zealand Falls huts are open on a caretaker basis. (For more on the AMC huts, see Chapters 9 and 17.) Furthermore, shortly after entering the Presidential Range, the hiker going south on the AT comes to Pinkham Notch and the local AMC Headquarters, which is not only open year-round with food and bunks, but equipped to advise on travel conditions.

SENIOR THRU-HIKERS

Probably the most famous older thru-hiker was Emma Rowena Gatewood, the legendary Grandma Gatewood. Mother of 11 children, and having put in a lifetime of domestic and farm work, she learned about the Appalachian Trail from a *National Geographic* article about Earl Shaffer's thru-hike. Thus inspired, she journeyed to Maine, took off from Mount Katahdin in July 1954, and promptly got lost. After several days she was rescued by the Maine Forest Service, which did not invite her to return. Undaunted, but

somewhat cowed by the Maine Forest Rangers, the following spring she started at the southern end of the trail and duly finished that fall at Mount Katahdin. She thru-hiked again in 1957, and finished a third end-to-end journey in 1964. Her first two hikes were each completed within one year. She had, therefore, thru-hiked the AT at the age of 67 and 69, and finished a section hike at the age of 74.

The oldest thru-hiker for which I have specific references was George Miller, who hiked the AT in 1952 at the age of 72. According to John P. Cowan in the 1953 bulletin of the Potomac Appalachian Trail Club, Miller was an experienced man on his feet, having once walked from Farmington, Missouri, to New York City. Like Grandma Gatewood he carried a minimum of weight, which he said never exceeded 26 pounds. On the trail he walked about 14.5 miles per day, completing the thru-hike in 138 days. Grandma Gatewood and George Miller are joined by very few over-70 hikers to successfully complete a thru-hike. Recently, however, there is an interesting trend—women seem to be walking away with the seniority prize. For example, Verna Soule, who thru-hiked the AT in 1987 at the age of 62, in February 1995 was gearing up to tackle it again at the age of 70. Unfortunately, a fall near Hot Springs, North Carolina, ended this attempt. Even veteran thru-hiker Bob Sparks (up to five end-to-end traverses) has observed that long-distance hiking for senior citizens is something of a woman's world. Sparks finished one of his hikes in 1992 at the age of 73, noting at the time that two women, ages 65 and 70, were also finishing.

Cindy Ross, in writing about older hikers, notes in her book *Hiking*: "They have all stayed consistently active through the years, kept busy, and have been 'participants' in life, not 'spectators.' Besides staying active, the hiking seniors contributed their backpacking ability to good health habits. They did not smoke, they practiced moderation in all things, and ate healthy foods. Did they stretch? No, they did not. One commented that it was a waste of time. Another said, 'No! Something might snap!' And another said, 'No. People my age didn't know we had to.' They didn't have to. All they found they needed was a good, slow walking pace in the morning that would sufficiently loosen their muscles. 'After the first good climb,' one commented, 'the juices would seem to flow and I could get this machine up to cruising speed.'"

The main differences between older and younger backpackers were speed, recovery rates, and perceived aches and pains. With respect to the latter, older people sensed that it was important not to talk about them—particularly with young people. "Nothing is as boring nor makes less satisfying conversation. No young person can imagine what it is like, and the topic is unproductive."

Young people can pile on extra mileage or a 25-mile day and bounce back after a good night's sleep. The wise senior hiker would not be as likely to "pour it on," sensing that reserves were limited. Cindy Ross reported that 67-year-old Alan Adsmond, who hiked the entire AT with his son, said, "After 1,000 miles on the trail, my rate of recovery definitely deteriorated. I was still 'roaring to go' in the morning, but by the middle of the day I was 'roaring to stop' but unfortunately couldn't."

Cindy Ross noted that, aches and pains aside, there is very little age barrier between older and younger backpackers. Whether skinny-dipping, hitchhiking, or looking for water, they are all dealing with the same elements, and older hikers tend to melt into the company of younger hikers with no effort. Bob Sparks, with his many years of being the oldest, or almost the oldest, hiker on the AT, described the relationship between senior hikers and their junior friends along the way. "A hiker is a hiker, and age doesn't make any difference. People are just happy to see you."

Several seniors noted a twist in the support they received from their young colleagues (ages 20 to 35): In general, the young people on the trail simply did not seem to notice any difference between themselves and folks who could have been their grandparents—whereas hikers in their 40s and 50s were downright eager to have their older friends make good mileage and do well on the trail. Why? Perhaps, in peeking around the corner of old age, middle-aged hikers see that the time they might be old is no longer infinitely distant. They don't want to even contemplate slowing down, much less giving up backpacking. They want models who promise them just as good a time as they are now having, 10 or 20 years hence. Even if they do not voice such thoughts, it appears to be part of the bond between the old-timers and the middle-aged long-distance hikers.

The performance of older hikers, like that of women, has been the subject of prejudice in the past. Before World War I it was commonly considered inappropriate for women or old people to engage in something as strenuous as mountain climbing. Miriam Underhill, the most famous American woman mountain climber in the mid-20th century, had to make many of her pioneering climbs without the benefit of male guides, as she recounts in *Give Me the Hills*. In her book *The Challenge of Rainier*, Dee Molenaar observes: "In 1913 a group of seven men and three women started up the Nisqually for a climb via the Kautz route. Dr. Meany was an old man then (Meany was

51 at the time) and with two of the women he stopped at the 6,500–7,000-foot elevation and returned to camp in Paradise Valley." In my own case I climbed Mount Rainier with my son Ted leading the rope in a party of four, including one woman. At the time I was 57 years old, and it was the day after I had been tactfully rejected as a candidate for the climb to the top by the local climbing school. In the November/December issue of *T&T,* I wrote, "It was nice to think that now Mount Rainier was not the exclusive province of rockjocks and mountain guides, that women's horizons had now expanded to the windy mountaintops. . . ."

OTHER OPTIONS FOR OLDER HIKERS

Whether you like it or not, there is a limit in mileage per day that a hiker can comfortably keep up month in, month out wearing a heavy backpack. In Chapter 12 I describe how by stretching the seasons (hiking from March 15 to October 15), a hiker need cover only 12 miles per hiking day to complete the trail in one year. This would be fine for hikers 50 to 60 but increasingly tough to keep up as the hiker approaches 70. Although, of course, there are exceptions, the age of 70 is about the oldest even an experienced and highly competent hiker/backpacker can be and hope to thru-hike without an extraordinary effort or good luck. The truth of the age limitation appears borne out by the unadvertised failure of a number of thru-hikers who were not able to repeat their earlier thru-hike when they tried it in their 70s.

Fortunately, there are alternatives that preserve almost all the mystique and special magic of a thru-hike.

A TWO- OR THREE-YEAR AT HIKE

That complete immersion in the project, the simplicity of the life, and the special trail friends are pretty much the same when hiking for two- or three-month stints as they are in a six-month thru-hike completed in one year. David Corriveau reported that one of the oldest hikers to complete the AT was John Oiley, who did it in two years. John spent his 80th birthday on the trail in August 1994. Despite bad knees and putting in grinding 12-hour days, he truly became the successful "Old Man of the Trail."

Cindy Ross reports that Kay Wood raised her three children, cared for her dying mother, buried her husband, sold her eight-room house for a mobile home, and headed to Georgia to begin the AT. She was 71 years old when she finished the two-year stint on the Appalachian Trail in 1989. And in the mid-1990s, Kay is still out there walking her daily five to six miles.

Doing the AT in two or three years as Oiley and Wood did is pretty much like the one-year thru-hike. Being on the trail three months or longer is long enough to put the urban world out of mind. It is the same rugged, simple, physical life with its limited cast of characters. It is made to order for the older hiker.

SECTION HIKING

In this survey, more than 80 percent of the end-to-enders were thru-hikers, doing the traverse in less than a year in a more or less uninterrupted effort. About half the remaining 20 percent took two or three years. The remainder were section hikers, people who bit off a piece of the trail every year or so, typically two or three weeks at a time. The section hikers had been on the trail anywhere from 4 to 23 years. Historically, several hikers have taken more than 50 years to finish.

Breaking up the trail experience and taking more than three years to hike it in sections is a thoroughly satisfying and interesting life project, but it is very different from thru-hiking. On the one hand, since the typical duration of the hike is not more than two or three weeks, most backpackers never reach that ultimate condition of feeling perfectly fit on the trail. Another difference is that the bonding with others on the trail, so marked in the accounts of thru-hikers in recent years, is not as strong. Finally, that feeling of being completely estranged from a now distant civilization is not likely to develop. However, section hikers can still see and taste, if not be engulfed by, the experience. They are more likely to cook and eat interesting meals, spend time with local inhabitants, and take it easy as they learn about the countryside. James and Hertha Flack spent eight years doing the whole AT, taking a total of 244 days and averaging 8.6 miles per day; they later reported about their experience in the book *Ambling and Scrambling on the Appalachian Trail*. They traveled neither all north nor all south, but "followed no set pattern . . . segments here there and yonder."

In her publication *Appalachian Trail in Bits and Pieces*, Mary Sands described her 16 years of hiking the AT in sections as a "leader, teacher, mother, and friend to 135 Girl Scouts," shepherding various small groups over the 2,000-mile trail. She had a thousand experiences, not only learning about the mountains herself, but with loving care indoctrinating those 135 young women in the wonders of the Appalachian Trail.

Like thru-hikers, the section hikers experience the feelings of great adventure. This approach suits those who can take the time off from the busy world only in short bites.

TABLE 4-1.
AGE OF BACKPACKER COMPARED TO TYPE OF HIKE

TYPE OF HIKE	AVERAGE AGE OF HIKER
THRU-HIKE	32
END-TO-END IN 2 OR 3 YEARS	33
LONG-DISTANCE, BUT NOT THE WHOLE AT	39
SECTION HIKE, END-TO-END (4 TO 23 YEARS)	50

As such it can provide a yearly escape from the stress of home and work.

The statistics compiled from the 136 AT thru-hikers in the survey show that thru-hikers are the youngest group on the trail and those who hike it in sections are the oldest (Table 4-1).

Note that half the section hikers were over 57 years old. In general, the statistics bear out the finding that older hikers increasingly undertake the AT in shorter pieces.

HIKING THE AT WITH VEHICLE SUPPORT

There is a final, small group of AT end-to-enders who hike the trail one or two days at a time. Except in Maine's 100-mile wilderness, the AT is rarely more than a day's walk from a road, and even in the wilderness it is possible to get out. Such end-to-enders have been supported by a loyal spouse, friend, or family member and walk the AT carrying a daypack. At the age of 67, Lucile Gustafson averaged 9.2 miles per day in 1988–89, walked six to seven hours per day, and completed the trail in 233 days. Her husband Gus drove approximately 30,000 miles and made arrangements for spending 190 nights in motels (at an average cost of $50 per night). Lucile spent 75 nights in shelters, 28 in a tent, and the rest in motels. She fell and broke her wrist, dealt with bears, snakes, and mice, never cried, and found it no problem to be a lone woman on the trail.

In contrast to doing it alone, 67-year-old Ray Brandes thru-hiked the AT in 1990 as part of a vehicle-supported expedition led by Warren Doyle (AT veteran of nine end-to-end hikes and then-Director of the Appalachian Trail Institute). According to Doyle's February 1990 article in *Backpacker* magazine, he trained the members of his expedition in advance with 60-mile hikes taking three days, and dayhikes of 12 to 17 miles (and longer) in all kinds of weather. By virtue of this rigorous preparation and the fact that hikers needed only to carry daypacks, the expedition covered the whole distance in only 126 days, averaging about 16 miles per day.

Moxie Bald Mountain, Maine. One of the AT's last fire towers

A final category of vehicle-supported thru-hiking is under circumstances where a hiker or runner is attempting to do the whole trail in record time; this is described in Chapter 12.

IS THIS FOR YOU?

Depending on your age, ability, and timing, you can probably find a way to hike the whole AT. And by taking plenty of time, the rewards can be reaped even by those for whom an athletic feat might normally be unthinkable. The end-to-end hike is a challenge and opportunity for a great adventure and is within the reach of almost anyone really eager to try. The reward isn't really for toughness but for commitment, a willingness to learn the tricks along the way and not give up. Toughness will come with the miles, savvy with the days that go by, and both rain and wonderful friendships will be plentiful all along the trail. Requiring only lots of time, curiosity to learn, and a little money, everything else required can be picked up along the way.

If you think you are not up to the physical challenge of 2,000 miles alone, then neither was Bob Barker, who despite multiple sclerosis clipped along over the mountains on crutches. And if your eyesight makes it difficult to drive at night, remember blind Bill Irwin, who turned over the responsibility of finding the trail to his dog Orient.

PHYSICAL CONDITION AND INJURIES

How experienced are the hikers when they start their trip? In my own case, I felt well prepared when I reached the shelter on top of Springer Mountain that snowy evening on April 7, 1989. After all, I had been backpacking and mountain climbing most of my life. I jogged regularly and got outside for skiing, gardening, and wood chopping. But as I looked around at the 25 other hopefuls in the shelter, I noted that they neither looked nor acted like neophytes. The answers to questionnaires bears that out: The typical thru-hiker had been backpacking several weeks each year. About one in twenty was a career hiker, logging many hundreds or sometimes over a thousand miles yearly. But there were some extremes at

> *I was fat and sassy—for I have always done my conditioning on the trail.*
>
> —George L. Ziegenfuss, in response to questions about training for his AT thru-hike

the other end, too. About one person out of every five said he or she had never been backpacking at all, and another 10 percent had only experienced dayhiking.

This diversity in hiking experience seems enormous. Almost one-third of the successful thru-hikers were beginners. And were they physically fit? Jack Steppe described his condition as "awful," and Bill Maracinkowski said his training program had consisted of "moving my things out of a four-story apartment building that didn't have any elevators." But most of the hikers had been physically active, keeping fit with some kind of regular exercise or training program, as described later in this chapter. However, on the average, hikers were not athletes. And physical fitness is not the key to success on the trail.

How do long-distance hikers of the AT typically prepare for this arduous feat? About half the hikers in this survey had undertaken a program of special training before they attempted the hike, such as jogging, swimming, doing calisthenics, running up stairs, stuffing their packs with 50 pounds of bricks for a climb up the local hill, and taking extended walks. Another group, about one-quarter of the long-distance hikers, were in such excellent shape that they required no special pre-hike conditioning. These are typically athletes who take part in competitive sports or engage in vigorous activities such as long-distance backpacking or mountain climbing. Some have jobs that require a high degree of physical conditioning, such as house framer, longshoreman, or forest ranger.

Physical conditioning is obviously an important factor in determining whether a hiker stays on the trail. Helen Bynum wrote in a 1992 letter to the *Appalachian Trailway News*: "My husband and I started a thru-hike in 1986. It took only five days to find we weren't in as good shape as we had thought, and we had to leave the trail." The hikers discussed in the following pages had all been on the trail for a considerable period, usually weeks or months, or had finished it; so, we are measuring the records of backpackers who have gone beyond the initial breaking-in period.

Of these experienced backpackers, many were clearly already in good physical condition or undertook serious efforts to be in good shape—but not all. About one-quarter of them made no special effort to get ready, and in some ways these are the most adventurous hikers of all: If they are aiming to complete the AT in one year, they have to move faster later on. How do these poorly conditioned hikers fare on the trail as compared to those better prepared? Does being in shape before starting the AT pay off over the long months? Is there a relationship between physical condition before hiking the AT and the quality of the thru-hiking experience? This chapter will address these and other questions about the role pre-trail physical conditioning plays in thru-hiking.

MEASURING PHYSICAL CONDITIONING

In order to measure physical readiness, hikers taking part in the survey were asked to report their condition at the start and any special training program they undertook. Based on these two answers, I developed a 10-point scale where "1" reflects very poor shape and "10" superb physical condition, "5" being average for a nonathletic general population. The physical condition reported by the group ranged from desk-bound and smoking two packs of cigarettes per day to competitive athletes and men and women with as much as 10,000 miles of backpacking experience.

Those rated "1" through "3" were out of shape, below the general population for their age and sex. Hikers described their pre-hike condition as: "Thin, not muscular,

smoked." "Had a lazy winter." "Out of condition, barely able to walk back and forth from my electric wok to my bed." Those rated "4" and "5" got a little more exercise: "Walking through the fields at night for fresh air." "Basketball and walking, but overweight and aerobically out of shape."

The overall average of hikers was "7," people who regularly take part in vigorous outdoor activities and sports at least several times per week, but are not in the range of athletes. Hikers rated "6" and "7" said: "I was in good shape but undertook no specific physical training." "Took a 50-mile shakedown hike." "Walked four miles daily, no pack." "Bad shape, weighed 236 pounds; but Nautilus, Stairmaster, and climbing hills with 60-pound pack of encyclopedias on my back [did the trick]."

The "8" and "9" hikers had undergone specific physical training for the trip and were in tip-top shape: "One hundred miles of shakedown hikes in the month before my start." "Walked 6–8 miles per day to and from work for six months prior to the trail." "Hiked daily with weights and blocks in my backpack." "Ran up and down 18 flights of stairs twice a day." "Not bad for an old fart—averaged three hours per day bicycling, running, skiing, hiking, snowshoeing."

The "10s" were athletes, outstanding physical specimens: "I am a competitive runner and triathlete." "Have run 13 marathons." "Walking at 3.5 miles per hour on an inclined treadmill with a pack on, increasing the weight of the pack weekly—also running 4–6 miles four to five times per week and weight training." "Have run regularly for about 15 years and used a Nordic Track trainer as a supplement; winter camped six or seven weekends prior to the AT in April." "I'm a long-distance bicyclist, a runner, cross-country skier, snowshoer, hiker, etc.—average three hours a day."

EFFECT OF PHYSICAL CONDITIONING

Did the hard work of getting into shape pay off on the trail? Yes and no. If we look at the average miles per day walked *in the first month*, the well-conditioned hikers did about 4 miles more per day than those not in the pink. This difference is evident from the data in Table 5-1.

Being in good physical condition before starting on the AT clearly enables hikers to cover more ground during their first month on the trail. And probably many of those who drop out in the early stages of the hike were in poor physical condition. But there is no minimum daily mileage required for a start. If 10 miles per day is too much, then fewer will do to start the gradual buildup of muscles and conditioning.

A number of hikers have emphasized that long-distance hiking is a natural self-conditioning experience. Alan

TABLE 5-1.

EFFECT OF CONDITIONING ON MILES PER DAY, FIRST MONTH

Starting Physical Condition	Given Rating	Miles per Day
Poor to average	1–6	9.5
Good	7	12.8
Excellent	8–10	13.3

TABLE 5-3.

PHYSICAL CONDITION AND WEIGHT LOSS

Starting Physical Condition	Given Physical Rating	Average Weight Loss
Poor	Below 5.1	22.0 pounds
Fair to good	5.1–7.9	15.0 pounds
Excellent	Above 7.9	12.7 pounds

Strackeljahn, writing on the basis of more than 3,000 miles of backpacking, notes, "I knew from experience that the only preparation is doing it." Bill Grace writes, "The only training that will help prepare you for the trail is the trail itself. Be kind to yourself. Start at half of what you think you need." In the end, the statistics bear this out. *After about the first month there is no difference between the weak and the strong beginners, at least in how far they hike each day.*

Careful readers will note that miles-per-day figures in this chapter are slightly higher than those in Chapter 12. This is because the population containing the details of any single factor varies slightly; that is, not all questions were fully answered in the questionnaires. In every case, the subpopulation containing *all* the information being studied has been used. I believe the different trends and interpretations reported here are valid. But in general, the miles per day figures are only significant to the nearest mile.

Only 3 percent of respondents felt they were in good hiking condition at the start. By the time they had been on the trail for a month, 50 percent had reached this point, and at two months 80 percent felt fit. By the end of the trip 98 percent felt they were in good condition, although three of the hikers in the survey trudged to the end without reaching "peak condition," apparently an unachievable Holy Grail.

Those in poor physical condition at the start paid for it primarily in slower initial travel and more discomfort. Carol Moore said of her preparation, "I walked the hills near my home with weights and exercised at a gym," and although she was in good condition, she reported, "it wasn't enough." Similarly, Emilie Jeanneney was in reasonably good condition before starting, but wrote: "I was running daily and taking weekend hikes to test my equipment. The preparation was not enough." Tom Pappas, who did the whole trail in 1989, said that despite "running, lifting, and basketball—I wish I had trained more." Finally, Buddy Newell, at 56 one of the older hikers on the trail, claimed that his lack of initial training was a "bad mistake" and that he should have climbed stairs with a full pack 100 times daily for at least a month before starting.

Almost all long-distance hikers lose weight, but those who are initially in poor shape lose much more that those who are fit, as shown in Table 5-3.

About two-thirds of this weight is shed in the first, shakedown month. One is tempted to speculate that hikers in poorer physical condition have relatively less muscle tissue, and more fat to burn. This fits with the image that the highly trained, physically ready hikers would lose less weight. See also the section "Nutrition and Weight Loss" in Chapter 14.

A final question readers might ask is whether pre-hike physical conditioning will improve the chances of completing the trip. Looking at the records of 20 hikers who did not go as far as originally planned, they were only slightly less physically ready than the successful thru-hikers (their physical-condition rating was "6," compared to "7" for the successful group)—not sufficient to be considered an important factor in not finishing.

One thing almost every hiker reported is that once fully conditioned to the trail, whether it took three days or three months, there was an incredible feeling of the body operating at close to perfection. For me, it meant understanding what my body could, and could not, accomplish. If I pressed hard one day, the next day I would find myself saying, "This is no fun. I need more rest." But when I was hiking at a comfortable, consistent pace day after day, I would awaken with the dawn, ever eager, supple, and ready for another glorious day.

PREVIOUS HIKING EXPERIENCE

Since a hiker's starting physical condition has only limited influence on the miles hiked each day, I was curious to ex-

TABLE 5-2.

MILES PER DAY, AFTER THE FIRST MONTH

Starting Physical Condition	Given Rating	Miles per Day
Poor to average	1–5	16.0
Good to excellent	6–10	16.0

plore whether his or her background experience in hiking might be a factor. There was certainly a wide range: Some successful thru-hikers had never backpacked at all, selecting equipment on the advice of the clerk in a sporting goods store and learning the hard lessons along the way. They had suffered cold and wet nights and terribly overloaded packs, but survived with a sense that their achievement was, if anything, greater than that of the experienced old-timer. Jim Shattuck, whose pioneering Maine-to-Georgia trip kept him on the trail through the winter of 1966–67, was described at his start as "a man in his late 30s, carrying an 88-pound pack, utterly exhausted, and staggering." He finished the AT triumphant—and carrying a pack that weighed 35 pounds.

The typical starter had about 1,000 miles of lifetime backpacking experience. Yet it turns out that there is no difference between the most and the least experienced backpacker in how fast the hiker travels (see Chapter 12) Some 20 percent of the hikers in the survey had no experience, often not even one night out, prior to their starting the AT; but their initial average of 10.8 miles per day was the same as that of the most experienced career hikers. After the first month, all hikers, beginners and experts, built up to the same 16 miles per day.

CONCLUSIONS

Most long-distance hikers, when compared to the general population, are in fine physical condition. Notwithstanding the pre-hike groans and self-deprecating remarks, about three-quarters of those in the shelter at Springer Mountain the night before the hike started were quite ready for what lay ahead. As for those 15 to 20 percent hikers who had started in poor shape or had absolutely no backpacking experience, after the first month they were hiking just as fast as than those who were experienced and initially fit.

Although this may seem to offer evidence that anyone in any condition can successfully complete a long hike, it does not say that the chance is equally good regardless of the hiker's starting condition. If all who attempted the trip had been queried the day they started, the results would have been very different. What the data do say is that among 136 long distance hikers who survived at least several weeks, and usually much longer, a remarkable "trail conditioning" took place, putting all the hikers on a more or less equal basis once the first month was past.

Thru-hiking and long-distance backpacking are intensely physical activities that reward the participants with a wonderful feeling of well-being. Yet although the hikers rate the physical challenge the most important obstacle to

overcome, we see again and again that physical condition before the hike is not the sine qua non for staying on the trail. As many hikers observed, the trail itself is a fine conditioner. Given a little extra time, and a real commitment, even the faint-muscled and nonexpert have the capability of thru-hiking the AT.

INJURY ON THE TRAIL

Judy Gallant wrote: "My feet were in such pain at the beginning of the trail, I often wondered if the pain would ever go away. It limited my mileage for a while. My new boots were very wide; I bought Spenco insoles in Waynesboro, Virginia. My knees also hurt a lot the first few days, probably because my pack was too heavy. A fellow hiker gave me his walking stick, which I named 'Bill' after him.

"Then in Pennsylvania I fell and got a huge lump on my forehead—but continued on the way. My knees felt better after a while. I ditched the stick on Mount Liberty in the Whites. Just before Stratton I fell and tore a ligament in one knee. I was carried off the mountain and tourists took me to a medical center. The doctor told me to get off the trail, to rest it for six weeks. I took five days off in Manchester Center, icing and elevating it, wearing a knee immobilizer. I then made up by slacking the section I had missed.* It was a real emotional time. Oxford and Purple Rose were unsure whether they should wait for me, or if I'd be able to make it. So we slacked until Hanover, and I carried a lighter pack (Oxford and Mr. Worcester took some of my weight). Without the emotional and physical support of my friends, it is unlikely I would have finished. My knee continued to be painful for three months after the AT."

In regular life Judy is an ICU nurse. She had some rather traumatic accidents along the way, but her trip was not atypical. Some 90 percent of all the 136 long-distance hikers reported bouts of illness and injuries, from head (six stitches after a fall crossing a rocky stream) to toe ("I lost most of my toenails and had numb toes for the next year").

Despite the fact that most hikers experienced injuries along the trail, injuries do not usually result in the hiker's giving up the trip and going home. Accident and injury did, of course, terminate some treks. When Troy Warren slipped on the steep, muddy trail going into Sams Gap, Tennessee, he broke his leg and was unable to move. Fortunately, another hiker found him after an hour. His res-

*"Slacking," or "slackpacking," means thru-hiking without full equipment. Most thru-hikers occasionally travel this way when arrangements can be made for support down the trail. O.d. Coyote has suggested the term be reserved for a leisurely style of hiking.

cuer dropped his own pack and ran down the trail for help. A paramedic team carried Troy out on a stretcher, but it was many months before he could walk.

Still, catastrophic injury like Troy's forced only four hikers in my sample off the trail. That so few gave up because of injuries is more a tribute to the commitment of the backpackers than proof that there are no hazards on the trail. It is just one more bit of evidence that they are a determined lot. For example, take Robie Vance. In response to my question on sickness and injury, he reported laconically that he took "12 days off the trail for an emergency appendectomy in Blairsville, Georgia." Later, upon looking back at his trip, he noted the greatest thing he got out of it was "enjoyment of the adventure—but it was not as exciting as I thought it would be."

Almost no one can escape at least some trouble with a body suddenly expected to develop the ability to go burdened over mountains day after day for six months. But most of the troubles—the blisters, black toenails, wobbly knees, and diarrhea—could be walked through. Maybe you would cut back on your mileage a little, quit early, wrap it up in the afternoon and take some painkiller. But it became serious when you had to stop hiking for a whole day or more. I have, therefore, considered injuries that required a day or more off the trail as a different category from all lesser ailments.

In my sample, about 40 percent were forced off the trail at some time or other, usually only for a day or two, to obtain medical help or rest; most of these were due to gastrointestinal ailments (see Chapter 13). A few game backpackers returned to the challenge after being off the trail with injuries for as long as a month or two. Not many were as dedicated as Joyce Vorbeau. Joyce fell and broke her arm, walked out to a hospital, got it set in a cast, and decided she did not dare stay off the trail. So, cast, pack, and all, she resumed her hike that afternoon. (The three other hikers with broken bones had to give up the trip.)

Among the 40 percent with difficulties requiring taking off one or more days was Bev Finnivan, hiking with her husband. She wrote: "My knees swelled up on the fourth day out; the swelling went down three months after I had finished. I ripped ligaments in my right foot, which was swollen and purple for 350 miles. I could not hike for three days because the foot would not fit in the boot. Blisters required a doctor, as did knees and foot. The sores on my hips bled for about half the trip. I injured my back and was immobilized with pain despite morphine substitute."

Usually hikers with blisters, "foot rot," "hiker's hobble," broken toes, stress fractures, or swollen ankles continued on their way with the aid of bandages, braces, aspirin, and Advil. Only a few hikers rated their trip entirely trouble-free. The litany of problems included bruised heels, hyperextension, pulled hamstrings, sprained ankles, tendinitis, inflamed arches, losing toenails, ripped ligaments, and the repeated complaint, "My feet hurt all the time."

Problems with feet were endemic. Half of the hikers experienced blisters at the start; many of these were attributed to thrusting tender feet into stiff, heavy boots (the relationship between blisters and boots is described in Chapter 7, Table 7-4). During his first few days in Georgia, one hiker was forced into a hospital for an entire week with so many serious blisters that his trip was terminated. And even later when hikers' feet became toughened, the combination of rain, heavy boots, and wet socks meant trouble for one out of five on the trail. One foot-troubled backpacker reported having seven blisters at one time. And more than one hiker, squirming out of boots, was horrified to see socks soaked with blood.

After being on the trail a while, the feet become tougher, the boots soften (or are replaced), so blisters are less of a problem. It seems that the worst problems come from *wet* boots. But blisters also turn up in new unwelcome places such as hips and shoulders.

One stalwart recommended going barefoot as much as possible before starting the trail, to toughen up the feet. The three weeks of not wearing shoes apparently did the trick, for he reported that he never had a blister. But it did nothing for his ankles, which were "always sore."

Shin splints are usually associated with runners and joggers, but more than a handful of my sample complained of this ailment. It was my only injury requiring time off the trail. Although rest helped, it was changing boots that did the trick for me (see "Durability," Chapter 7).

In response to the questionnaire, long-distance hikers reported the following major areas of troubles and injuries:

TABLE 5-4.
HIKER INJURIES

PROBLEM AREA	PERCENT OF HIKERS REPORTING PROBLEM	
	INITIALLY	LATER ON
BLISTERS	51%	21%
KNEES	35%	40%
ANKLES	20%	16%
HIPS	17%	11%
BACK	10%	5%

Along the Hausatonic River in Connecticut

As the months go by, most ailments subside, but not all. Blisters heal, ankle problems decrease somewhat, hips and back cause much less trouble. In general, injuries are anywhere from one-quarter to one-half less common at the later stages of the hike. But knee problems get worse, and orthopedic surgeons note that women are particularly at risk. In an article in the October 16, 1991, *New York Times,* Jane E. Brody wrote: "Women are more vulnerable to knee injuries than men, even in the same activity. For example, a study of university basketball players showed that women suffered 60 percent more knee injuries." The hiking data from my study also shows a higher susceptibility to knee problems for women; on the average, 34 percent of the men reported knee injuries compared to 46 percent of the women. Surgeons ascribe the greater vulnerability to wider hips, which cause the thigh bone to turn slightly inward, putting added pressure on the knee joints. But Brody also points out that the difference in injury rate disappears as the women become conditioned, and on the AT I found a similar result: It was the men who had progressively more trouble as the hike continued; the rate of knee trouble for the women did not increase. There are a number of similar areas, such as susceptibility to minor ailments on the trail, where the women, once rolling, seem to get tougher than the men.

The only injuries that resulted in experienced hikers giving up early were knees and broken bones. And the ultimate test for knees is the steep downhill sections in New Hampshire and Maine, a stretch of trail that has crippled many an otherwise tough thru-hiker. In addition, knees often are exposed and legs bare, so one fall ended up requiring 12 stitches. One hiker put it simply, "I blew my knees out in Maine."

As for other ailments requiring time off the trail, insect bites were a problem for some (for more on insects and repelling them, see Chapter 16). One thru-hiker had to take off six days after being stung by "bees" (probably wasps, hornets, or yellow jackets); another with a brown recluse spider bite that would not heal was forced to seek medical aid. There was also a case of snakebite in my sample (see Chapter 15).

Considering the fact that the trail is lined for miles with poison ivy, particularly in the mid-Atlantic states, it is not surprising that this is the worst poison of them all. Many is the hour I spent gingerly evading stretches of poison ivy, even to the extent of retreating to the roads to get around an infamous stretch of this little plant. One can only pity the hikers suffering this misery, particularly the fellow who hiked a week without pants when afflicted in the region of the crotch. There were actually two such cases, one resulting in a trail name that is mercifully buried in the shelter registers (where messages and trail thoughts are recorded in the evening).

In general, thru-hikers carried very limited first-aid supplies, reflecting the rigorous weight limitations. Pain killers, small bandages, body powder, mole skin, and a few favorite nostrums were often the full extent of the medicine kit. However, sharing of first-aid supplies was common, and often the best-supplied travelers were not thru-hikers but weekenders.

AVOIDING INJURIES

Are trail injuries avoidable? Can one proceed prudently and avoid taking chances? To find out, I examined some of the factors that might contribute to such injuries.

One might suppose that poor physical conditioning before the hike would contribute to a greater vulnerability to injuries and minor ailments, at least during the first month, but I found that the poorly conditioned thru-hikers had no more troubles than those who were best trained. The explanation may lie in the circumstances of trail conditioning. The untrained hikers do almost 40 percent fewer miles per day in the first month than those who are well conditioned; this slower rate may hold down their injuries and ailments to the same general frequency as the others. As they become stronger, they hike more miles and do not suffer any greater frequency of troubles. All of this appears to imply a kind of balance exists between mileage and stress. It is also evidence of the hiker's dictum that the trail itself is the best conditioner.

What about speed and distance, the number of miles covered each day? Certainly the agile backpacker leaping from rock to rock might be expected to be more vulnerable than his or her timid partner crawling over every obstacle and taking no chances. But the statistics do not bear this out. How fast you hike does not seem to make any difference in your chance of getting hurt. I would guess the factors are compensating: On the one hand, the fast hikers are presumably more athletic, and even if more likely to fall, they are probably quite tough. Slow hikers are presumably more careful, but possibly more fragile. Note, however, that the above comparisons are *per mile*. Per hour, the slow hikers fall less but must hike longer to cover the same distance.

Carrying a hiking staff did not seem to make a significant difference in preventing falls and hiking-related injuries; see "Hiking Staffs," Chapter 11.

There is another seemingly logical factor: weight. The pressure on knees and ankles, the squeezing and bruising of the feet, the sore shoulders and hips, even the degree of stability in steep places and over the rocks, would seem to be affected by total weight. Surely the ankle strain of a 200-pound man carrying a 50-pound pack is greater than that of a 115-pound woman with a 25-pound pack. (And note that the only thru-hikers who manage to travel in sneakers or running shoes are light in weight.) However, in my sample neither the number of serious injuries nor minor ailments seems to be affected by variations in total weight. Our 250-pounders do just as well as the small woman in tennis shoes.

All this leads to considering injuries rather stoically, seeing them as a problem you can't avoid on the trail. In the course of taking five million steps, it simply is not possible to avoid a misstep. It is toughness of mind, then, rather than toughness of body, that will lead to a successful through-hike.

Friendships form along the trail

TRAIL NAMES

Having been passed the word by a southbound hiker that Marshmallow was already ahead at the next shelter, any hiker would increase his or her speed a little. "Marshmallow" is the trail name of Nancy Tremblay, and like many other hikers she acquired it more or less by chance as she thru-hiked the AT. As she tells it:

"My trail name, 'Marshmallow,' came about at Rainbow Spring Campground. There were about nine hopeful thru-hikers there, and we decided to have a feast, complete with roasted marshmallows for dessert. I ended up eating most of them out of the bag while dinner was cooking, and a hiker named Lon accidentally called me 'Marshmallow.' They tasted so good that from that point on, I carried marshmallows with me and ate them for lunch with peanut butter. The name really stuck after that!"

Trail names have not always been a tradition on the AT; in fact, they appear to date back less than 25 years. Sto-

The name you give yourself means much more than the name you were born with.

—from the film
The Rainmaker

ries of thru-hikers prior to the mid-1970s do not mention trail names; there were never more than a handful of thru-hikers on the trail in any single year, so it was a highly individual experience. The long-distance hikers gathering at campsites and shelters were the odd few among many short-distance backpackers. A thru-hiker would be meeting different people each night, and there was little opportunity to develop deep friendships.

With the sharp increase in interest in thru-hiking in the 1970s, the number of starters at Springer Mountain increased to about a thousand, and in the early weeks of the trip the thru-hikers dominated the evening camping and shelter gatherings. In the 1970s, the number of yearly thru-hikers edged up toward 100, and it averaged about 150 in the 1980s. Those who stayed on the trail often became fast friends, forming small groups for hiking during the day or often traveling alone and meeting for a break and making camp. Then, too, the trips into town, the close quarters at hostels, sharing motel rooms, shopping, showering, laundering, and supplying often became group activities. Thru-hikers shared not only the same goal but almost everything in their lives—except during the solitary miles on the trail.

Dick Hurd, one of the "Three Blind Mice" who are working their way northward several weeks each year, writes: "I view [trail names] as a bit of whimsical fantasy, like the old West—you can lose or choose your identity. It goes somewhat with the summer-camp atmosphere I associate with the Trail. I suspect analysis will show broad categories such as pure fantasy, quirks, physical traits, anatomical oddities. Our own group name may be unique: 'Three Blind Mice,' from the nursery rhyme—relating to a particular hike on which the trail guide was less than useful and we felt like the blind leading the blind.

"I heard a female hiker relate how she got her sobriquet of 'Jiffy Pop' after losing some of her gear to the depredations of a bear on a cold night; some fellow hikers wrapped her in several aluminized tarps, and someone noted the resemblance to a package of Jiffy Pop popcorn. And last year we and a fellow hiker had all hiked out from the Loft Mountain Campground store, restored by beer, when a mile down the trail our friend realized in a panic that he had forgotten his little black book at the phone booth. He dropped his pack and ran the full distance back, recovering his treasure, and we immediately dubbed him 'Lost 'n Found.'"

Stimulated by Hurd's questions, a tabulation of trail names indicated the following categories: About one-third were for a hiking or personal trait; one-quarter derived from home, family, personal history; another quarter were whimsical or fantasy names; and the rest resulted from a single trail incident.

HOW THRU-HIKERS ARE NAMED

Thru-hikers are about evenly divided between those who were dubbed by others and those who chose their own name. About a quarter of the hikers brought along a trail name from earlier life, as in the case of "Old Hickory," who carried a name with generations of history behind it, or "Mr. Bee," who kept seven hives at home. Three-quarters of the names were significantly modified or downright acquired on the trail, often in the first few weeks.

Jean Cooley certainly did not invent her trail name: "I acquired the name 'The Bag Lady' during my first trip on the AT, in 1983. I left Springer on March 19 and two days later, in a cold rain, pulled into Gooch Gap shelter to find a shelter full of wet hikers who nevertheless found room for me somewhere. They were all sitting against the back wall of the shelter in their sleeping bags for warmth, and I got the impression that they found me and my obvious status as a trail neophyte rather amusing. This was my first serious hike, and all the research in the world can't substitute for experience. I had thought about the problem of keeping one's gear dry and decided for budgetary reasons not to buy a pack cover, but to keep everything inside my pack in plastic bags. I am also quite a disorganized packer and somehow whenever I want something in my pack, it is inevitably at least two-thirds of the way to the bottom. So I sat at the edge of the shelter, with its audience, and tried to make myself some dinner, emptying my pack and scattering its contents, with plastic bags blowing everywhere in the wind. My audience watched me in fascinated silence. Finally, someone broke the quiet by saying, 'We ought to call you the Bag Lady.'

"I like the name because I didn't think it up but acquired it spontaneously, and it also has the added meaning of a person who carries all her worldly possessions with her. It's a name that turns up used by other people occasionally, but I like to think I'm the one-and-only, truly original 'Bag Lady'!"

A trail name may be intimately associated with the hike, but not necessarily with the world beyond the mountains. Consider, for example, "Pooh" (Greg Knoettner): "I went by the name 'Pooh,' as in the bear. I received the name at Neels Gap, just after Blood Mountain, because of a penchant for carrying large amounts of honey (two or three pints). It seemed to give me a burst of energy that I could not get from any other food. Otto and Peter saw me reading *Winnie the Pooh* as I was taking honey shots, and the name was formalized. None of those guys finished, but the name endured. Now in off-trail life, it has all but died."

Often, however, the trail name persists and is included with the regular name as an a.k.a. (also known as). This is common in trail registers and in post-trail correspondence with hiking friends.

One of the happiest outcomes of a thru-hike is meeting someone with whom you decide to spend the rest of your life. For Lou McLauren, a thru-hiker who married her partner Randy, the trail names were not only an integral part of the trail experience but have extended into their marriage and lives beyond the AT:

"Both Randy and I were familiar with the mythology of trail names before starting our hikes. I also knew that traditionally they were acquired once a hike had started, but I chose a name before even reaching Springer. For no good reason other than I love them, I decided to take the name 'Mystic Mint,' a decadent Nabisco cookie. In retrospect, a number of other more applicable names probably would have arisen from my hike, especially since many register entries focused on my blisters and various aches and pains. However, 'Mystic Mint' stuck. My current license plate even reads 'MM RR,' and MM is on my engagement ring to Randy and one of his wedding bands to me.

"Randy's trail name went through an evolution on the AT, and he ultimately ended up with a very appropriate label: 'Ranger Randy.' When I first met him he was going by the cumbersome moniker 'Das Wanderkind,' or 'Wandering Child' in German. He had lived in Germany for the past four years, and this was an endearment given to him by his then-fiancée. The name went well with the heavy woolen hiking hat he wore, but both the name and the hat seemed a little out of place on the AT. Soon after we met he sent the hat back home, along with discarding his German name for a trail-inspired name.

"We met at the Natahala Outdoor Center and then spent the next two months hiking together. Throughout the Smokies he offered little nature lectures to me, as he had a well-developed knowledge of natural history and the environment. I, on the other hand, was an innocent when it came to these things. As a result of his lessons, I began to call him 'Ranger Randy.'

"Even now in civilian life the name is used. Randy works for the Nature Company, and his store sponsors monthly events. About every quarter, 'Ranger Randy's Art Classes' are given, attended by children of store patrons. My parents gave us shirts with our trail names monogrammed on them, and with his German hiking hat Randy is all decked out."

Selecting your own name is not only prophylactic to avoid a nonflattering moniker, but a chance to project the image of how you see yourself—an opportunity to have a name that reflects something of your inner person.

Don Allen knew that he wanted to select his own trail name and that it would play an important part in how he wanted other people to see him: "I first heard about trail names when I visited Harpers Ferry in January 1989 and was given a list of several other hikers (and their trail names) to contact about hiking information. I also purchased the *Five Million Steps* video, and noticed that many of the thru-hikers had names having to do with food. During April, I took a 70-mile shakedown hike from Dick's Creek Gap in Georgia to Amicalola Falls. While hiking, I met a couple of new thru-hikers who had trail names that weren't too complimentary, and I decided I'd better make up my own before starting the AT. (I was very glad I had done this when I met 'Nutless' in New Hampshire.) Anyway, after considering names such as 'Rambling Reck' and

'Yellow Jack,' I chose one of my favorite snack foods, that emphasized the fact that I like to surprise people (since each package says 'toy surprise inside'). When I got back from my shakedown hike I purchased a few boxes of Cracker Jack, and really liked two things it said on each package: '100% Natural' and 'When you're really good, they call you Cracker Jack.' I have also found that along with leaving positive and well-composed register entries, it gives the people behind me a good feeling about the type of person I am; they seem to like the type of person who would call himself 'Cracker Jack.'"

Matt Cross writes, "Picking a new name for yourself is the ultimate fantasy. You have the opportunity to be, or create, a sort of alter image. . . . I was not Matt on the trail; it was 'Maverick.' Usually the name is the opposite reality; I mean, by literal definition I am not a Maverick at all, but [having] a cool name . . . completed the adventure." As "Ranger Rick" put it, "Trail names can be so much a part of you that people you see every day don't know your real name. "

But there is also the trail ethic that rejects self-assumed names. As Catherine Eich writes: "I've been called 'Cat,' short for Catherine, for some years. In Maine in '77 a thru-hiker saw me flying up a steep grade, I've always been strong on the ascent. 'You're not a cat, you're a bird!' he called as I blew by. At the stop that evening I was dubbed 'Catbird.' I loved it.

"The folks I met on the AT in the 1970s claimed that thru-hikers were supposed to be named by their companions or acquaintances along the trail—not by their own choosing. You had to wait until somebody came up with a nickname that you liked, and then you could use it in the registers."

Bill Harrison reflects this view: "You cannot really choose or assign yourself a true trail name—they arise out of actions, events, or observed characteristics of the hiker himself and reflect how he is seen or experienced by others.

"Very often the best names are spontaneous, and the *very* best names also have some element of double entendre or a secondary meaning. One example is my own moniker, 'The Wild Turkey.' In the early years of my long-distance hiking, I had tentatively used several nicknames that had no basis in the hiking experience, but none was really comfortable. Around '84 or '85 I developed a taste for Wild Turkey 101 whiskey and decided that it was worth carrying on our hikes. On one trip, after a hard day, I pulled out the bottle, took a long swig, and let out what was to become my trademark yell. Lee looked over and

Four days to Katahdin!

said, "Well, that Wild Turkey sure does make you gobble!" From thence forward I have been 'The Wild Turkey.'"

Many of the trail names evolved as the long journey continued, as happened for Tina and Greg Seay: "We began our hike about two weeks after exchanging our wedding vows; small wonder we were dubbed 'The Honeymooners.' There were about three other couples with the same name, though, and that sort of confused things. . . . Through the course of a hike, through the highs and lows, the trail magic, and the rain, the blisters, and the cool spring water, one fact made itself increasingly clear: What matters most when you're living like that is going on right where you are, right when you're there. Now we sign the registers 'Here and Now.'"

Bob Schroeder wrote, "I think the interesting part about trail names on the trail is they are entertainment. Life on the trail is in its simplest form—hell, a candle is entertainment. The first people I met on the trail took a couple weeks before discovering their trail names. Sometimes we had quite a few people trying to help—that was fun. Jon and Jackie finally decided on Cold Beer and Fried Chicken. We were relieved once they had their trail names."

Some hikers also develop a logo that accompanies the register entries. It may be initials, as for Dave Bally:

Or a picturesque cat as signed by Craig Mayer:

The whimsical thread is particularly noticeable among logos. For example, Tim Novak's logo depicting his and Andrea Berberian's hike, Half Ass Expeditions '87. He writes: "To be a 'Half Ass' hiker you must leave camp after 11:00 A.M. and you must make stops to enjoy your surroundings. Also you mustn't be concerned with miles unless you're counting them until your next beer or pizza!"

Dennis La Force walked with a rubber stamp signing the registers "The Old Goat of Manchaug."

About one-quarter of the trail names are brought to the AT from the past, usually carrying a story, as in Bob Schroeder's case: "My dad was in the egg business. My job was delivery. When entering the back door of grocery stores, restaurants, and other places with a case of eggs balanced on my shoulder stamped 'EGGS,' someone was almost sure to holler, 'The eggman's here!' So when I went cross-country driving as a trucker, what else for a CB handle—'Eggman.'"

Schroeder used "Eggman" as his trail name as a thru-hiker in 1989, then returned to trucking, name and all. "The days are long and hard and lonely. At nighttime I roll into a shelter—I mean 'truckstop'—and have a bite to eat and maybe talk to someone named 'Drifter' or 'Donald Duck' and then get back out and hit the trail—I mean road—again."

In addition to CB handles, nicknames are also common at summer camps, on computer bulletin boards, and in the military. Nicknames turn up under a number of special circumstances, often marking a phase of life where the person is removed from usual surroundings. Adopting a trail name seems to be part of the bonding taking place among this small group of thru-hikers striving to achieve a common goal. The rigors of the task and large number of dropouts along the way lend an air of the elite to those who finish. The survivors sometimes refer to themselves as the "AT class" of the year in which they finish. It is an exclusive society with a strenuous initiation, and the graduates gather and reminisce like the graduates of Padunk High School, the Yale Class of 1940, or the 374th Air Force Bomber Wing.

Perhaps no single factor has contributed more to the trail name phenomenon than the shelter registers. There is happiness in reading that those ahead are worrying about your progress, or perhaps chagrin when it turns up that a rival is unexpectedly *ahead* or that someone takes exception to the blue-blaze route you have chosen. And always the registers are filled with cartoons, wisdom, opinions, stories, adventures—and trail names. Many a long-distance hiker is known only by his or her trail name.

TABLE 6-1.
THRU-HIKERS WITH TRAIL NAMES

YEAR OF THRU-HIKE	% WITH AT TRAIL NAMES
1988–1989	92%
1983–1987	82%
1978–1982	45%
1973–1977	30%
BEFORE 1973	0

Old trail registers have now become treasured collectors' items, being replaced by new blank books as they become filled.

So, trail names have become an integral part of the thru-hiking experience. They seem to mark the emergence of thru-hiking as a social institution, and because there are relatively few thru-hikers, trail names tend to identify and reinforce their owners' status as members of a hiking elite. The organization of thru-hikers, the Appalachian Long Distance Hikers Association (ALDHA), was founded in 1982, reflecting the development of a social culture of a special kind among long-distance backpackers. According to a tabulation of 141 ALDHA members who thru-hiked in 1988–89, some 130, or 90 percent, used trail names. The actual fraction of ALDHA thru-hikers who reported trail names rose from none to 92 percent at the end of the 1980s (see Table 6-1). Doug Frackelton notes: "Prior to the AT, I would have thought trail names a little tacky, but now I think they may be a rich source of association, unique to a singular experience and shared really only in the context of the trail by the anointed."

TABLE 6-2.
AN AMUSING SHORT LIST OF TRAIL NAMES

TRAIL NAME	GIVEN NAME	NOTES
BAREBUTT	TED PARKE	FROM AN ARRIVAL AT NIGHT IN RAINCOAT, HEADLAMP, PACK, BUT NO PANTS. (AS TOLD BY AVANTAGGIO AND DECAVALCANTE) (O)
BARKILLER BOB	BOB ALCOTT	FROM THE WESTERN MOVIE STARRING RICHARD BOONE (S-O)
BIKER-HIKER	MAURICE MCCASLIN	MAC IS A MOTORCYCLE ENTHUSIAST (S)
BILL x 2 + KIM	KIM KNUTI BILL GRACE BILL MARCINKOWSKI	TWO BILLS AND KIM STUCK IT OUT IN A RARE THREESOME TO DO THE WHOLE AT (S)
BLUE RIDGE RANGER	DEAN AHEARN	FROM THE ALBUM OF THE 1960s (S)
THE CAROLINA FLASH	JACK STEPPE	THE ORIGINAL PROPONENT OF "ENJOY YOUR HIKE"; TRAIL-NAMING AT ITS WHIMSICAL BEST (S)
CHOO-CHOO	BILL CRAWLY	HIKED IN A LONG BEARD AND RAILROAD ENGINEER'S CAP, AS TOLD BY NOEL DECAVALCANTE (O)
CLOCK-WORK KISSER	DENISE DANIEL	HER HIKING PARTNER'S WATCH BEEPED ON THE HOUR—TIME TO STEAL A KISS (O)
CONNIE COFFEE	CAROL COLLINS	FROM THE PINT THERMOS OF HOT COFFEE ON HER BELT (O)
THE COOKIE MONSTER	JIM HEWINS	THIS 1987 THRU-HIKER WAS NOT THE ONLY ONE CRAVING SWEETS
DOBIE MA	TRUDY WHITNEY	"MOTHER OF THE DOBERMAN" (S)
EGG	ADAM TICKNOR	FROM THE NICKNAME EGGHEAD IN SCHOOL (O)
FLATFOOT DAVE	DAVE CHIRNITACH	SIZE 14 AND FLAT FEET, AS TOLD BY NOEL DECAVALCANTE (O)
GEARCHANGER	DOUG FRACKELTON	FROM CHANGES IN HIKING GEAR IN VIRGINIA (S)
GINGERBREAD MAN	DAVID SHIMEK	NAMED BY A FRIEND WHO NOTED HE WAS RUNNING TOO FAST—"LIKE THAT OLD GINGERBREAD MAN" (O)
GONZO	ALAN STRACKELJAHN	FROM THE MUPPETS CHARACTER—"HERE WE GO! (S)

TABLE 6-2. (Continued)

TRAIL NAME	GIVEN NAME	NOTES
HIKE-A-HOLIC	DENNIS HILL	HAD HIKED 9,000 MILES BY 1989 (S)
HIGH-TECH HACKING HIKER	BRUCE MCLAUREN	CARRIED A Z88 LAPTOP COMPUTER (S)
HYDRO	CRAIG PHEGLEY	SWEATS LIKE A HYDRO PLANT GENERATING WATER, AS TOLD BY DECAVALCANTE (O)
I'M MIGHTY THOR	FREDA HILES	FROM "I AM MIGHTY SORE." SHE HIKED WITH GONZO AND WITH CASSI THE WONDER DOG (S)
IRISH ROVER	JOHN HENEGHAN	NAMED IN AN IRISH BAR ON SAINT PATRICK'S DAY (O)
IRISH SETTER	SIOBHAN PERRY	"JUST SETTIN' AROUND" (S-O)
J WALKER	JUDY GALLANT	"I LIKE THE IDEA OF CROSSING THE STREET WHERE I WANTED TO CROSS IT" (S)
J.J. FLASH	ROBERT STARBUCK	FROM THE ROLLING STONES SONG AND BEING ON THE TRAIL ONLY 115 DAYS (S)
JUMP START	ROBIE HENSLEY	STARTED HIS THRU-HIKE WITH A PARACHUTE JUMP TO THE TOP OF SPRINGER MOUNTAIN (S)
KEYS	ALFRED J. LEMIRE	NAMED FOR A MIDNIGHT LOCK-OUT OF HIS CAR AND A TRIP FOR NEW KEYS (O)
LAGUNATIC	CAROL MOORE	"LAGUNA BEACH, CALIFORNIA, PEOPLE ALREADY CALL THEMSELVES BY THIS NAME BUT THIS WAS THE FIRST ON THE AT" (S)
LONE EAGLE	J.W.P. ROBERTSON	A RETIRED MARINE CORPS COLONEL, HE ALREADY HAD THE NICKNAME (O)
LUCKY, LUCKY, LUCKY	PAUL HOLABAUGH	THRU-HIKED FROM MAINE SOUTHWARD AMID BEAUTIFUL WEATHER (S)
MA FROM PA	MARY ANN NISSLEY	MARY ANN CALLS IT "JUST A PRACTICAL NAME" (S)
MAINE MOMMA	NANCY KETTLE	HIKING TO VISIT SON AT THE UNIVERSITY OF MAINE (S)
PROFESSOR HOARTENANCKLE	KARL KRAUS	FROM CARPOOL DAYS (S)
RAGS	TED MURRY JONES	ALREADY A NICKNAME OF THIS COUNTRY & WESTERN SONGWRITER, A.K.A. RAGGEDY MAN (S)
RAINMAN	BOB RZEWNICKI	ENDURED 55 DAYS OF RAIN ON HIS AT TRIP (S)
RANGER RICK	BRUCE HARATY	FROM A STORY HE TOLD OF HIS PARK RANGER DAYS IN OREGON (O)
RERUN	ROBERT SPARKS	SPARKS FIRST LONG-HIKED THE AT IN 1980 AND HAS HIKED THE WHOLE TRAIL ABOUT FIVE TIMES
ROCK KICKER	GREG LOHMUELLER	TRAIL NAME ACQUIRED IN GEORGIA, IT STUCK LONG AFTER HE STOPPED KICKING ROCKS (S-O)
THE SINGING HORSEMAN	NOEL DECAVALCANTE	FROM THE TRANSLATION OF HIS GIVEN ITALIAN NAME, "SINGING CAVALRY" (O)
SIX FEET	KENNETH MILLER	KEN WAS ONCE WARNED BY A FEMALE TRAIL WORKER TO "KEEP SIX FEET AWAY" (S-O)
SKIDDAH	DAVE HORSFALL	OR MR. SKIDDAH, FROM HIS HOME STATE OF MAINE'S LOGGING SKIDDERS (O)
SMILE IN MY HEART	HELEN GRAY	"KNOWING FULL WELL I COULDN'T KEEP A SMILE ON MY FACE FOR 2,100 MILES" (S)

TABLE 6-2. (Continued)

TRAIL NAME	GIVEN NAME	NOTES
SONNY DAYZ	DAVE WALP	"BECAUSE IT SEEMED LIKE I ALWAYS HAD GOOD WEATHER" (S)
STATS GODRIC	BILL GUNDERSON	FROM A HISTORICAL BOOK AND HIS STATISTICAL BENT IN GATHERING AT FACTS (S-O)
THE SWALLOW	KURT SEITZ	"I COULDN'T THINK OF ANYTHING I WOULD RATHER BE THAN A SWALLOW" (S)
TAPEWORM	JEFFREY BRODERICK	THE GREAT HUNGER OF THIS 1988 THRU-HIKER IS STANDARD AMONG LONG-DISTANCE HIKERS
THE TENAFLY TRAMPER	PAUL WITTREICH	HE HIKED THE AT OVER A PERIOD OF 44 YEARS
VAN GO	BILL HOSTERMAN	ARTIST HOSTERMAN TRAVELED TO GEORGIA IN A VAN BEFORE BEGINNING HIS HIKE (S)
WEST VIRGINIA WINNEBAGO	JACK BETTLER	FROM HIS BIG PACK COVERED WITH PATCHES (S)
WILBURY (GIRL WILBURY)	LAURIE MACK	A LOOSELY KNIT 1989 GROUP, PROBABLY NAMED FOR THE BAND "TRAVELING WILBURYS" (O)
WINGFOOT	DAN BRUCE	ONE OF THE BEST-KNOWN "CAREER HIKERS" ON THE AT. THRU-HIKED IN 1985, AND ANNUALLY DURING 1987–92
XO	BILL BERTHONG	HAD JUST DEPARTED THE NAVY FOLLOWING YEARS OF DUTY AS EXECUTIVE OFFICER ("XO") ON SHIP

(S) = Self-named

(O) = Named by others

(S-O) = Arrived at by interaction

Meadows, Virginia

FOOTWEAR

Only one item of equipment is so vital that its failure, all alone, can bring a long-distance hike to an unhappy end: footwear. Even among experienced back-packers walking 1,000 miles or more, there are boot-related disasters, as we have seen in Chapter 5. Carol Moore noted, "Between blisters and damaged nails I had to leave the trail in Pennsyl-vania." Joe Finnivan, in reply to how long his footwear lasted, replied simply, "longer than my feet." Randall Gates didn't even get out of Georgia. He reported that his feet, but not the boots, were broken in by the time he reached Unicoi Gap: "I thought I was going to die." Several of the hikers reported that they had foot problems for virtually the entire AT trip.

About 60 percent of the hikers even-tually worked out a satisfactory footwear

Although the sport of backpacking rides on footwear, technology at the boot/body connection isn't as cut and dried as with the rest of the gear. Too many variables: feet, fit, flex, form, fashion, philosophy.

—Steve Howe

solution. The 136 sample hikers reported wearing 238 pairs of boots and shoes of various kinds, most of which they wore out completely. Grandma Gatewood wore out seven pairs of sneakers and shoes on her first thru-hike, and several of the hikers in the 1989 sample needed four pairs to tra-verse the AT. On the other hand, a hand-ful of owners of sturdy boots, wearing everything from "cheap Sears work shoes" to $250 Limmer boots, did the entire hike in a single pair.

Thru-hikers provide a unique col-lection of experiences for evaluating boots. Since they are out for months and months at a time, they actually wear out their footwear. They are also often of modest financial means and expect their equipment to last the whole trip. So they are critical when soles delaminate, leather rots, support disintegrates, or the boots "bend up in the middle and squish my toes. . . ." For boot tests, manufac-turers typically involve a few hikers who are out for a short time. Rarely do they undertake lifetime tests of their products. At best, some guide, ranger, or long-distance hiker will wear (and perhaps wear out) a pair of boots given to him or her for evaluation—hardly the way to develop a broad-based, unbiased consumer report.

The 136 hikers in this sample walked 250,000 miles, which would be like one person spending 50 years hiking and testing boots. So, their evaluations of various categories of boot types and makes, gathered and presented here, would seem to offer a wealth of unbiased, honest appraisal.

The generalizations that follow were usually made only if there were at least 10 pairs of boots in a category—amounting to 5,000 to 10,000 miles of backpacking. In a few cases where the results appear to be especially interesting, a category of only about five experiences has been included—with due warning that this may well not be significant statistically.

As Steve Howe pointed out in his *Backpacker* magazine article of March 1993, "There are simply too many variables." None of this prevents writers from preparing evaluations, even when based on absurdly limited quantities (such as one). A recent magazine article reviewed 11 makes of light leather boots on the basis of the experience of six rangers walking 650 miles; this is a total of less than 60 miles per pair of boots, all of which were different. By comparison, the minimum sample for boot comparisons in this chapter covers the hiking life of 11 pairs over about 10,000 miles. And even so the reader must be chary, for when it comes to boots there are many variables, and what works well for some might not for others.

It should also be noted that the following comparisons may include lumping together somewhat different boots in a category. A single manufacturer usually makes at least a dozen different kinds of boots; here they may be lumped as being the same brand, or of the same weight category, even though the boots may not all be identical.

What's Available?

There is a mind-boggling variety of footwear out there for you to wear in the wilderness. A review of equipment in the March 1993 issue of *Backpacker* listed no fewer than 350 models of hiking boots and shoes ranging in cost from $40 to $300. The single most important variable is weight, which, after fit, is usually the first thing considered when out hunting for a new pair of boots.

Why all the emphasis on reducing boot weight? Tests by the U.S. Army Research Institute of Environmental Medicine determined that carrying 1 pound on the foot used as much energy as carrying 6 pounds in the pack. Other studies confirm these measurements and provide evidence of the heavy price paid in expended energy as shoe weight increases. Controlled tests based on oxygen uptake reveal the energy cost is equal to about 1 percent per 100 grams of increase in shoe weight (100 grams equals about 3 ounces). This is true for walking, with and without a pack, for both men and women. Because the difference between light running shoes and boots will range from 1 to 3 pounds, wearing the heavier alternative will require the backpacker to put out anywhere from 4 percent to a whopping 14 percent extra energy. Translated into an equivalent increase in backpack weight, two independent studies indicate that the energy cost of carrying the additional weight on the feet is in the range of 5.8 to 6.4 times the weight on the back. Thus, the shift from heavy boots to lightweight boots, reducing the foot load by 2 pounds, is like reducing the pack weight by 12 pounds.

Historically, mountaineers, loggers, hunters, trappers, and guides wore heavy all-leather boots studded with nails. These boots provided excellent traction on ice, snow, and, surprising though it may seem, on wet rock. Many a mountain hostel and backwoods tavern floor suffered irreversibly from the stomping of such hob-nailed boots. At home they were removed upon entering.

The era was brought to an end by an Italian inventor, Vitale Bramani, who in 1935 concocted a hard rubber lugged boot sole containing carbon, known as Vibram. The resulting trail grip was superior on every hiking surface, with the possible exception of wet rock; it was also much easier on the kitchen floor. From then through the '60s, long-distance hikers used a variety of boots such as L.L. Bean hunting boots, work boots, surplus Army boots, and even sneakers. In the years after World War II practically every boot designed for outdoor climbing and hiking had a Vibram sole (and, half a century later, the Vibram sole still dominates the boot market). Boot construction became considerably refined, but boots remained all leather (rubber was good for hunting but not for strenuous hiking).

By the 1970s, however, a much lighter boot, with a fabric upper, typically nylon or Gore-Tex, made its debut. The lighter-weight boots evolved by taking a leaf from the rapidly expanding sport-shoe industry.

It is convenient to break hiking footwear into four categories, as in Table 7-1.

The weights given in the table are for women's size 7 and men's size 9. Typical actual boot sizes of those answering my questionnaire were women's 8½ and men's

TABLE 7-1.
CATEGORIES OF HIKING FOOTWEAR

Category	Description	Approximate Pair Wt. (lbs.)	Approximate Life (miles)	Approximate Cost ($)
Running shoes	Tennis shoes, basketball sneakers, etc.	1	700	50
Lightweight	Fabric plus split leather	2	1,000	90
Medium-weight	Reinforced fabric and leather or split leather	3	1,050	122
Heavyweight	Full-grain leather	4	1,600	150

size 10 and over—and weight goes up sharply with size. In my own case, I have hiking footwear in all four categories, and in my size, 14, boots weigh 1 to 2 pounds more than for the advertised size 9.

WHAT DID THEY HIKE IN?

Of the 238 pairs of worn/worn-out footwear, two-thirds were light or medium weight. The degree of hiker satisfaction for each category is listed in Table 7-2.

Thus, we see a preference for lightweight boots among almost half the hikers—and they are slightly more satisfied with their choice than those buying heavy boots. The very high satisfaction expressed by those hiking in running shoes or sneakers is worth noting, but is not statistically meaningful.

Common sense would lead you to think that the softer and lighter the footwear, the fewer the blisters. But the data do not indicate this is the case. There were over 60 cases of blisters among those in the sample, but the percentage of afflicted hikers (about 29 percent in the early days of their hike) was the same whether they were light, medium, or heavy boots. Although blister troubles decreased greatly as feet toughened up, there was still no difference among the various boot weights.

Ankles are particularly vulnerable, requiring protection and support. It would seem that the stiffer, heavier, and more supportive the boot, the fewer would be the ankle injuries. However, here again the numbers do not bear out the hypothesis. About 10 percent of the hikers initially had ankle problems, and about 5 percent later on. But heavy boots were not better in this respect than the lighter models.

Only four hikers wore sneakers or running shoes, so a statistical answer is not meaningful; but, for what it is worth, they reported no blisters and just one case of "little ankle problems." With respect to ankle problems, there is an important factor that may have influenced the negative finding that heavy boots are no help: Unlike blisters, which are notoriously unpredicted, many people with ankle problems know about this weakness in advance, so they might well opt for heavier, more supportive boots at the time of purchase, avoiding light shoes with no ankle support. It is possible, then, that the people wearing sneakers intrinsically have strong ankles and that people who buy heavy boots have among them more cases of problem ankles. Thus, you cannot blame the heavy boots for additional problems reported on the trail.

Do older hikers tend to wear heavy boots because that is what they were brought up with? Or, conversely, are

TABLE 7-2.
HIKER SATISFACTION WITH FOOTWEAR IN VARIOUS WEIGHT CATEGORIES

Category	Percent of Hikers	Satisfied with Footwear	Comment
Running shoes, sneakers, etc.	2%	(100%)	Only a few, but they were uniformly satisfied
Lightweight	46%	60%	The difference between lightweight and medium is probably not significant
Medium-weight	17%	64%	
Heavyweight	34%	48%	

older hikers more sensitive to carrying extra pounds on their feet and perhaps more eager to eliminate every possible pound? A review of the numbers indicates that the average age of hikers in medium and heavy boots is about 10 years younger than hikers going light. Gordon Gamble, a rather lightweight thru-hiker, was in his late 60s when he walked the AT. He wore sneakers with plastic bags to keep his feet dry. Although the older hikers show a preference for the lighter footwear, the survey indicated that hikers of all ages carry about the same-weight packs.

Backpackers are understandably more conscientious about breaking in heavy boots than light ones. Thus, 78 percent of those wearing heavy boots had broken them in, 71 percent of those in medium-weight boots had done so, but only 32 percent of those who chose lightweight boots had broken them in. No one in sneakers or running shoes bothered. Several hikers lamented that they had not broken in their boots sufficiently; this seems to be borne out by the high rate of blisters, 27 percent, in the early days on the trail, dropping to 6 percent later on when boots were softer and feet tougher. Some hikers took the opposite tack; instead of softening the boots, they suggested toughening the feet. Alcohol baths were tried but did not seem to help. Several echoed Christian Lugo's advice: "I recommend *not wearing shoes* much in the weeks before starting the trail. It toughens your feet."

BOOT SATISFACTION BY MANUFACTURER

As shown in Table 7-2, lighter boots had a slightly higher hiker-satisfaction quotient than heavy boots, but the difference is small. If boot weight is not critical, then what about the difference between brands? Using a threshold of 10 as the minimum number for comparison, there were enough replies from seven manufacturers to permit calcu-

lating hikers' satisfaction and troubles. Table 7-3 summarizes these results.

The boot brands are listed in order of the percent of hikers who said they were satisfied with the boots, ranging from 81 percent for Hi-Tec to 36 percent for Danner. Two additional measures of boots are the frequency of blisters and ankle trouble. Presumably the higher the percentage here, the poorer the boot. Reported separately from the boot satisfaction questions, these responses reflect only two measures and ignore many factors such as durability, tread, and cost. Blister problems ranged from a low of 26 percent for Vasque to 55 percent for Danner. Ankle problems ranged from 2 percent for Vasque to 35 percent for Merrell.

No boot is perfect, and even the best-rated footwear resulted in about 25 percent of the wearers getting blisters. But since the lowest-rated boot had twice that percentage, if you have tender feet the difference may be worth considering. The same is true for those of you with trouble-prone ankles: You might prefer risking a boot where only 2 percent of those reporting had ankle problems to a brand where 35 percent reported negatively.

In many cases, the total number of a brand of boot was too small to make comparison. (The total number of replies included 30 different brands.) But some interesting insights can be gleaned as to the miscellaneous categories in Table 7-4, one of which represents reports from only four hikers wearing running shoes. As for the Sears and Limmer footwear, although the total number covers only five and six users, a number too skimpy for any real confidence in the results, it is worth noting in view of the consistency of the reports.

It is not surprising that the made-to-order, hand-crafted Limmers receive high marks, but the favorable accounting for the mixture of Sears work and hiking shoes is a pleasant surprise. The last three categories in Table 7-4

TABLE 7-3.
HIKER SATISFACTION WITH VARIOUS BRANDS OF FOOTWEAR

MANUFACTURER	NO. OF PAIRS	HIKER SATISFACTION	BLISTERS	ANKLE TROUBLES
HI-TEC	32	81%	31%	13%
MERRELL	20	80%	40%	35%
FABIANO	14	57%	29%	14%
VASQUE	50	54%	26%	2%
RAICHLE	16	38%	37%	12%
ASOLO	14	36%	36%	14%
DANNER	11	36%	55%	18%

TABLE 7-4.
HIKER SATISFACTION WITH FOOTWEAR IN MISCELLANEOUS CATEGORIES

Category	No. of Pairs	Hiker Satisfaction	Blisters	Ankle Troubles
Limmer	6	83%	33%	0
Sears	5	80%	20%	0
Running shoes	4	100%	0	0
Lightweight	18	68%	6%	12%
Heavyweight	20	45%	10%	0

bear out earlier-noted trends that hiker satisfaction increases as weight decreases.

DURABILITY

As noted in Table 7-1, the durability of footwear on the AT varies widely and is a function of boot weight. Backpackers' results are scattered, but on a per-mile basis it costs about 7 cents for sneakers or running shoes and about 12 cents for medium-weight, fabric/leather models. Heavy, all-leather boots run about 9 cents per mile, although they may require new soles, the cost of which is not factored in. There are plenty of horror stories on the subject of boot life: Soles drop off, leather rots, and support melts away. However, compared to weight, fit, and comfort, durability is not an important factor in the boot-selection process. Furthermore, some manufacturers of boots, like the makers of packs, cringe at publicity of their equipment wearing out on its first trip, even if the trip is 2,000 miles long. Several hikers whose boots failed apparently due to poor manufacture reported that they were sent replacement boots free of charge in response to their collect call from the trail. However, this is not universal policy. The ATC keeps a thru-hiker's corner in its Harpers Ferry headquarters with notebooks and information for the grapevine. One of the notes in October 1993 read, "Fabiano *will not* accept collect calls about their boots."

How many miles you walk per day may have a small overall effect on how many miles you get out of your boots. Hikers averaging 13 miles per day or less get an average of 1,150 miles, while those averaging 16 miles can expect 15% fewer miles over the life of the boot, below 1,000 miles.

One durability factor not always outwardly apparent is the slow breaking down of the heel and arch support. For example, as I crossed Vermont near the end of my hike, I developed an excruciating case of shin splints—which I recognized from having experienced this trouble in earlier years when running. The shin splints were so severe that I took a week off at home. The orthopedist found nothing alarming, and the pain eased but did not go away entirely. Following a hunch, I shifted to a new pair of lightweight boots, identical to those I had been using for 900 miles. The shin splints disappeared within 24 hours. In retrospect, it seems that the breakdown of the internal boot structure was more pronounced than the outside signs of wear—and I needed that support. Similar experiences on the effects of weakening boot structure (leading to knee and foot tendinitis and shin splints) crop up from time to time in the reports of long-distance hikers.

CHANGE IN SHOE SIZE

Six months of pounding along the Appalachian crest brings about a long-term change to many a hiker's feet. Aside from temporary swelling, changes as great as an increase of two sizes have been reported, a case in point being Grandma Gatewood. Based on a sampling of the long-distance hikers, some 30 percent of the men finished the hike with feet averaging over half a size greater than at the start. Women suffered more: Some 80 percent reported an increase between a half and one full size. All of this offers another reminder that in the purchase of hiking footwear, a little too large is safer than a little too small.

SOCKS, SPARES, AND CAMP SLIPPERS

There is a standard sock protocol that calls for a thin, snug-fitting liner, usually polypropylene, Orlon, or nylon, and a thick wool outer sock. In theory, the rubbing all takes place between the two pairs of socks and not at the skin. About two-thirds of the long-distance hikers followed the protocol, although not without introducing their own styles, such as silk or cotton liners and Thor-Lo or Wigwam oversocks. And although three-quarters of the hikers wore two pairs of socks, 15 percent wore only one (usu-

Crossing the West Branch Discataquis River, Maine

ally wool), 7 percent wore three, and at least one hiker stated he wore four pairs of socks. One iconoclast wore running shoes and *no* socks.

Cotton socks are generally excoriated for hiking because cotton has no insulating value when wet and it dries slowly. Yet despite the dire warnings, about 10 percent of the long-distance hikers sneaked their toes into cotton socks each morning—and none reported the worse for the experience. Despite this flaunting of accepted practice, no one was casual about the importance of always having a spare dry pair of socks. Just a few of the hikers took only two or three pairs with them, 84 percent carried three to six pairs, and some 15 hikers did not feel safe without carrying seven to ten pairs of socks.

After a long day on the trail, it is a luxury to get out of hiking boots for the evening. About three-quarters of the hikers brought along footwear to act as "camp slippers." The favorites were sneakers, flip-flops, jogging or tennis shoes, and various types of sandals. At least one enterprising hiker wore plastic bags over socks when in camp.

WATERPROOFING

There is no element of comfort so dear to the hiker as dry feet, nor any goal more fruitlessly sought. In the summer and along the middle states you can start with dry feet, but if you are wearing carefully waterproofed boots and sweat from head to toe, at day's end your feet will be clammy, if not downright wet. Those same boots might keep you lovely and dry for a day or two of rain, but given a week of daily storms, overflowing brooks, deep mud, and damp nights in a shelter, they too will fail.

There are intrinsic differences between leather boots and footwear that is partly or all fabric. We can, without further ado, dismiss the "breathing fabric" phenomenon: Even if it worked perfectly when brand new, long before the first few hundred miles are over those microscopic little pores will be all clogged—plenty clogged to prevent real foot "breathing," but never so clogged as to prevent outside wetness from seeping in.

A good pair of all-leather boots will keep your feet warm and dry for a day or two even in mud, rain, and snow. If they have been carefully waterproofed not too long ago, this will help. If you get to a warm cabin or home by the second or third day, you will probably be happy with your waterproof boots. But if you are a long-distance hiker, and conditions stay bad, by the third or fourth day the boots will be as if you had just removed them from the bottom of a pond. And they will resist drying with the same stubbornness that they resisted getting wet. Of

course, if you are making and spending an evening by a fire in a cabin, or can make a hot fire outside your shelter, those boots can be dried—but only with painstaking care. The stories of hikers who had to limp out of the woods with melted, warped, twisted, and burned shoes are legend.

Reed and Jacqueline Benet tried both approaches and put the lesson down neatly: "Leather hiking boots: Got wet, stayed wet, got blisters. Canvas-top boots: Got wet, dried quick, no blisters."

Judy Gallant reported the worst-case scenario for heavy leather footwear: "The boots grew a fungus in them which magnified foot odor. Finally got rid of the odor in Andover after two applications of Lysol."

The first time I hiked in light fabric-and-leather boots, I had a somewhat shocking experience. The path that morning lay across a large dewy meadow, a traverse that in my leather boots would have been no different than a sidewalk stroll on a sunny day. But in those fabric boots my feet were soaking wet before I got to the other side of the meadow. And then came the surprise: After an hour of walking, lo and behold the boots were dry again. And even when spending a night in a damp shelter, by putting on dry socks in the morning it was just about as good as hiking in completely dry boots.

Manufacturers of all-leather boots recommend waterproofing treatments. How-to-backpack books echo this advice with statements such as "Devoutly follow the directions for the waterproofer you purchase." But Dan Bruce, one of the most experienced hikers to repeatedly traverse the AT, notes in *The Thru-Hiker's Planning Guide*: "As for waterproofing your boots, none of the popular products on the market will keep water out of your boots for long, but they will deter it." Experienced backpackers in my study echoed this state of affairs; some flatly commented that waterproofing was a "useless undertaking," or that "When it rains you still get wet." The survey reveals that hiker willingness to undertake this somewhat messy job is a function of the kind of boots they wear (Table 7-5).

I guess this shows that waterproofing is a "rite of leather," long followed and of at least some value in leather

TABLE 7-5.
WATERPROOFING BOOTS

TYPE OF FOOTWEAR	PERCENTAGE WATERPROOFING THEIR BOOTS
RUNNING SHOES, ETC.	0
LIGHTWEIGHT	22%
MEDIUM-WEIGHT	64%
HEAVYWEIGHT	95%

boots for some circumstances. On the other hand, water-proofing appears to be virtually useless for boots containing fabric. In the words of one hiker, "You get wet anyway."

GAITERS

This hiking accouterment, used primarily by mountain climbers, skiers, and hikers in very cold or wet weather, is usually a waterproof fabric overshoe that covers the boot or ankle and extends partially up the leg. Its most obvious function is to keep rain, dirt, and particularly snow from running down between boot and sock, keeping legs and feet drier and warmer. Gaiters are a must for truly extreme conditions, such as northern winter mountain climbing. They also provide additional protection against poison ivy, ticks, snakes, and underbrush.

Among the long-distance backpackers surveyed, only half wore gaiters. Of these, one might expect that those wearing running shoes or lightweight boots would be most likely to opt for the additional protection of gaiters; however, Table 7-6 shows that those choosing gaiters are pursuing a more conservative course, seeking the most complete foot and leg protection possible. Half of those

TABLE 7-6.
GAITERS AND FOOTWEAR

Type of Footwear	Percent Wearing Gaiters (including part-time wear)
Running shoes, sneakers, lightweight boots	32%
Medium-weight boots	50%
Heavyweight boots	58%

who report using gaiters do so only part of the time. They wear them initially, when it snows, when there is poison ivy, or simply "on and off." As John Swanson put it, "Gaiters . . . great for briars and nettles, but I found my boots got wet anyway, so I stopped wearing them."

Thus, gaiters turn out to be one more reflection of hiker personality and individuality. If you want that extra bit of protection, they certainly will help. But it means increasing your load by about half a pound, and when they are on your feet it is like having three extra pounds in your pack.

At a shelter in Virginia

PACKS, TENTS, STOVES, AND GUIDES

As with footwear, long-distance hiking is not only an extended test of backpacker endurance, but in many cases a durability test for equipment. Unfortunately, not all items of gear and equipment survive the trip or provide satisfactory service. As the miles and months pass by, some tents prove to be unendurably small and others too heavy. Straps on packs break once, twice, and three times. Stoves blow up. Snakebite kits, compasses, and underwear get sent home. A

*P*robably no area of thru-hiking planning is more misunderstood by the long-distance hiker novice than the gear requirements for the hike.

—Christopher Whalen,
The Appalachian Trail Workbook for Planning Thru-Hikes

trusted guidebook recommends closed hostels and relocated trails. Items are discarded and replaced; new things are bought, not always because the old ones "failed," but because the older items were unsatisfactory in a subtle but important area.

Within the last several years, a number of excellent planning books for long-distance AT hiking have been issued, covering a wide range of important subjects from whether to wear a wristwatch to tips on obtaining a hiking partner. One of the best is *The Thru-Hiker's Planning Guide* by Dan "Wing-foot" Bruce. For equipment selection, the most up-to-date and thorough survey of major items such as footwear, tents, sleeping bags, stoves, and packs is *Backpacker* magazine's annual *Buyer's Guide,* listing well over a thousand items. But although the advice in books and magazines comes from experienced backpackers, it is still based largely on the backpacking experience of one person or a handful of people.

The equipment coverage that follows here is limited and based primarily on the evaluations of the 136 experienced hikers included in the survey. If there is one lesson that comes out clearly, it is the great divergence of opinion, at least in some areas. Consider hiking in the rain: Some hikers claimed they "loved it," most simply got wet, and a fair number found it the worst single thing they had to put up with. Although my opinions are freely included, they are labeled and sometimes (as in the case of internal- versus external-frame packs) clearly not in line with others in the survey. But, despite the varied opinions of this highly individualistic group, there was also sometimes a strong consensus. As to cooking methods, for example: Although one hiker cooked over alcohol poured on a plate, almost half of the hikers bought their stoves from the same manufacturer, and almost no one ever built a fire for cooking. Hence, the equipment selections and evaluations reported here provide a broad consensus, but leave it to the reader to suit him or her self on the basis of the arguments presented.

PACKS

There are only two equipment items absolutely essential for long-distance backpacking. The first is adequate footwear: Even the world-acclaimed Nepal sherpas and porters wear something on their feet when the going gets tough. The second item is a pack. It is true that John Muir carried his goods in a sack, and Grandma Gatewood also initially carried things in a canvas sack, but no one recently has been so inclined. George Miller, the extraordinary 72-year-old who thru-hiked the AT in 1952, designed, built, and carried his own "balanced" pack made up of two cylinders, one on his back and one across his chest. (No one, to my knowledge, ever copied Miller's dual-pack idea.) The backpackers in this survey mostly carried a considerable load, about 45 pounds—and all on the back. There were two exceptions where close vehicle support let the hikers carry just a light daypack. In one case a faithful spouse provided daily support; the other was a member of one of Warren Doyle's group hikes. But most of us are not so fortunate to have Warren Doyle to plan our trip or a spouse standing by.

The problem of selecting the most suitable pack is certainly not due to a lack of choice. The equipment buyer is literally overwhelmed. The clerk may or may not have ever put on a pack, and selection may be only a trifle less arbitrary than buying a lottery ticket. The sheer volume of products available is daunting. The 1994 *Backpacker* magazine *Buyer's Guide* lists a total of 414 packs offered by 49 manufacturers. How is anyone going to pick out his "best"

match from 12 pages of detailed pack specifications? One could try by selecting a suitable name: Astronomers might be intrigued by REI's "Evening Star" or Lowe's "Total Eclipse"; those with a physics background could opt for Quest's "Big Bang." Good picks for psychologists would be Natural Balance Design's "Essential Rapport" or "Vital Experience." Mexican food enthusiasts can buy Mountain Tool's "Enchilada Grande," and a macho type might like McHale's "INVEX Bayonet." But, best of all, for top corporate executives, Gregory's "Chairman of the Board" would seem to be a must.

A better way to select a pack is by brand, making a careful scrutiny of the manufacturer's product line. Although specific designs vary year by year, the tradition, quality, price range, and general characteristics of packs change slowly. Like automobiles or designer clothes, certain brands appeal to certain people.

The 136 long-distance hikers in the survey used a total of 162 packs manufactured by 25 companies, ranging from 8 to 36 packs per company. However, most of the packs came from only seven sources; these are listed in Table 8-1 in the order of the hiker's "satisfaction" evaluations—that is, how many hikers answered "Yes" to the question "Were you satisfied with your pack?" The adjacent column rates "praise," the percent of hikers who went out of their way to comment favorably about their choice. The next column gives the rate of repair or replacement for each brand. (Note that this is an inverse rating: The lower the percentage, the less trouble.) The last column itemizes the numbers of internal- and external-frame designs evaluated.

As might be expected, hiker praise decreases along with the general satisfaction rating, and the repair/replace index goes up as the satisfaction rating goes down. It should be noted, however, that the four companies with the highest ratings sold primarily *internal*-frame packs, while the bottom four represent mainly *external*-frame packs; thus, these brand ratings may be heavily influenced by the greater popularity of internal-frame packs. In addition, the top four companies' packs were represented in fewer number and their packs were significantly more expensive than those of the four companies represented on the bottom half of the table.

For those unfamiliar with packs, it should be noted that the two major types are very dissimilar. Chris Townsend explains the differences in his book *The Backpacker's Handbook*. Classically, the backpack was simply a sack or basket carried or tied to a rigid heavy wood frame with straps over the shoulders. These packs served Indi-

TABLE 8-1.

HIKERS' SATISFACTION WITH VARIOUS BRANDS OF PACKS

Manufacturer	Satisfaction	Praise	Repair/Replace	Number Evaluated
Gregory	100%	33%	7%	15 internal frame
North Face	92%	23%	23%	8 internal, 5 external
Lowe	83%	40%	7%	14 internal, 1 external
Mountain Smith*	81%	25%	13%	8 internal
Kelty	68%	14%	31%	3 internal, 33 external
Camptrails	63%	22%	26%	5 internal, 18 external
Jansport	47%	0%	47%	15 external
All others	57%	7%	24%	12 internal, 17 external
Average	**66%**	**17%**	**23%**	**Total 65 internal, 89 external**

*The total number of Mountain Smith packs evaluated falls below the arbitrary minimum of 10 usually observed in this book as a cutoff for generalizations, so the ratings here should be regarded as less indicative.

ans, guides, soldiers, and trappers well, but all the weight fell squarely on the shoulders and back. Then, about 40 years ago in a brilliant innovation, Kelty combined a modern, curved aluminum frame with a strong, wide hip belt into what is usually called an *external* frame pack. Depending on adjustments, most of the weight could now be carried directly on the hips.

However, the new pack's external frame, by design, hung away from the body, only loosely connected at the shoulders. Technical climbers could not tolerate the loosely connected frame. So, in the late 1960s, a pack was developed with a somewhat flexible *internal* frame, permitting the pack to be tightly bound to the climber.

Gregory packs came through with an admirable rating: Each of the 15 purchasers was satisfied, and a third added specific words of praise. Repair frequency was low, with only one case of restitching required. The next three brands—North Face, Lowe, and Mountain Smith—also had high approval and praise ratings, though higher repair and replacement. By way of contrast, of the 15 persons reporting on their Jansport packs, fewer than half were satisfied, none praised them, and almost half of the packs needed repair or replacement.

It is much to their credit that pack manufacturers universally will quickly replace worn-out parts such as straps, or even broken frames, on the basis of a telephone call from the thru-hiker. Several hikers have noted that they obtained repairs and replacements for packs more than 10 years old. In only two cases, Recreational Equipment, Inc.

(REI) and Wildness, did hikers report a hassle over getting such service. However, it is clear that many packs are not designed for the wear and tear of 2,000 miles of trail. There were 51 reported cases of repair/replacement, amounting to about 40 percent of all the packs carried. External-frame packs had a higher failure rate (47 percent) than internal-frame packs (34 percent).

Following the conventional wisdom, guidelines for selection would appear to somewhat favor external-frame packs for the long-distance AT: They are better for heavy loads, hot weather, general convenience, and where more extreme conditions such as steep grades, technical climbing, or winter weather are not expected. Thus, in their initial purchase, 58 percent of the survey respondents chose external-frame packs, and only 42 percent were carrying internal-frame packs. Despite the statistics, however, in the long run there is a trend toward internal-frame packs. There appear to be several factors at work. Age makes a difference: Hikers carrying internal-frame packs averaged six years younger than those carrying external-frame packs. Or, hikers may be influenced by what *Backpacker* magazine authors Getchell and Howe refer to as the internal-frame's "mountain jock" image. At any rate, the cost of the internal-frame packs, item by item, averages almost twice that of external-frames.

As in buying footwear, purchasing a suitable pack means choosing among literally hundreds of brands and models available. Also, in both cases the purchaser must initially make one major decision. In footwear, it is how heavy the shoe. In packs, it is internal versus external frame. Consulting knowledgeable friends, clerks, magazines, and books can be very misleading, for, as the survey shows, individual opinions vary widely.

Cost is a consideration. Whereas both internal- and external-frame packs can be purchased for less than $100, external-frame packs generally run about $150 to $200. Internal-frame packs are sometimes available for less than $200, but usually cost over $300 (1996 prices). My son Kim, a psychologist, notes that in understanding opinions about packs, the concept of cognitive dissonance may be a factor (see Chapter 17); that is, because hikers paid twice as much for their internal-frame packs, their evaluation is influenced by a need to justify the expenditure.

General satisfaction was significantly higher among those carrying internal-frame packs (80 percent) than among those carrying external-frame packs (51 percent). In 21 cases, packs broke down completely or were discarded because of extreme discomfort. Three hikers changed packs three times. Seven hikers replaced external-frame packs with internal-frame packs; in only one case did a hiker shift in the other direction.

Enthusiastic comments and praise were almost three times as frequent for internal-frames as external-frames, 27 versus 10 percent. The more favorable experiences with internal-frames was not due to the fact that such packs were more lightly loaded; the difference in reported mid-trail pack weights (halfway between replenishment stops) was not significant.

The appeal of the internal-frame pack cannot be denied, but is not entirely obvious. When hikers were questioned as to why they preferred the internal-frames, the word "comfort" was the most common answer. Particularly, it was their feeling about the pack when the going got rough. Having the pack act as part of your body, instead of a wobbly, carefully balanced load, seems to be extremely appealing. The choice appears to be in the huggy-teddy-bear category and is not very quantifiable. Thus, if you find an internal-frame pack that has a user-friendly feel about it, and you can afford to buy it, do so. You are more likely to be happy with your acquisition than cold logic might predict. And in the 1990s, an ever-increasing number of hikers are carrying internal-frame packs.

By 1997 backpack designers had developed some highly sophisticated models of internal-frame packs, some of them custom fitted, and there appears to be a market for such packs. They are highly praised for their comfort but are expensive, costing $500 and up.

TABLE 8-2.

AVERAGE WEIGHT OF PACK (AFTER THE FIRST MONTH; INCLUDES ALL GEAR)

	MEN	WOMEN
BEFORE PROVISIONING	35 LBS	34 LBS
AFTER PROVISIONING	47 LBS	45 LBS
LIGHTEST PACK	20 LBS	30 LBS
HEAVIEST PACK	75 LBS	65 LBS
PERCENT OF BODY WEIGHT (WITH HALF OF THE PROVISIONS CONSUMED)	25%	28%

How Heavy the Pack?

Few areas reflect the diversity of backpackers so much as the amount of weight they choose to carry. Since the long-distance hikers in this sample were mostly experienced, we do not have the tale, so often retold, of grossly overloaded starters shedding tens of pounds of equipment over the initial days of their trip. Nevertheless, even these experienced men and women did lighten up some in the first month. On average, after they had settled into a hiking routine, they had reduced their pack load about 6 pounds.

The usual procedure is to stop and go into town for provisions about once a week. Hikers may leave town a few ounces lighter from washed-off dirt, but they are carrying about 12 pounds of new provisions to get them to the next stop. They have probably also put on a pound or two from feasting on ice cream, pizza, and beer. The pack weights for the long-distance hikers in this survey are listed on Table 8-2.

Despite the fact that they usually weigh less, women carry almost the same weight as men. This results in a slightly greater load measured as the percentage of body weight. Two-thirds of the long-distance hikers carried packs that weighed between 20 and 30 percent of body weight, roughly between 40 and 60 pounds. This goes along with the results of tests carried out almost 100 years ago in Germany before World War I, which determined that German infantry troops on marches of 12 to 45 miles should not carry loads heavier than 44 pounds.

Tents

For the Appalachian Trail thru-hiker, the tent plays a very different role than in backpacking elsewhere. This is due to the existence of over 250 shelters spaced strategically along the AT. The hikers in this survey slept in shelters 70 percent of the nights while on the trail.

Compared to a shelter, a tent can be more comfortable: It can be staked out in grass, leaves, or pine needles. It is warmer on cold nights, protects against insects and wandering skunks, and provides privacy. Best of all, when it isn't practical to reach a shelter, or upon finding one filled to overflowing, it provides an alternative. If necessary, you can set it up right on the trail.

But putting a tent up and taking it down takes time. It is impossible to cook—or even to sit up—in some tents. And packing a soaked tent is a pain. Even the strongest hiker deliberated the weight penalty of a big, comfortable dome tent with room for cooking. Most thru-hikers wanted a simple, small, two-person tent. With few exceptions they were satisfied with their choice. The most common complaint (9 percent of the responses) was that the tent was too heavy. Tent weights ranged from 1.7 to 8 pounds, the average being 4 pounds. Tina and Gregory Seay carried an 8-pound North Face Mountaineer, but it was their "honeymoon suite."

Weight appears to be the primary consideration for going without any tent at all. About one in five hikers omitted tents, with 10 percent relying on a tarp, 3 percent using a plastic tube or bivy sack, and 7 percent firmly venturing forth with none. This latter group obviously relied on getting to one of the 250 shelters, a hostel, pavilion, barn, B&B, motel, or sleeping with a friend. (Sleeping arrangements are discussed further in the next chapter.) But along with Grandma Gatewood, who initially curled up under a plastic shower curtain at night, these hikers report an occasional unpleasant night in the rain.

Most hikers were happy with their tent (or no tent) selection. Many preferred the tent with its privacy and coziness. But no one enjoyed having to pack a wet, heavy tent. Warmth was not a significant consideration in using a tent, but the protection against insects was. And, while you might think long-distance hikers purposely traveling without a tent would be especially sensitive to pack weight, that was not the case. These hikers apparently made up the saved 4 pounds in other items, because their packs weighed the same as those with tents.

A number of hikers brought one-person tents, which weigh a pound or so less than the lightest two-person tents. However, for any purpose beyond slithering into and sleeping, they are too cramped and confining. Eight hikers (7 percent) complained that they were too small. Personally, I was delighted with the 3½-pound Sierra Design Clip Flashlight tent. But, eager to save a pound, I exchanged it for a North Face Mayfly. My first night in the new tent, I found getting in and out was difficult, and somehow all the wetness of rain, dew, and condensation scraped off on me on the way out. But that was nothing compared to the second night: A rainstorm broke late that day, and I erected the Mayfly just in time. Covering my pack quickly with its waterproof cover, I squeezed into the tent as the torrent descended. I was warm and dry. But the rain continued steadily. As it grew dark I realized that even if I grabbed some cold supper and retreated to the tent without getting thoroughly soaked, I could not eat—there was not enough headroom to crouch or sit up, much less eat and drink. So I unhappily hunkered down to a night without dinner. I transferred back to my Clip Flashlight the next week.

Aside from being too heavy or too small, there were few serious faults reported with the tents. Only three leaked, one lost grommets, and one broke, out of a total of 109; there were only a few cases of complete failure and replacement. Most changes were due to tent weight and size. Compared to boots and packs, where up to half of the equipment was unsatisfactory, hiker satisfaction with tents was distinctly high. The satisfaction ratio (those who specifically stated they were satisfied) averaged 70 percent and varied only a few percent from brand to brand. Furthermore, in contrast to boots and packs where product approval varied widely with brand, there was little difference in how happy the hikers were with various tent brands.

Compared with about 250 different backpacking tents listed in *Backpacker* magazine's *Buyer's Guide* (1993), only

TABLE 8-3.
TENTS AND ALTERNATIVE SHELTER CARRIED BY THRU-HIKERS

MANUFACTURER	NUMBER	PERCENT OF TOTAL
TENTS		
SIERRA DESIGNS	39	29%
NORTH FACE	29	21%
EUREKA	16	12%
ALL OTHERS (16 BRANDS)	25	18%
TOTAL	**109**	**80%**
NON-TENTS		
TARPS	13	10%
TUBES, BIVY SACKS, ETC.	4	3%
"NONE"	9	7%
TOTAL	**26**	**20%**

44 different tents made by 19 manufacturers were used by the 136 hikers surveyed in 1989. As shown in Table 8-3, 62 percent of all tents used were made by Sierra Designs, North Face, or Eureka.

Sierra Designs' Clip Flashlight, a "tight fit for two men," was far and away the most common tent carried on the trail; it was used by 32 of the long-distance hikers. The Clip Flashlight also received high praise from many of its occupants; for example; "absolutely outstanding," "the only tent to have," and "the choice for long-distance hikers." Sierra Designs' heavier Meteor Lite was also lauded.

North Face tents were of a bewildering variety, with eight models represented on the trail from among the 29 available. The North Face Tad Pole was rated by one couple as "best out there," but the smaller Mayfly was too tight for some (including me).

Eureka was the third most popular brand (16 tents), with at least a dozen different models. Eureka owners complained somewhat more than the other groups about their tent leaking or its being too heavy.

The final advice on buying a tent for long-distance hikers would seem to be that the specific brand is not very important—nor was waterproofness or durability much mentioned by the hikers in the sample. The tent one buys should not be too small (which rules out most one-person tents) nor too heavy (with 4 pounds about the limit). All this would seem to be a green light in most cases to buy on sale, when marked down, or possibly secondhand. Save your dollars and spend them where they buy quality, as in packs.

STOVES

Although fairly small Primus cooking stoves were carried into the Arctic and Antarctic more than a century ago, common use of small stoves on the AT dates back only about 25 years. Pioneers like Dorothy Laker made their own cooking fires for every hot meal, cup of coffee, and bowl of soup. But it takes time to make a fire, effort to scrounge the forest for dry wood, and consummate skill and patience if the wilderness is really soaked. These days, long-distance hikers will make a fire to sit around and visit, but cooking over a wood fire seems primarily to be undertaken by those out for a few days of good eating and modest hiking.

In the survey, out of 126 responses to queries on stoves, only four hikers said they were carrying none. And in all but one or two cases, the person was traveling with close companions and might expect to share use. So, although not as vital as boots, pack, or sleeping bag, the stove comes close to being considered a necessity. Hikers are hungry much of the day, and the prospect of a hot evening meal has spurred on many a weary backpacker.

The stoves being carried on the AT came mainly from three manufacturers: Mountain Safety Research (MSR), The Coleman Company (Peak 1), and Optimus (SVEA). Table 8-4 summarizes what hikers took with them.

As for the satisfaction rating for stoves, those who answered "Yes" to the question "Were you satisfied with your stove?" reveal a pattern similar to tents and different from that for boots and packs. The satisfaction rating for stoves was high and varied little among different brands. The total range for stoves was only from 77 to 83 percent; this compares with 36 to 81 percent for footwear and 47 to 100 percent for packs.

The MSR Whisperlite was by far the most popular stove among the long-distance hikers. This stove was the first model to incorporate the aluminum fuel bottle as an integral part of the operating stove. A special hose connected the bottle and stove, thus saving the weight and trouble of two fuel containers in the pack; by the early 1990s most stove manufacturers had come out with a similar arrangement. The Whisperlite weighed less than a pound, cost under $50, and ran quietly (many of the other early stoves sounded like a blowtorch). It was reliable enough for most users to put up with its one major shortcoming, a tendency to clog and the resulting requirement of skill and knowledge for maintenance. Several hikers had to give up on their old Whisperlites and simply bought replacements when they could not fix their old stoves. Most mastered the secrets of cleaning, even though this required special tools, knowhow, occasional parts, and sometimes an expert friend. Because of this clogging problem, Whis-

TABLE 8-4.
STOVES

MANUFACTURER	NUMBER	PERCENT OF TOTAL	FAILURE RATE
MOUNTAIN SAFETY RESEARCH	59	47%	15%
COLEMAN PEAK 1	26	21%	8%
OPTIMUS/SVEA SUUNTO	19	15%	5%
VARIOUS BUTANE/ PROPANE	12	9%	17%
VARIOUS ALCOHOL	6	5%	0
NONE	4	3%	—

perlites racked up a 15 percent "fault rate." Whisperlites also completely defied simmering—they either ran at full blast or faded out. Whereas 47 hikers carried MSR Whisperlites, a handful chose the more expensive MSR "International" or XG6 models; these were also highly rated but received comments such as "frequent cleaning problems" and "short life." Early in 1994 MSR announced that its new International 600 model incorporated a weighted needle that made unclogging possible by simply shaking the stove. In general, MSR stoves of one kind or another were carried by about half the AT long-distance hikers.

The second most popular stoves (about 21 percent) were the Coleman Peak 1 and the more expensive Peak 1 Multifuel. They weighed about 1½ pounds (not including the necessary fuel bottle) and cost in the range of $65 to $80. A few cases of "temperamental behavior" were reported, but most users were pleased and some noted with satisfaction the stoves' excellent simmering capabilities. Peak 1 owners reported an 8 percent fault rate. When my Peak 1 failed after several years of use, Coleman replaced it with a new one without charge.

The third most popular stove brand was the historic Optimus and SVEA family (now Suunto), which accounted for 15 percent of all the stoves carried. Most of these were the venerable SVEA 123, a tiny rugged brass stove weighing only a little over a pound (not counting fuel bottle). It has a strong reputation for reliability, and hikers reported carrying models 30 years old. The SVEAs stem from the original Swedish Primus, which is even older. My friend George Schindler says his still works. I myself own several operating Optimus models; the oldest was purchased in Sweden in the 1950s. Hikers become very attached to their SVEAs despite the stove's not being able to simmer and its high noise output—always seemingly a contradiction in the peace and quiet of the deep woods. Users reported a low 5 percent fault rate.

As with most equipment, long-distance hikers displayed rather individualistic preferences in stoves. About 10 percent carried a variety of butane/propane stoves, such as Bleuet, GAZ, and Hank Roberts propane. Users liked the ease of stove operation but found it difficult to purchase the special fuels on the trail. The fuel containers for such stoves present a solid waste problem, and many long-distance hikers object to them for ecological reasons. Their fault rate was also rather high, at 17 percent. A final handful relied on the classic camper's fuel, alcohol. Several carried the Trangia stove, although they found it rather bulky. One hiker relied on Sterno, and one rugged individualist burned alcohol in a plate. Alcohol is clean and handy but

packs only about half the heating power of gas and is not easy to purchase along the trail.

In the 1990s an ecologically attractive idea hit the backpacker's market: a small, lightweight stove suitable for tiny twigs and bits of wood. The secret lay in a battery-powered fan which made possible a hot, pot-sized fire. It worked, but never really caught on. The overwhelming problem was that it required a continuous feeding of wood chips to keep going. Turn your back for more than a minute, and what had been a roaring little inferno was hardly an ember among the ashes. The stove's unquenchable appetite was its undoing. In addition, there was the need for a charged battery and dry, carefully selected fuel. Regrettably, there were few backpackers willing to fuss with the hungry little monster, and there went a good idea.

Stoves are still evolving in the 1990s as weight is pared down, simmering capability improved, and multifuel use introduced. Cloggability reduction is another thing. It certainly is not promising when the oldest stoves on the trail, such as the SVEA 123, have the *lowest* record of clogging. And don't be misled by easy-sounding recommendations on the use of a repair kit, cleaning needle, extra burner jet, and preheat-tube assembly. Repair instructions may be easy to follow given tools, know-how, and a warm, well-lighted room. However, not a few hikers have been reduced to tears trying to coax a stove into working in cold, wet, and dark conditions. Your best bet on a long trip is to have a true expert (meaning he or she has lived with and relied on a stove for months) *show* you what to do when things go wrong.

Except for troubles with clogging, most stoves will faithfully provide hot meals at modest cost in time, weight, and dollars. Hot food can be a tremendous morale booster—which is why 98 percent of the long-distance hikers carry stoves.

AT TRAIL GUIDES

One of the most marvelous features of the AT is that the only absolutely essential element to finding the way is the white blazes. There are thru-hikers who have traveled its full length without consulting a map, reading a trail description, using a compass, or knowing in advance what is around the next turn. Although even today, due to trail relocations, the blazing may occasionally seem capricious, the average thru-hiker rarely gets lost, and then not for long. Thousands of volunteers from the 21 supporting clubs clear away the brush, build water bars (to divert water flow off the path), erect bridges, and paint those wonderful blazes.

The trail in New Jersey

TABLE 8-5.
USEFULNESS OF GUIDES AND REFERENCES

INFORMATION SOURCE	HIKER RATING	USES	NUMBER OF RESPONSES
APPALACHIAN TRAIL DATA BOOK	8.0	LOCATING ROADS, FOOD, SHELTERS, LODGING, CAMPS, AND HIGHLIGHTS	77
PHILOSOPHER'S GUIDE (THRU-HIKER'S HANDBOOK)	7.3	IN-TOWN PLANNING, PERSONAL INFORMATION, FOOD AND LODGING	80
TRAIL GUIDES, STATE-BY-STATE	6.8	DESCRIPTIONS AND DETAILS OF THE TRAIL, FINDING WATER	53
TRAIL GUIDE MAPS, TOPO AND PROFILE	6.2	KNOWING JUST WHERE YOU ARE	69

Almost as useful as the blazes is a hiker coming from the opposite direction. And if he or she has come a long distance, the information is likely to be reliable because the judgment is seasoned. Trail contacts are also more up-to-date than any other information source. This is important, for the trail conditions are dynamic: A storm creates blowdowns, beaver dams cause flooding, or a driving late-spring snow may obliterate all evidence of the trail.

Another unofficial but helpful source of information is the trail register. Almost every shelter has a copy, and it contains all the latest news of trail and hikers, sometimes in a display of real artistic or literary talent.

Local inhabitants rarely can provide accurate information. On several occasions when I halted on my journey up the AT and talked with local fishermen or hunters, they did not know they were on the AT—nor did they know which way was Georgia and which way Maine. Local inhabitants seldom wander more than a few hundred yards off the roads, and the primary advice they offer is to beware of snakes. Although some homeowners can redirect the lost wanderer to the trail, many have no idea what you are asking about.

Although you can hike the AT without any references or guides, for most people it is more fun, satisfying, and comfortable to be able to plan the trip. The three big requirements are food, water, and shelter. You can carry your own shelter, but there are some stretches where for miles there is not a flat spot to erect a tent. You must find water, because it is heavy work carrying it—and becoming dehydrated is no joke. And it takes at least 2 pounds of food per day to fuel the pack animal, so no one plans to go more than 10 days before taking on fresh victuals. Thus, knowing where there is a spring, a campsite, a grocery or post office, and how large the mountain you must climb to get there, reduces uncertainty and increases enjoyment.

Every one of the 136 hikers in the survey seems to have taken at least one kind of reference material; most took two or three. Table 8-5 summarizes the four most common references used by long-distance hikers, in order by rating. They are all available from the Appalachian Trail Conference at stores near the AT from Georgia to Maine.

Approximate cost for non-members of the Appalachian Trail Club is $4 for the *Appalachian Trail Data Book,* $9 for *The Thru-Hiker's Handbook* (which replaces the *Philosopher's Guide),* and about $136 for all 10 trail guides with maps. Late in the year the ATC sometimes offers "The Famous Guidebook Special," when members can get books and trail guides all for about $110.

THE DATA BOOK

The Appalachian Trail Data Book, rated 8.0, is updated and reissued each year. It is the indispensable source of information on the trail, linking distances and important destinations (including campsites, shelters, groceries, lodgings, restaurants, water information, significant sights, and the like) in a very compact and efficient format. Most importantly, it covers not only road intersections, but how far down the road one must travel for service. Important landmarks, mountains, gaps, lakes, and geographical features are also noted. Its compactness (it weighs 4 ounces) and form permit easy reference use. Over two-thirds of the hikers carried the *Data Book,* and the rest all seemed to ask for information from those who were carrying a copy!

THE PHILOSOPHER'S GUIDE/NOW ISSUED AS THE THRU-HIKER'S HANDBOOK

The *Philosopher's Guide* filled a gap left by the *Data Book.* Rated almost as highly as the *Data Book,* it contained personal information about services, conditions, and people. First prepared as information notes in 1981 by Darrell Maret, it was expanded and rewritten yearly. In the words of the author, it was "a guide with the 'inside' scoop on what the AT is really like and with helpful hints and advice on how best to succeed." Maret held that his guide was "the only ATC publication to admit that it really does rain on the AT." He withdrew from the project after 1990, and in 1993 a similar guide series was started by Dan Bruce, a 25,000-mile veteran of the AT. *The Thru-Hiker's Handbook* is now issued yearly.

APPALACHIAN TRAIL GUIDE BOOKS

Ten official trail guides are issued by the Appalachian Trail Conference, providing maps and detailed trail information from Maine to Georgia. Reissued periodically by local clubs, they provide background on each section of the trail, general hiking information, history, and an almost painfully meticulous description of the trail itself.

Many hikers find the trail guides to be too detailed and seemingly more appropriate for weekenders picking their way over a few miles to the top of the nearest mountain. One of the problems with the detailed information is that forest landmarks, like "jumbled rocks," "narrow footpath," and "old woods road" are often difficult to recognize and can become obscured in the intervals between guide publications. However, hikers do appreciate the extraordinary detail when it comes to locating water. Guides were rated 6.8 in the survey and were carried by 40 percent of the hikers. Actually, many hikers did not carry the whole guidebook but cut out or copied that portion of the trail they were on. This saved only about half a pound but is indicative of the care taken by many to minimize pack weight.

TRAIL GUIDE MAPS

Each of the 10 trail guides is accompanied by a series of trail maps, printed separately and carried by hikers more frequently than the books themselves. The trail maps are invaluable if you need to know where you are with reference to the outside world. They greatly facilitate reentering civilization after immersion in the wilderness, and vice versa. They are mostly, but not always, accurate. Relocation of the trail away from encroaching roads and private property (more on this in Chapter 17) is the primary cause of confusion. A unique feature of the maps is a parallel "Trail Profile Map" which plots the vertical scale versus mileage. This has been a brilliant innovation, since the trail difficulty is not obvious from a regular topographical map. Trail difficulty is heavily dependent on steepness, notches, gaps, water crossings, and flatness. When planning for the next day's hike, backpackers focus mostly on the profile map.

Because the profile maps are drawn by translation from regular topographic maps, a relatively small change or error in the perceived trail location can result in wholesale changes in the profile. I carried an altimeter, which I carefully calibrated. Knowing my altitude sometimes permitted picking out my exact location, but occasionally it also left me hundreds of feet in the sky, or underground, on the profile. The rating given by users (6.2) was a little lower than that given the other guides, possibly due to these problems. But two-thirds of the hikers used the maps, and most would not consider leaving the shelter without them.

Sunrise over Lower Jo-Mary Lake, Maine

SLEEPING ON THE TRAIL

Besides its being the longest continuous trail and along a wonderfully interesting route, the Appalachian Trail's most distinguishing feature is its extensive system of shelters. Approximately 250 such shelters are nestled along the trailway on ridges, mountaintops, overlooking meadows and lakes, and buried deeply in the forest. They provide warmth and cover. They are the social centers, the communication crossroads, and protection from what sometimes seems interminable rain and wetness. A few still have dirt floors, leaking roofs, or teenage beer parties; but a massive building and relocation effort in recent years has resulted in a succession of clean, dry, well-located shelters. Most long-distance hikers spend their nights in these shelters (Table 9-1).

Since more than half the nights are spent in shelters,

> *The silence that is the starry sky.*
>
> *The sleep that is among the lonely hills.*
>
> —William Wordsworth

the life there—from dusk to dawn—could quickly fill a sociologist's notebook. Physically, the shelters vary a great deal, with uncrowded space for as few as four or as many as 25; typically they fit from eight to twelve people. Some have two bunk levels, a few have double bed–size bunks. Most shelters are open on one side with board floors and wood bunks. They are usually "broom clean."

Occupation of shelters is on a first-come, first-served basis. If you really want to stay at a shelter, you may have to arrive by mid-afternoon—particularly early in your trip when the crowds are greatest. But sometimes you happen upon an empty shelter. On my trip I spent over 20 nights alone in shelters. And most hikers are extraordinarily generous, particularly if it's raining; they will make room if it is humanly possible. Occasionally someone brings selfish manners along, but most space problems are resolved with good humor. Latecomers expect that they may have to set up tents. People eat and sleep on their own schedules, cooking food singly or in pairs. Conversation is quiet and usually is centered around the fire.

TABLE 9-1.
WHERE DID THEY SLEEP?

ON THE TRAIL	PERCENT OF TOTAL DAYS OF THE TRIP
SHELTERS	56%
TENTS	20%
TARPS	2%
IN THE OPEN	3%

OFF THE TRAIL	PERCENT OF TOTAL DAYS OF THE TRIP
HOSTELS	8%
MOTELS/HOTELS/B&BS	6%
WITH FRIENDS	3%
AT HOME	2%

Thru-hikers go quietly to sleep by dark; you may be surprised at how many are already asleep when you turn in.

When it is raining, dinner can be cooked under the shelter's ample overhang, and usually the stormier the night, the cozier the shelter seems. In contrast, nothing can match the task of setting up a tent in heavy rain and trying to keep the vital contents of the pack dry. Few backpack tents are large enough to cook in (or have suitable vestibules), and some are so small that you cannot even sit up to have a cold supper. Tent dwellers in the morning have the prospect of packing and carrying wet gear. At best the tent is perfection and privacy, the comfort of soft grass, leaves, or pine needles. But even under ideal conditions, locating a spot, grooming it, and erecting and packing the tent take an extra half hour out of the busy day.

A few hardy souls carry tarps and tubes (3 percent of the nights), and about 2 percent spend their nights under the stars. But this leaves one open to the experience of being awakened in the wee hours as the first ominous drops splash on the sleeper's face.

On a few parts of the trail, particularly in New England, closed cabins replace the three-sided shelters, providing protection from the weather. The longest stretch is the series of AMC "huts" in the White Mountains. These are not crude sleeping shelters, but rather are staffed accommodations geared especially for families, the inexperienced, and the short-trip hiker. Reservations are necessary; a night's stay including dinner and breakfast can cost as much as $60. The thru-hiker can be a misfit in this environment. The problem is discussed from the thru-hiker's standpoint in Chapter 17.

On average, hikers spend one night out of seven in town, when they shop for food, visit the post office, and get themselves and their clothes clean. Most often (8 percent of total nights, and almost half of all nights not on the trail) they will stay at one of about two dozen hostels on the trail, many of which charge nothing; others ask only a modest contribution or fee, usually in the range of a few dollars. The hostels most often mentioned were Graymoor Monastery in New York, Shaw's Boarding Home in Maine, Rusty's Hard Times Hollow in Virginia, The Inn at Hot Springs in North Carolina, and Tillie's Woods Hole in Massachusetts. Some, like Shaw's, Rusty's, and The Inn, are filled with loving, caring people who make the in-town stop as memorable as the AT itself. Others, like The Place and Doyle's Hotel in Pennsylvania, are more like having a shelter stop in town where hikers congregate.

Hostels can be crowded, noisy, and not always completely secure from petty theft. But they are universally rated as one of the great bargains of the AT, and are unique—no other park, mountain, or trekking region offers so many places to spend a sheltered night at so little cost. Hostels are maintained by friendly churches or public organizations (fire departments, hiking clubs). Many of the most extraordinary hostels are the creation of private individuals friendly to the long-distance hiker who are willing to contribute time and money to provide a home-away-from-home. Hostel life can be beguiling, and more than one hiker tarries longer than just the night. As far as I know, the record is a six-week stay at Rusty's.

Some of the "elite" hostels even serve meals, although most provide only bunk space, showers, and accommodations to allow hikers to prepare their own food. Several ATC publications including the *Handbook* include detailed information about hostels.

There are also many stopping places for hikers that fall between the extremes of the free hostel and the luxury of a tourist motel room. Such places may charge anywhere up to about $10 per night for shower and bunkroom, somewhat more for private quarters and cabins. Hospitality may include wonderful cooking, as offered at Shaw's Boarding Home in Monson, Maine. Occasionally a hiker short of cash can do chores, but this is not common.

If they can afford it, hikers will spend "in-town" nights at a motel (6 percent of all nights, about one-third of the time when off the trail). In the South, motel accommodations can be delightfully inexpensive, as low as $20 per night for a single, or less than $10 per person if hikers combine with roll-aways and double beds. Up north hikers must take care, as the trail sweeps past the outskirts of big cities or through popular tourist areas. Here the per-night cost for a single can run $40 to $75, and in Kent, Connecticut, hikers reported room costs were $90 to $100. For those relatively few couples with energy left over after a day's hike, a hostel can be too public and the tent too confining for intimacy. Nothing can beat a motel shower and a double bed.

Then there are the accommodations of friends, relatives, and even some strangers, located in the vicinity of the AT. I spent about a dozen wonderful nights eating delicious home-cooked meals, making use of showers and laundries, and luxuriating in a soft bed. My hosts eagerly asked questions and listened to the stories of life on the trail. They usually picked me off the trail at a road crossing late in the day and deposited me back, clean, fed, and restored, the next morning. Few are the hikers who have not been invited for a meal or the night at the home of some casually met tourist or local family.

Finally, many hikers sneak off for a few nights at home—probably more than the 2 percent indicated in the table. (Longer stays at home, for a week or more, are not uncommon but are not included in these statistics.)

In historical accounts, several thru-hikers, including Garvey himself, have reported becoming so used to the primitive sleeping accommodations on the trail that they slept on the floor when visiting civilization. In my survey such preference is rare, with only about one person in a hundred not opting for a soft bed.

WHERE DO LONG-DISTANCE HIKERS MOST LIKE TO SLEEP?

Table 9-2 summarizes the hikers' overall favorite places to spend the night on the trail, according to various conditions.

More than half the surveyed hikers (53 percent) would choose a shelter, good weather or bad, but only if it was not crowded. Given good weather and good sites, about a third of the hikers would put up a tent, preferably in a meadow or where there is a view. And despite the trauma of being awakened by unexpected rain, 10 percent would risk going to bed under an open sky as their ideal way to spend a night on the trail.

The ultimate is to pitch your tent on a mountaintop or bald summit or overlook, and watch the sun go down in the west and come up in the east next morning. On April 26, 1989, I did just that, climbing to a peak over 4,000 feet above Brown Fork Gap in North Carolina. I sat alone, watching the sun go down, and then retired to my tent to experience the strangest meteorological phenomenon of the whole trip. Starting around midnight, the wind increased from calm to almost 30 miles per hour, then died back to total calm, in about 15 minutes. For the next several hours the wind would follow this strange 25-minute cycle—blowing hard, dying back, and then building up again. By morning all was calm and the meteorological "breathing" had stopped. No one has offered an explanation for this curious all-night cycling of the mountain wind.

WHERE DO THEY HATE TO SLEEP?

When you ask hikers this question, they list two worst-case sleeping arrangements: being caught in the rain, and being stuffed in an overcrowded shelter. Table 9-3 tells the story.

TABLE 9-2.
HIKERS' FAVORITE SLEEPING ACCOMMODATIONS ON THE TRAIL

IN SHELTERS	
WHEN NOT CROWDED	33%
IN THE RAIN	14%
ON A BEAUTIFUL NIGHT	4%
WHEN NO ONE ELSE THERE	2%
IN TENTS (IN GOOD WEATHER)	
LOCATED ON GRASS, PINE NEEDLES, NEAR WATER	29%
ON MOUNTAINTOP OR BALD OVERLOOK	4%
IN THE OPEN	
WHEN CLEAR, NO RAIN OR BUGS	7%
WITH VIEW	2%
IN HAMMOCK	1%

TABLE 9-3.
THE WORST SLEEPING ARRANGEMENTS

IN SHELTERS	
CROWDED	31%
HOT, BUGGY, SNORERS	12%
LEAKING, WIRE BUNKS, BAT FLOORS	10%
REMOTE FROM THE TRAIL	3%
IN TENTS, UNDER TARPS	
IN THE RAIN	36%
BUGGY	4%
OTHER PLACES	
AMC HUTS	3%
WAYNESBORO FIRE STATION	1%

Hilltop in Maine

In recent years heroic efforts on the part of maintaining clubs have reduced the number of leaking shelters and those with wire bunks or "baseball bat" (made from small logs) floors, so that only about 10 percent of the hikers made a point about such discomforts. It should be noted that the "baseball bat" floors in Maine lean-tos were not a problem when the shelters were originally built. At that time it was accepted backpacking practice to cut armloads of fresh pine boughs to place underneath the sleeper. It did not matter whether you were sleeping on the ground, small logs, or a bed of nails—the result was as good as a hay loft. Today, of course, the typical hiker has only an inch or so of thin pad between sleeping bag and lean-to floor or the ground.

Heat, bugs, and the snoring of other hikers also make for some miserable nights. Finally, a few hikers were not happy to stay in AMC huts in the White Mountains, for reasons described in Chapter 17. And last of all, there is the report of the hiker who spent an unforgettable night in the Waynesboro Fire Station where it was necessary to sleep with all lights on.

SLEEPING BAGS

All the long-distance hikers in the survey carried sleeping bags in cooler weather. There were four individualists who gave up sleeping bags in the heat of the summer, wrapping themselves in a blanket or flannel sheet.

The 1993 *Backpacker* product review "Bagging It" lists about 300 makes of sleeping bags, but the hikers in our sample carried about 100, and among these there were few complaints regarding quality, warmth, getting wet, or feathers oozing out between the stitches. They were generally satisfied with their choices, irrespective of manufacturer, shape, filling, or design.

About 57 percent of the bags carried were fiber (primarily Hollofil, Polarguard, and Quallofil), 35 percent were down, and about 8 percent of the respondents used both, depending on the time of year. Conventional wisdom holds that the fiber bag is significantly better under wet conditions, losing less insulation power and drying faster. This wisdom, plus the significantly lower cost, was probably the reason hikers on the rather wet AT more often selected fiber. But conventional wisdom has been challenged by some hikers and also by Jack Stephenson, outfitter extraordinaire, whose high-quality but expensive outdoor equipment is widely acclaimed. He wrote in the Fall 1991 Stephenson's equipment catalog: "If a bag gets wet (almost *always* from *inside* due to lack of vapor barrier), synthetic bags lose insulation much faster than down bags, until added water is about 3 times the insulation weight. Then the synthetic bag is miserably cold and down is still warm. Water fills up spaces between synthetic fibers and conducts away heat, while down absorbs moisture within fibers and keeps insulating air spaces open. Much more moisture is needed to collapse down, and that happens only if the bag is carelessly dunked in water."

Although Stephenson's view may appear extreme, he is an authority on vapor-barrier clothing and outdoor equipment. The manufacturers of artificial fibers do not hesitate to advertise the water-absorption performance of bags with their brand of fiber insulation. Ducks and geese have no such lobby and probably no interest in donating their down, but they do have impressive experience in dealing with a wet environment.

The tremendous increase in body metabolism stemming from daily backpacking, plus the fact that AT thru-hiking does not normally include the winter season, means that bags that are rated down to 10 to 20 degrees F (−12 to −7°C) are usually more than adequate. Note, however, that in cold weather if for some reason you spend the whole day sitting or lying around camp, the night cold will appear to be 10 degrees lower than when climbing into the bag after a hard day's hike.

With respect to sleeping bag temperature ratings, *Backpacker* notes they "are about as reliable as a used car salesman's prattle." Actually, a group of us sitting around a campfire on a cold night agreed on how the temperature ratings of sleeping bags were determined: The manufacturer's rating is the temperature at which, when friends try to wake you in the morning, you will not awaken!

The prospective buyer is best advised to pay little regard to descriptive jargon as to the bag's construction; this allows you the freedom to seek out a good bargain, deciding on your own what is a low enough temperature rating, with reasonable confidence that the bag will be a satisfactory companion during those long nights on the trail.

A final word on washing bags: *Don't.* Yes, it is right to keep the bag clean, and even if you are dirty, it helps to wear clean sleeping gear to keep dirt off the bag. But washing seems to do terrible things to the insulating ability of a sleeping bag, and dry-cleaning is worse. If you are willing to take the trouble, a bag liner will help keep a bag clean. At any rate, the life of a bag seems more a factor of how many times it is washed than how many times it has been slept in. If you still must wash your bag, heed special instructions.

SLEEP PADS

No specific survey questions were aimed at sleep pads, but it can be noted that practically all hikers carried them, reflecting the very high gain in sleeping comfort (softness, warmth, and dryness) obtained at relatively low cost in dollars and pounds. The self-inflating Therm-A-Rest pads, costing from $40 to $110 and weighing up to several pounds, were carried by many of the long-distance backpackers. Without exception, the pads commanded rave reviews. If sleeping comfort appears elusive, it seems clear that the restless sleeper should invest in a Therm-A-Rest pad. The standard for the trail, however, was a simple closed-cell foam pad, the Ridge Rest, weighing a pound or less and costing around $20. It was the pad I carried and all I ever wanted. It almost lasted the whole AT. The record for pads seems to be held by the "Three Blind Mice," three Georgia hikers doing the trail in segments: For each sleeper they carried the ultimate collection of two or three Ridge Rest pads plus a Therm-A-Rest.

A final observation is with respect to saving weight by buying the three-quarter-length version of a pad. In cold weather, it is the feet that are last to warm up. Thus, they need insulation not for comfort, but for protection from the cold ground. This is best provided by a pad that reaches to the far end of the body.

PILLOWS

I spent the night of April 27, 1989, at the Birch Spring, Virginia, shelter, which I shared not only with the most aggressive mice on the AT (for more on mice, see Chapter 15), but with several agreeable college students out for a few days. The following morning we all headed north at the same time. I fell into last place. As we climbed the long hill, I became aware of a buzzing sound that seemed to come from the pack of the man just ahead of me. I asked him and he immediately exclaimed, stopped, and took off his pack. His battery-operated vibrating pillow had accidentally been turned on. He explained that backpacking always gave him a sore neck, and the best solution was to take along his vibrating pillow.

The experience illustrates a very special affection between hiker and pillow, a kind of "I can sleep anywhere in anything as long as I have my own special pillow." In recognition of this, a single outdoor catalog lists no fewer than eight different trail pillows, and convertible stuff sacks with a fleece surface have recently become available.

Despite the fact that in my survey three tough hombres insisted they slept with no pillow, and two others claimed that an arm was a sufficient pillow, most others lovingly stuffed a clothes sack, T-shirt, or pants leg with clothes for a pillow before retiring. Many made sure to use a down vest, fleece pile jacket, or sweater to make it soft. Both a teddy bear and a live dog served as pillows. Several hikers had their own special hiking pillows, contoured or down. Two hikers simply folded flannel sheets, and one utilized "Stephenson's clothes sleeping system."

NOTES ON SLEEPING

Equipped with a comfortable sleeping bag, pillow, and soft pad, your physical requirements for a good rest have been met. Most hikers are bone-tired from 10 hours and 15 miles of backpacking. With stomachs contentedly full of macaroni-and-cheese and a Snickers Bar, sleep comes quickly. Dave Getchell noted, "Perhaps the greatest pleasure in the great outdoors is curling up for a good night's sleep." My hiking friend Dick Walker used to say that the only time he got enough sleep was during the long nights when winter hiking in the White Mountains.

On the AT, the practice among long-distance hikers is to follow the sun. As darkness would settle, I would look around the crowded shelter and discover that hiker after hiker had quietly slipped into his bag and was already asleep. Perhaps one person was perched in a corner, a candle flickering, as he wrote in his journal. No one said "Good night," no one admonished, "It's time to get to sleep, the sun is setting"; everyone knew we all needed lots of sleep and the time to start was now. Typically, hikers get at least nine hours of sleep.

But many of those with whom one shares a shelter are not thru-hikers. They are out for a few days or a weekend. Their whole concept of their trip in the wilderness is different. They eat extra well, including cooking steaks over a real fire; bring wine and beer; and often sit around the fire deep into the night enjoying the companionship. Less integrated are the young people equipped with a powerful boombox. For them the woods is an escape from supervision. At the bottom of most thru-hiker lists are the outing clubs, scouts, and church groups, who in gatherings of one, two, or three dozen, take over a whole shelter or campsite. They are often polite and fun-loving, and I have shared many a lean-to with them. But they are also often noisy, undisciplined, and rambunctious. If possible, the best answer is to move on a mile or two and find an alternative site.

There are also a number of less extreme alternatives that assist in getting a good night's sleep. The first is to purchase a little pair of soft ear plugs. They are comfortable and cheap, and they effectively shut out a noisy world. A second alternative is to carry your own set of earphones and radio (for more on radios, see Chapter 11).

There is the matter of soreness, aches, and pains. It seems that almost everyone suffers from these, especially in the first days and weeks. Aspirin, Advil, Tylenol, and other non-prescription drugs are widely consumed; they have changed many a hike from painful to pleasant. Taken before retiring, they offer a significant soothing plus a placebo effect.

The last alternative applies particularly to older hikers, for whom the adjustments to wilderness sleeping may be more difficult. Many backpackers who sleep like a log once they are acclimated to the trail have a terrible time the first few nights in the woods. When you make that last visit to your friendly family physician, preparing yourself for a trip with such invaluable prescription drugs as Lomotil for diarrhea and Cypro antibiotic, you might ask for a prescription for a benzodiazepine drug. These relaxing-sleeping pills (such as Restoril) work quickly and wear off completely by morning.

White Mountains, in New Hampshire, after an October snow

CLOTHING AND RAINGEAR

Whalen's advice on hiking pants (see right) is followed overwhelmingly by the hikers in my survey. Andrew J. Giger, a 1969 thru-hiker with strong opinions on many subjects, wrote in James Hare's *Hiking the Appalachian Trail*: "Shorts were worn 99.999 percent of the time while walking. . . . Long trousers . . . were used occasionally when entering a town. They came in handy after a day's walk to help ward off mosquitoes. They were comforting on cool evenings before turning in. . . . Leg protection didn't seem even remotely worth the burden of hiking in long trousers . . . they cause extra work in friction at every step."

> *While hiking, even though the temperature is low, a pair of shorts is your best bet. You will stay warm on all but the coldest days.*
>
> Christopher Whalen,
> *The Appalachian Trail Workbook for Planning Thru-Hikes*

Thru-hikers 25 years later are practically always found in shorts; it is simply the way to go. They wear shorts in nice weather, in the rain, and sometimes even in the snow. Notwithstanding brush, nettles, poison ivy, snakes, and ticks, the hikers in my survey overwhelmingly—95 percent—preferred shorts. More than 20 percent of the 136 hikers *never* wore anything but shorts. Less than a handful usually wore long pants, and only two habitually covered their legs.

The overwhelming popularity of shorts on the trail is due both to comfort and to the freedom from knee drag. Unless protection from the cold demands it, the practice is to leave the legs bare and step ahead in freedom. In recent years polypropylene long johns have become a popular halfway step, and of course the European tradition is to wear knickers. When I was hiking in the Alps some years ago, my Swiss hostess confessed to being embarrassed by my short pants. We were hiking after the September 1st "deadline" for wearing shorts. I therefore bought a pair of knickers, which are still safely stored in my closet.

The most surprising finding of the survey is that King Cotton is not dead. No hiking material is so consistently inveighed against by the "experts" as cotton, because it provides little insulation, absorbs moisture, and is slow to dry. Yet many people like the feel of cotton next to the skin, and it is a common choice for undergarments and light wear. There are certain conditions in which cotton is not best, but most of the time it is thoroughly comfortable. As Roald Hoffmann put it in the January/February issue of *American Scientist,* "I (no better than most people) really think that a cotton shirt feels better. I believe it, without even trying it on."

Starting in the 1970s, the popularity of jogging and other individual sports brought about the development of lightweight synthetic-fabric shorts with built-in liners. Now, 20 years later, this type of clothing is increasingly the choice for long-distance hikers. These shorts dry quickly when wet, are cool in hot weather, and require no underclothing; indeed, the survey in 1989 revealed that 60 percent of the men and 40 percent of the women were not wearing underwear. (No one, however, has matched Colin Fletcher's Grand Canyon hike; he noted in his book *The Man Who Walked Through Time* that he traveled in the canyon for several days in just boots and pack.) The new clothing is rather less rugged than that worn in the wool, canvas, and leather era, but since it is lightweight one can carry plenty of spares—which brings us to the subject of rain.

HIKING IN THE RAIN

"A rainy day is better met
by those who don't mind getting wet."

—Don Hirsohn, *The Appalachian Trail*

From my journal, May 5, 1989, Great Smoky Mountains National Park:

Gradually the rain became heavier, the weather colder, and the wind stronger. But with primarily a downhill hike ahead and peak ridges behind me, there was no choice but to go on. I was correctly and heavily dressed this time, but the driving rain eventually soaked my wool corduroy pants higher and higher and then I noticed my shirt and arms were wet, despite my long Gore-Tex rain jacket and hood. By 3 P.M. there was not a dry bit of clothing on me. I had to stop five minutes to eat a candy bar and drink some water,

for I simply could not continue walking all day without something.

I pulled into Cosby Knob shelter at 4 P.M., being greeted by a delightful Canadian couple who fed me hot soup and shelter-cooked bannock. We were the only three in the shelter that night. It was glorious to have enough space. I changed every scrap of clothing I had, putting on all the dry items left in my pack (two T-shirts) and made a tremendous hot dinner for us all (chicken, cocoa, cookies). I was asleep at 8 P.M. It was a cold night, right down to freezing with the wind blowing directly into the shelter.

We all slept, but I did have to get up to sacrifice my down vest, which I was using as a pillow, to put it on and get warmer. I used a few socks and underwear as pillow; nothing else was dry.

May 6, 1989. What a time I have been having! What weather! Right now I am still in Cosby Knob shelter, dressed with every bit of clothing I own. It is 40 degrees outside, storming, hailing, and the wind blowing hard. There is heavy intermittent rain and flashing lighting with scary thunder. Awful.

In the shelter registers, in journals, and in grim conversations as they splash the soggy trail, thru-hikers would tell each other, "If you want to get to Maine, you have to hike in the rain." And in 1989 rain it did, as Randy Gates tabulated: "I had 69 days of rain in my first 100 days."

Some common reactions to the subject of rain: "You just accommodate yourself." "I wasn't going to let the rain end my dream." "I got used to it since it rained every day." The vast majority of hikers simply carried on stoically. A few, in a demonstration of either extreme adaptability or genuine toughness, professed to enjoy the rain. In response to the questionnaire statement "How did you deal with the problem of rain while you were hiking?," they responded testily, "What problem of rain?," "I just kept right on hiking," or "I did not treat it as a problem—it made sunny days that much more enjoyable."

Hikers employed a number of strategies; if worst came to worst, retreat was possible. For example, after three soaking days in the Smokies, I took my load of wet clothes off to a motel in Gatlinburg and simply dried out for 36 hours. Others also reported that they had on occasion "wimped out." It was also possible to modify hiking plans, and if the company was good a group stayed on in a shelter, waiting it out with friends. The opposite is to wear as little clothing as possible, take few breaks, and walk fast. Such an approach does work but appeals primarily to the toughest hikers.

Despite the gung-ho attitude exhibited by some on the trail, hiking in the rain is generally not a very popular sport. The going is usually slower due to wet rocks, gooky muck, and slippery roots. There are no views and few animals. (The animals are not so dumb. When it is wet they take cover and stay warm and dry.) With each passing hour of rain the wetness penetrates arms, legs, shoes, and eventually soaks into the innermost pockets. Only the pack and its precious contents of dry clothing and sleeping bag can be completely waterproofed by using a cover. One thru-hiker described her all-too-human reaction: "I cried a lot. I hated to walk in the rain." Another wrote, ". . . the cold ice rain in the spring was horrible."

Love it, tolerate it, or hate it, all long-distance hikers agree on how best to manage clothing when hiking in the rain: If at all possible, get to a shelter for the night, change out of your wet clothes, and if cold, get into your sleeping bag. Next morning, carefully stow away those lovely dry items and pull on the wet clothing from the night before. (Short of hours by a fire, wet clothing never dries overnight.) With luck and a little sun, you will hardly notice the cold wetness after half an hour of brisk hiking, and if the air is dry the clothing will become dry in just an hour or two. Cindy Ross has published a short but helpful guide for staying comfortable while hiking in the rain: "Shower Power—How to Stay Happy When the Sky Dumps on You" appeared in the May 1990 issue of *Backpacker* magazine.

Unfortunately, staying comfortable in the rain is impossible under some circumstances. The sad consensus is that no matter what you wear, you will get wet. But the subject is too important to simply be ignored. Most hikers have settled on a two- or three-step defense depending on the following conditions.

WARM OR HOT WEATHER

In temperatures above 60 degrees F (15°C), no problem—wear your skimpiest nylon shorts, a cotton or blended T-shirt, tank top, or nothing, and let the rain pour over your body and legs into your boots. After a while your boots will squish with each step, and soon you won't hesitate to walk right in the middle of the trail, which by now is a running stream. This is easier than walking like a crab along the sides.

COOL WEATHER

Temperatures from 35 to 60 degrees F (2 to 15°C) are difficult. You will try to wear clothing to at least keep the trunk of your body dry. A highly waterproof jacket that really keeps out the rain will eventually become unbearable as you lug that 45-pound pack up the next mountain. Almost all hikers agree that it is better to get wet from rain than from sweat. So, you equip yourself with a "breatheable" rain jacket; in 1989 this meant Gore-Tex, by far the most popular rain jacket carried by hikers.* If you don't climb the mountain too fast, the jacket is new and loose, the storm does not last more than an hour or two, it doesn't rain too hard, you will do just fine. But this is all middle ground. If the bad weather lasts, after three or four hours of pouring rain the wet will somehow penetrate that magic fabric, and you will get wet, wet, wet—on the second day if not the first. As one hiker reported it, in wet weather "I used a perfectly useless Gore-Tex anorak." But if you move slowly, with a light pack, and downhill, you may stay dry at least for a while.

About 10 percent of the hikers prefer a poncho, despite its one glaring shortcoming: A poncho in the wind is not only ineffective in keeping out rain, but in a storm with high winds it may self-destruct. If you can hike along a quiet valley with the rain pouring straight down, a well-fitted poncho may be the answer. Because ponchos are by nature rather loose, they usually allow enough air circulation to prevent the wearer from drowning in his own sweat. A few hikers carry both poncho and rainsuit.

COLD WEATHER

Below 35 degrees F (2°C), the choices are not so difficult. Getting wet and soaked through is dangerous because of hypothermia, so clothes that will keep you dry are essential. Many consider this rainsuit weather. The problem of getting sweaty is reduced and the danger of getting chilled is increased. Most hikers wear a rain jacket plus either rain pants, wool trousers, or quick-drying synthetic pants. An increasingly popular cold-rainy-day outfit is tight-fitting polypropylene underwear, shorts, and a rain jacket. The poly may get wet but retains some insulating ability and dries quickly. Hikers are wearing this combination in all kinds of weather. One problem is that the tights are rather fragile. When the precipitation changes to snow, the situation is not so critical and the hiker can pile on any available clothing that will not trap body moisture.

Kenneth Miller, a 1989 thru-hiker, reported that he

---

*However, in Cindy Ross's May 1990 *Backpacker* magazine survey of hikers whose experience totaled 140,000 miles, the verdict on Gore-Tex raingear was disappointment: "Perhaps the harshest criticisms were reserved for Gore-Tex because of high expectations and matching prices."

Big Rocks, New York state

had bought a "good rain jacket and pants. I got wet." So Miller ended up usually hiking in shorts and T-shirt when it was raining. If this sounds all too familiar, it is. In *Hiking the Appalachian Trail,* editor James Hare quotes Raymond Baker saying the same thing some 25 years earlier: "I found raingear not worth carrying on the trail. By not allowing your body moisture to escape, you wind up wetter and more uncomfortable than if you wore ordinary clothing."

Actually, it is not only the complex and expensive layering that supposedly keeps the wearer dry after a long exposure, but the durable water repellent treatment (DWR). But an extensive series of tests conducted by Dave Getchell and reported in the September 1995 issue of *Backpacker* magazine indicates that "once the inexpensive DWR wears off, even owners of the most luxurious raingear will start using language as foul as the weather."

The inescapable conclusion is that backpacking in comfort in heavy and protracted cold rain is one area where modern technology—unlike the rain—has not penetrated. And this is a condition more likely to be met on an Appalachian Trail thru-hike than in most areas of the world. It is not that a rainsuit, poncho, gaiters, Gore-Tex jacket, or rain hat are not helpful; it is simply that they do not make for a complete solution. There is, however, one item that works and is critically important: a waterproof cover for the pack. Happiness, if not downright survival, depends on having dry clothes to change into at the end of the day.

When having to endure these miserable conditions, several thru-hikers recommended singing in the rain as the answer. And at least two hikers seem to have found the perfect solution: Nancy Kettle carried an umbrella, and so did Laurie Adkins, "The Umbrella Lady." An umbrella is an ideal combination of a walking staff and rain protection with ventilation. But it does run contrary to the "tough it out" tradition of many long-distance hikers.

On the edge of the Smokies, North Carolina

COMFORTS AND AMENITIES

Along with 40 pounds of prescribed equipment and food, a few ounces of personal trivia for pleasure and comfort completed the pack of most long-distance backpackers. Table 11-1 (page 75) lists some of the more common items taken along.

CAMERA

The 15 percent of hikers who did not bring a camera sometimes expressed regret. One sturdy male even carried a camcorder. Nothing can beat bringing back in pictures the extraordinary, and the ordinary, happenings on the trail. Friends, family, and many others enjoy following the long trek vicariously through slide shows, photo albums, even illustrated articles.

> *"The time has come," the walrus said, "to talk of many things."*
>
> —Lewis Carroll, *Alice's Adventures in Wonderland*

One thing to consider is whether the extra quality and versatility of really fine camera equipment is worth lugging. If you are a true photographer, then take along tripod, telephoto lens, and that super 3-pound SLR camera. Remember that most scenery and mountaintop views are best captured with a wide-angle lens. If you are not a pro, save the weight. A small 35 mm camera, as automatic as you can afford, should be under 1 pound. I bought a 12-ounce lightweight camera for the hike and took over 1,000 pictures. I sent the rolls to processing and then home as I hiked.

A second factor is even more critical: How do you carry your camera? Every hiker agrees that a camera in the pack stays there. Even in an outside pocket, access is severely restricted. Not only is the camera hard to get at, but many of the best photo opportunities occur when you and your pack are not together. On the other hand, a camera carried loosely over the shoulder is an intolerable nuisance, and when one hiker dropped his loosely carried camera into a spring the second time, the photographic record of his trip was finished. Special camera har-

TABLE 11-1.
OTHER PERSONAL ITEMS CARRIED

ITEM	PERCENT OF HIKERS WHO CARRIED
CAMERA	85%
JOURNAL-WRITING MATERIALS	80%
HIKING STAFF	65%
PICKED UP ALONG THE WAY	35%
SPECIALLY MADE	20%
SKI POLE	10%
READING MATERIAL	60%
COMPASS	50%
RADIO	40%
SNAKEBITE KIT	30%
ALCOHOL	15%
TOBACCO	12%
MARIJUANA	5%+
MOUSETRAPS	5%
HARMONICA	3%
WHISTLES (SAFETY)	2%

nesses do the trick but do not complement the various straps of the ever-shifting backpack. There are two other possible spots: on your belt or in a belt pack in the front. I carried my camera in a little leather calculator case fitting right on my belt. It came out of its holster almost as fast as Billy the Kid's six-shooter, and because it was part of my clothing it was with me during many photo opportunities when the pack was leaning against the shelter wall. Only a relatively small camera can be carried conveniently in this manner, so this argues again for buying or borrowing a compact 35 mm camera for the hike. Note that the small cameras achieve smallness partly by using wide-angle lenses, which is what you want for many of your pictures.

JOURNALS

"If you would not be forgotten, as soon as you were dead and rotten, either write things worth reading, or do things worth writing."

—Benjamin Franklin

Four out of five long-distance hikers, practically everyone—male, female; those out for just two weeks, thruhikers—maintained at least some kind of record of their daily struggles. Indeed, keeping a journal seems to be something of a tradition for end-to-end hikers. In 1973, when editor James R. Hare put together his two-volume monumental opus on Al end-to-end backpacking, *Hiking the Appalachian Trail,* there had been about 120 such transits. Hare collected 46 fascinating accounts from these pioneer thru-hikers. Some of these stories are in themselves books, and most are literate and interesting.

The most famous account of an AT traverse is Edward B. Garvey's 1971 book, *Appalachian Hiker: Adventure of a Lifetime.* It is the only AT hiking account I ever saw being carried on the trail. However, other excellent journals have been written and published, many privately. Several unpublished accounts of 1989 transits have been copied for me, including Mac McCaslin's diary. This features a daily log sheet modeled after that originally drawn up by Ed Garvey; it includes 13 items ranging from places stopped, travel conditions, weather, food, and miles, to people, animals, plants, and Mac's "main concern of the day." The following is a sample entry from Mac's diary.

1. *Date: Saturday, September 16, 1989*
2. *Log Entry: 132*
3. *Travel*
   From: Stony Brook shelter
   To: Cloudland shelter
   Beginning: 7:30 A.M.
   Ending: 5:45 P.M.
4. *Number of Miles Hiked:*
   a) By trail 17.8
   b) Other 0.5
   c) Cum. 1686.8
   d) Cum. 93.1
5. *Weather:*
   A.M. Mostly cloudy
   P.M. Rain
6. *Food:*
   B three granola bars (while curled up in sleeping bag—Brrr!)
   L three deviled-ham sandwiches
   S tortellini
7. *Condition of Trail: Up, down, struggle, up, down, up, down, stagger, crawl, crawl, roll, up, down, roll, down, straight, stagger, up*
8. *Shelter used: Cloudland shelter*
9. *People: None*
10. *Animals: Deer, chipmunk, cows, cat, pigs, large Rottweiler demanding to be scratched behind the ears*
    Plants: Wood sorrel, fern, aster, blackberries

Birds: Grouse, crow, woodpecker, warbler, duck, blue heron, turkey

11. *Money Spent: $0 (day); $1,143 (cumulative)*

12. *Notes of the Day:*

A.M.—*Got stung by a wasp. At least it got my arm hot. (It was freezing.) After I got moving I felt better. Coming down with a cold.*

P.M.—*Have seen a lot of birds today. Started raining about 4:30. Was glad to see the shelter. Hope Oscar found a warm place to sleep.*

13. *Main Concern of the Day: That Fran got my week's log sheets*

Writing in my journal consumed about an hour a day. I often gathered my thoughts and observations while actually walking, and when the mental register had filled up I would sit down on a log and write then and there.

Tradition aside, there are many good reasons to keep a journal. It is a friend that is always there—a place to confide your thoughts, feelings, discomforts. And it is a record of your experience that may someday jog a hazy memory. Many long-distance hikers give public slide shows when they return, and more than a few write articles for local papers, alma maters, friends, and relatives. Whether you venture the whole route or only partway, you'll have more than enough experience to write a little book—too few of which, unfortunately, are readily available.

One or two hikers reported bringing a pocket-sized tape recorder, another way to capture your experience and sounds along the trail.

HIKING STAFFS

Half of the female and almost two-thirds of the male long-distance hikers carried a hiking staff. Usually it was just picked up along the way, but sometimes it was very special or had been crafted to order.

About 10 percent carried staffs only at the start, but practically everyone picked up something for fording streams and other special purposes, such as protection. I can remember in Tennessee reading in a shelter journal that the trail ahead would take me through a valley where the inhabitants were known to think more highly of their hunting dogs than of backpackers; the next day was the only time I carried a staff from morning to night. In general, where there are many streams to ford, loose rocks, tricky downhills, mud, and dogs, more hikers carried a staff. Where the trail required the use of hands—as in the White Mountains—or was flat and smooth, staffs were less

common. Those with staffs were typically three to five years older than those without.

Is carrying a staff likely to help avoid falls and injuries? When I studied the 49 serious hiking-related injuries reported in the sample (including shin splints, swollen knees, foot problems, and lacerations and bruises due to falls; see Chapter 5), there was no significant difference in injury rate between those carrying a staff and those not.

READING

About 60 percent of the surveyed hikers carried reading material. A few avid readers carried books, some leaving paperbacks at the shelter for others to pick up and take along. Adam Ticknor finished 12 novels on the trail, and I found Tom Pappas at Bly Gap curled up reading a book in his tent as if he had just arrived by taxi. Bonnie Goulard improved her mind: She carried and studied a dictionary and learned new words. Mac McCaslin came across a *Playboy* magazine at a shelter in Connecticut. (He recorded in his diary that this brought about a change of plans, and he had decided to take a few days off and go home to visit his wife.)

As for me, other than writing in my journal, I found I was too busy during the day and too tired at night to read. It was the only extended time in more than 50 years that I did not read before going to sleep.

Did those hikers who gave up the literary world and concentrated on walking hike a longer day? The statistics indicate that they did, spending about half an hour longer each day—10.5 hours altogether—than those who were reading or writing in their journals.

COMPASS

Only half the men and a little more than a third of the women carried a compass for the whole trip. This can only be regarded as proof of the efficient blazing, maps, trail guides, and AT signs. About 10 percent of those originally bringing compasses never used them, and some sent them home.

For many others, like myself, a compass in the woods is a security blanket. And the highly damped, rugged compasses available in the range from $10 to $20 are much easier to use than those available just a few years ago. I sometimes followed the alternative blue-blazed routes, and on occasion the trail disintegrated into a bushwhack. In such a situation a compass is indispensable. I even used it to detect walking in the wrong direction on

In the Lemon Squeezer, Harriman State Park, New York

the AT (more on this in the next chapter). Under the rare circumstances when you are lost (or should we say, temporarily "disoriented"), the compass can be a life-saver. Even such old pros as Dorothy Laker and Ed Garvey got lost, the latter when going out at dusk in search of water. Yet the reality is that for most, a compass is not necessary to hike the AT.

RADIO

In our survey sample, 40 percent of the backpackers carried a miniature radio with earphones (weight about 5 ounces, cost $20 to $50). Although the excuse is usually to get weather forecasts, the hikers with headset radios mostly used them to fight boredom on a dull stretch and occasionally for relaxing in the evening. I used mine only two or three times a week when on a slow slog up a long mountain, in dull second-growth and scrub areas, or to fill the night world with my own choice of music when not sleeping.

A radio *could*, if you wanted, be used in weather forecasting. Not that the weather in the mountains actually has much to do with what is broadcast from the neighboring valleys; the weather predictions for local metropolitan areas are not very applicable to the AT, positioned as it is high along the mountain ridge. (For example, summer temperatures typically are 5 to 10 degrees cooler on the trail than in the valleys below, and as much as twice as much rain falls on the backpacker as on the farmer's fields below.) One wonderful characteristic of the AT is that shelters, campsites, and the trail itself are usually higher than the surrounding countryside, a boon for radio reception. I found FM reception remarkably good, and for those interested in classical music there was usually a loud and clear National Public Radio station nearby.

Local radio can be an education: At the start of my journey in Georgia, I listened to a stock car race one misty afternoon. I heard the entire Coca Cola 600 from start to finish as I trudged up and down the Stekoahs. It made me feel in close touch to the views and happenings of the people in the area I was hiking through.

SNAKEBITE KIT

Only 30 percent of the hikers bothered with snakebite kits, and some of these kits were subsequently sent home. Because of the depredations of generations of earlier visitors to the woods, one scarcely sees a copperhead or rattler anymore. Furthermore, the actual value and utility of the snakebite kits are questioned by most experts. See "If a Snake Bites You," Chapter 15, and note that none of the suggested steps requires a snakebite kit.

ALCOHOL

Back before the 20th century, the mountain explorer was often accompanied by a flask containing whiskey, brandy, or some other hard liquor. And since a gulp of the stuff was invariably "warming," a genuine medicinal value was ascribed to the beverage. Indeed, the view that strong drink can be helpful has not entirely died out, as chronicled by Sherman and Older in their book about their 1973 AT thru-hike, *Appalachian Odyssey*: "Whoever wrote 'I got my love to keep me warm' never slept on the Appalachian Trail in Georgia in early spring. We trembled with cold, squirmed and shivered, shaked and shuddered. We curled into each other, hugged each other, tossed and turned. We spent half the night playing single sack, double sack, sack in sack, all the while taking long swigs of Southern Comfort we brought to warm our blood."

A thru-hiker from Atlanta had a less fortunate experience with alcoholic warming in the White Mountains of New Hampshire, according to a November 14, 1988, *Insight* magazine article by Kathryn Hudson. A man had been hiking along the AT for six months when he reached the White Mountains in the summer of 1988. To cope in a cold spell, he reportedly mixed half of a fifth of vodka with orange juice in his canteen for snorts to keep him warm. Another hiker found him on a mountaintop hypothermic and violently ill; state Fish and Game officers were forced to rescue him at 3 A.M. Morgan pleaded guilty to a charge of reckless conduct and was fined $500.

Today the opinion is that alcohol dilates the capillaries, exposing the body to greater cooling and increased risk of hypothermia, in addition to the blurring of thinking and judgment. This view did not require the wonders of modern medicine. Over 100 years ago, M.F. Sweetser, in his guide to the White Mountains, recommended that mountain climbers carry cold tea and said unequivocally that "Strong liquors are weakening in their effects when such work as mountaineering is at hand."

On April 11, 1989, I tented in Slaughter Gap, Georgia, on my AT trip. There, spread along the ridge, were a dozen tents with a first-class cocktail party going on. The folks were just up for the night, and it was a lovely outing. A little alcohol seems both more common and more appropriate for the weekender's hike than for the serious long-distance backpacker. Like many others, I have had to move on when finding a drinking party underway at a shelter. And like many others, I was pleased to share a wee dram. For thirst and first aid, alcohol is not suitable, but as a hike amenity it has graced many a camper's evening fire.

About 15 percent of the long-distance hikers carried the makings for such an evening.

All this says nothing about beer, that favorite beverage of the hikers. Beer was mentioned by 39 percent of those in the survey as the food item they most looked forward to when getting off the trail, surpassed only by ice cream. Beer, accompanied if possible by pizza, was a major attraction of the local bar when visiting a trail town. And beer and bars appear to account for nearly 100 percent of the troubles that long-distance hikers occasionally got into. In response to the question about whether the hiker had encountered any trouble with drunks, several respondents wrote "Yes, me."

In general, beer is far too heavy to be included in the pack, except for the first few miles on the first day out of town. But more than once, an intrepid volunteer has taken on the errand of a round trip to town several miles away to bring brew back for a shelter party. The record goes to the hiker who crossed the wide Kennebec River in Maine twice one night to provide for the evening repast.

Except for beer at stops or when within striking distance of civilization, long-distance hikers are markedly abstinent: Almost 85 percent of the men and 92 percent of the women reported not carrying any alcohol. In general, Sweetser's dictum of a century ago appears to be a commonplace rule among those who would backpack a long distance.

TOBACCO

Although smoking is now recognized as a serious health hazard, it was a common amenity for 19th-century mountain climbers. In his book *Scrambles Among the Alps,* Edward Whymper, the first man to climb the Matterhorn, recorded carrying and smoking cigars on his epic attempts to scale that mountain.

About 12 percent of the hikers in this survey admitted to smoking, but not Noel DeCavalcante; he "quit smoking the day I departed Springer Mountain," never to light up again. A few hikers felt quite strongly about not smoking, regarding it as defiling the trail and the wilderness. The dozen or so who nevertheless did smoke often carried a pipe or, surprisingly, cigars; this included at least one woman.

MARIJUANA

In the survey, the question "Did you smoke?" elicited in a few cases the reply, "Do you mean tobacco?" Half a dozen (and probably a few more) of the hikers in the survey said they smoked marijuana. One of them described his solu-

tion to the problem of endless rain: "I smoked a joint and did my best to phase [the rain] out."

Hiking in the White Mountains in New Hampshire early October 1973 with my three young sons, we climbed Mount Carrigain and to the top of the lookout tower to admire the view. However, the air inside was far too dense to stay because of the smoke from half a dozen hikers celebrating their ascent. Notwithstanding a few such instances occasionally reported on the AT, the Mount Carrigain incident is the only time I have run into pot use, including my whole journey from Georgia to Maine. My own trip experience, however, may be somewhat biased since my senior status may have inhibited some hikers from partying. The typical age of thru-hikers, 25 to 35, matches the period when such smoking is relatively more common, and it is hardly surprising that an item so readily carried along might be enjoyed in the privacy of the woods. On the whole, however, it would seem that the recreational use of marijuana by long-distance hikers on the AT is quite limited.

OTHER LITTLE THINGS TAKEN ALONG

Hikers carried a variety of other personal items. Four took harmonicas; two took Bibles; and a few with scientific bent carried thermometers, altimeters, anemometers, and other instruments. Bruce McLaren lugged a Z88 computer the whole journey, but unfortunately it suffered a tragic memory loss in New England. A number of hikers, including myself, carried mousetraps and set them every night in hopes of reducing the population of mice at shelters (see "Mice" in Chapter 15).

Others carried whistles, field guides, binoculars, Frisbees, and Hacky Sack balls. Bev Finnivan had both a husband and a teddy bear along, while Nancy Tremblay carried a little troll. Some hikers collected items along the way, such as butterflies, feathers, arrowheads, and stones shaped like the state in which they were found. Two people transported pebbles and one carried an American flag from Springer Mountain to Katahdin. Joyce Vorbeau took along two modified milk jugs for doing her laundry.

Not withstanding such small, lightweight personal items, the discipline of carrying every ounce of goods on one's back results in a model of efficient selection. There is nothing quite like the prospect of weeks and months of backpacking to provide the incentive for extreme economy. The result may appear Spartan, but it leads to a simplified lifestyle so satisfying that many long-distance hikers regard it as one of the most profound lessons from their months on the trail.

A bend in the New Jersey trail

HOW FAST, HOW FAR

No matter how lovely the woods, how great the views, how deep the solitude, or how steep the trail, these are only passing impressions along the way. It is not the mountains and valleys, the snow and rain, the rocks, mud, bugs, and certainly not world events that dominate the conversation of long-distance hikers around the evening fire; it is "How many miles did you do today?"

Completing the AT requires commitment, but some 2,100 miles is too great a distance to conjure. What the thru-hiker *can* grasp is how many miles were completed each day. He may not know the name of the local wilderness area, what day of the week it is, or even what state, but he knows how far he went today, often to the nearest tenth of a mile. Those hikers who keep journals always record each day's progress.

Because it provides a key to the successful thru-hike, and since it is something the hikers usually keep track of,

> *We'll blow 'em right off the trail.*
>
> —conversation in a trail shelter

miles per day is probably the most significant single statistic of the long hike. This statistic also might show effects of trail topography, hiking experience, physical condition, age, sex, body weight, pack weight, and resting (time off the trail).

In researching this book, I received some twenty journals with detailed itineraries telling where each evening was spent, how far and how long people hiked, and often how lonesome or happy they were. Not only were journals and the answers to questionnaires detailed, but cross-checks reveal that they were generally surprisingly accurate. An example is the hiker's estimate of his or her average miles per day. It can be checked, because we know from the overall circumstances of the hike how many actual days were hiked by each individual. It turns out that 90 percent of the correspondents' miles-per-day answers were within 2 miles of the calculation based on total trip length. You have to be an optimist to thru-hike, so it is not surprising that most of the guesses were a little on the high side.

An interesting check on hiker accuracy occurred when Kim Knuti, Bill Marcinkowski, and Bill Grace did the trail as a threesome. Since hiking together they have moved to separate parts of the country, and they filled out their questionnaires independently. Nevertheless, on numerical items involving miles, hours, and days their answers are almost identical.

One of the few hikers I met who was not obsessed by numbers was Jack Steppe, the "Carolina Flash." Jack, a truly delightful trail companion, was on the way from Georgia to Maine but did not seem to care about miles. I twice caught him napping in the middle of the day, once in the center of a green meadow and once curled up on a flat rock. It was also Jack who counseled me as we climbed Blood Mountain in Georgia, "You know, Roly, the test is if you sweat going uphill, you're going too fast." But then, Jack wasn't the average true-blue thru-hiker.

DURATION OF THRU-HIKE

The typical AT thru-hiker takes 170 days from start to finish, or about 5.5 months. In a sampling of almost 200 thru-hikers between 1948 and 1992, about 40 percent took five to six months. Longer than eight months means hiking the Appalachian crestline in winter, an experience few will purposely risk—no more than two or three hikes out of a hundred. Even in the South, winter hiking can be daunting, as related in James Hare's *Hiking the Appalachian Trail* by Jim Shattuck, who succeeded in an extraordinary thru-the-winter hike in 1966–67:

"Lord, help me! Help me! I need your help!" In the early morning of March 1, 1967, this cry emanated from behind a slant rock outcropping and mingled with the sound of wind and drifting snow atop Sinking Creek Mountain. Yes, and I'm not ashamed to say that it was I who was doing the yelling. Fortunately, I did not know that an unofficial temperature reading of twenty-seven degrees below zero was being registered at nearby Mountain Lake. All I knew was that the cold in these southwest Virginia mountains had a peculiar penetrating effect. My numbed hands and fingers were behaving like uncoordinated, unfeeling claws as I tried without success to lace my boots.

Shattuck experienced this in the south, where presumably the winter is milder than in the north. In New England, hiking mountains in the winter is a specialized sport requiring skis or snowshoes, crampons, and ice axes and usually undertaken for a limited number of days. Add heavy packs, deep snow, and an obscured trail, which make hiking in these mountains slow and difficult, and you see why there are almost no winter thru-hikers in that region. Furthermore, Maine's Baxter State Park and Mount Katahdin are closed after the middle of October.

More recently, Kenneth Wadness risked the winter trek, thru-hiking from Maine and finishing in Georgia on February 8, 1991. Wadness started in June 1990 after his teaching year ended. He headed south, braving swarming mosquitoes and blackflies so thick that he did not dare to stop and chat with others on the trail for fear of being eaten alive. Crossing into New Hampshire he hit his first freezing weather, and by the time he was in Virginia temperatures ranged as low as 10 degrees F (–12.2°C) with winds of 40 mph along the ridges. When it was icy he clung to trees along the sides of the trail. When there was snow he slogged through it, 70-pound pack and all. He often traveled four or five days between meeting someone, and counted more than 100 days alone. Despite such rigors, he always rested on the Sabbath. Wadness's trip took 220 days; he averaged 10 miles per day.

The other extreme, walking or even running the trail as fast as possible, has been intriguing strong hikers for decades. Even Earl Shaffer, whose pioneering thru-hike in 1948 took 124 days—pretty fast under any conditions—later undertook a really speedy transit: In 1961 he hiked the trail a second time, in 99 days. In general, however, there have been few trips made in less than 100 days. Wardrow Leonard, carrying his own things and walking without special team support, completed the trail in 1990 in only 61 days, the fastest time as of that date. In 1991 there was a widely heralded "race" involving Scott Grierson and David Horton. Both had teams to support their effort, so neither needed to carry significant pack weight. Scott Grierson walked the trail in 55 days, and David Horton mostly ran it in 52 days.

Prior to 1973 there were at least a dozen transits under 100 days. Branley Owen's record 73-day hike in 1970 required 14 to 15 hours per day on the trail and averaging over 27 miles per day. He reached Katahdin 39 pounds lighter and exhausted. Owen carried a minimum of food and equipment, with a pack weight never exceeding 28 pounds. Four years earlier, young Eric Ryback had managed the distance in 82 days, carrying a mammoth pack weighing more than twice Owen's. Ryback, just out of high school, hiked south from Katahdin in June and paid the price in a trip made miserable by blackflies. In Hare's *Hiking the Appalachian Trail*, Ryback wrote, "My hands and neck were swollen twice as large as normal, and the stings hurt. This is the first time I have wanted to go home." Lost, dehydrated, crying, lonely, with broken and bleeding blisters, and hiking as much as 18 hours a day, it seems a miracle that he even finished, much less in record time.

A review of 35 thru-hikers, dating from Earl Shaffer's first transit in 1948 through 1972, reveals an average time of 144 days; this compares with an average of 170 days for hikers in 1989. These pioneer thru-hikers were a extraordinary lot, facing uncleared, poorly marked trails and frequently getting lost. But in fairness to today's thru-hiker, it should be noted that the length of the AT was then only a little over 2,000 miles, compared to a distance of over 2,100 miles in the 1990s. In addition, relocations (see Chapter 17) have moved the trail from hundreds of miles of roads and highways to the deep woods and ridge crests, substituting longer and usually rougher going (this also moved the trail away from small towns, country stores, farmers' barns, and mountain homes where the lucky early thru-hiker often was offered a free meal and shelter). Actually, the 35 thru-hikers in 1948–1972 walked an average of 14.0 miles per day. Thru-hikers in 1988–90, trekking over the longer and rougher distance, averaged about 12.6 miles per day. (Note that both these figures *include* the days rested, not hiked; the usual miles-per-day figure quoted in this book is higher because it excludes days rested and counts only days actually walked.)

No successful thru-hike of the AT could really be called leisurely; one cannot be casual about a regime that requires getting up before dawn and lugging a pack 10 hours a day over rocks and mountains, through heat and cold, for half a year. Worst of all is the certain knowledge that every day rested means another day added to the trip. Because of the length of the challenge, most thru-hikers take maximum advantage of the extended spring achieved by starting in the south at Springer Mountain (the favorite time in our sample being the first two weeks in April) and heading toward Katahdin.

An unusual aspect of this journey comes about because the backpacker is not heading just north, but northeast, traveling through the long summer across the time zone and also northward toward longer days. Thus, for many months the sun always seems to rise at the same time, around 6 A.M. However, in evenings just the opposite happens. The long, lighted dusk of Georgia and North Carolina quickly gives way as hiking days shorten alarmingly. On the whole, it is a slow-moving, benevolent seasonal experience, "the constant spring" that blesses the Georgia-to-Maine hiker. Some 90 percent of the 1989 sample thru-hiked in this direction, approximately half of them reaching Katahdin in early October.

It requires a rugged hiker and strong reasons to go the other way; only 4 percent of our sample thru-hiked north-to-south. Trails in the northern high mountains can be blocked and the path obscured by snow as late as June. And after the melting snows, mud is king. The earliest the brave venture forth in Maine is mid-June. And from then until mid-July, the blackfly reigns supreme. No traveler in those parts at that time of year ever speaks casually of the blackfly experience.

The remaining 6 percent chose various alternatives to the classic Georgia-to-Maine, one-year thru-hike; these are described more fully in Chapter 4. "Flip-flop" backpackers usually hiked northward until more than halfway, and then started at Mount Katahdin and walked south to where they had left the trail. Hikers in danger of being caught in an early Maine winter after Baxter State Park's closing date sometimes choose this option. I left the trail in southern Maine to go up to Katahdin and then hiked south.

TIME OFF THE TRAIL

Practically every thru-hiker welcomes some time off the trail. Only the few who seek a speed record, and two or three of the most rugged individuals, have hiked the AT without taking time off. Records show that about two hikers out of a hundred rest fewer than four days during an entire thru-hike. The average person takes off 24 days, mostly a day at a time. Fast walkers interrupt their journey about once every 10 days; others stop about once a week.

There are real reasons to stop. Even those who love the woods eventually need to get themselves and their clothing clean, obtain new supplies, rest up a bit, and eat, eat, eat. The typical long-distance backpacker is suffering from a significant calorie deficit while on the trail (see Chapter 14). However, in a glorious 24 hours in town he or she can absorb 6,000 to 7,000, or even 10,000 calories of ice cream, milk, beer, pizza, hamburgers, salads, fresh fruit and veggies. Although hikers rarely give "pigging out" as their reason for stopping, their enthusiasm about consuming tremendous quantities of food on off days is unequivocal.

Getting clean is another matter. In today's environmental protocol, dishes, clothing, and bodies are no longer to be immersed in springs, small streams, and ponds; there is likely to be someone drinking from that spot within a few hours, and in recent years hikers have universally regarded water as sacred. Of course, you can always take a pan of water off into the woods and wash, but the honest fact is that few care to do so after hiking 15 miles in a day. If clothes and hikers develop an offensive odor, few comment, for we are in the wide-open, sweet-smelling woods

—and all suffer the same affliction. I can vouch for one long-distance hiker who would disappear into the woods after a day's hike with a large container of water, even in cold weather, but I suspect he had inherited an unusual affinity for personal cleanliness not really shared by the majority of hikers. Most people on the trail only bathe when it is hot and a suitable large lake or stream is handy. More often, you are glad to simply find enough water to drink, much less to bathe in. And the day you find a perfect swimming spot is sure to be rainy and cold.

Few hikers spend much trail time washing clothes. Thus, a laundromat, along with hostel and food, is more than just a luxury. Should you ever wander into a laundromat close to the AT, you may witness an odd sight: There, standing around the various machines exchanging stories, is a group of oddly dressed young adults. They are often in bare feet or boots and, no matter how beautiful the weather outside, are in full raingear—every other piece of clothing is being washed and dried.

Most of the thru-hiker's days off are spent catching up with the feeding and cleaning chores. Sometimes they need time to duck a storm or to dry out after a wet journey. Some hikers will perform odd jobs (particularly at the AMC huts in the White Mountains) in return for room and board, but rarely will they be doing other work for a full day. About half the hikers will be off the trail for up to a week or so because of sickness or injury. Finally, there is getting back home, going to The Gathering (a reunion held in Damascus, Virginia, each spring), and an occasional wedding or funeral. One hiker joined his wife for six weeks in Europe, returning faithfully to finish the trail. Two unfortunate fathers reported they had to go home because of "children problems." But 86 out of every 100 days of their trip, thru-hikers were climbing up and down the mountains and getting closer to that final goal.

Do hikers take time off the trail when they are tired? Does resting a day renew them so they then hike faster? To find out, I studied the hikers' miles per day immediately before and after time off the trail. On the second and third days before stopping, hikers averaged 13.2 miles per day; on the last day before stopping, in an apparent burst of energy to reach a rest stop, they averaged 14.6 miles! But resting made no difference upon returning to hiking: After the stop, hikers averaged 13 miles per day.

MILES PER DAY

Since Mount Katahdin, or the end of the trail, is too distant to be an immediate objective, thru-hikers must focus on something closer at hand. For most of them, the prime

TABLE 12-1.
AVERAGE MILES HIKED PER DAY

MILES	PERCENT OF ULTIMATELY SUCCESSFUL THRU-HIKERS
10 TO 12	6%
13 TO 15	60%
16 TO 18	27%
19 TO 21	5%
22 AND OVER	2%

measure of progress is the number of miles hiked in a day. The hero around the evening campfire is the man or woman who covered the most miles. Table 12-1 shows our sample's average miles per day.

The overall average (not counting days off) for both male and female thru-hikers is 11.5 miles per day. But these averages fail to reflect the true picture. Individuals vary widely in hiking speed. Based on data recorded in their journals, we can compare three hikers moving at different speeds and note the wide variation in distance traveled on various days (see Table 12-2).

Relatively slow hiker Gordon Gamble thru-hiked in 1980, taking 194 days but spending only 7 days away from the trail. Gordon, a 66-year-old traveling alone, averaged 11.4 miles per 9.5-hour day. A gifted amateur photographer, he took some of the finest panoramic color slides that ever pleased an audience; more than a decade later, his slide show of the trip is still breathtaking. It seems his slow pace must have been due in part to the meticulous photography he took time for on the way.

Doug Frackelton's pace was typical for thru-hikers. He also walked 9.5 hours a day but hiked faster than Gamble, so he averaged 14.3 miles per day. At 58, Doug is in the range of older hikers who usually walk somewhat more slowly. But he ran counter to the statistics by being both highly experienced and in superb physical shape (running, ski track training, winter camping). As is often the case, there is no truly "average" day in his hiking record. He walked as few as 2 or 3 miles at times, and as far as 24 to 25 miles on several occasions. Frackelton reflects unusual confidence and competence. He surmounted all difficulties with apparent aplomb, and looking over his shoulder reported that the hike had been "not too difficult."

Ray Brandes made a fast trip up the AT under unusual circumstances, as a member of Warren Doyle's "1990 Appalachian Trail Circle Expedition," one of relatively few organized groups to do the whole trail. This was a carefully

TABLE 12-2.
HOW OFTEN HIKERS WALKED A GIVEN NUMBER OF MILES IN A DAY

MILES PER DAY	SLOW (GORDON GAMBLE) No. DAYS HIKED	MEDIUM (DOUG FRACKELTON) No. DAYS HIKED	FAST (RAY BRANDES) No. DAYS HIKED
1	1	1	0
2	1	1	0
3	4	2	0
4	5	0	2
5	5	3	0
6	9	4	0
7	11	5	1
8	10	2	0
9	16	2	1
10	15	8	6_
11	11 AVERAGE	10	4
12	17	13	3
13	26 MOST	12	8
14	14	15 AVERAGE	7
15	11	12	6
16	13	17 MOST	12
17	7	8	10 AVERAGE
18	6	10	12
19	3	9	7
20	1	4	13 MOST
21	0	3	10
22	1	1	8
23	0	0	7
24	0	2	6
25	0	1	1
TOTAL DAYS WALKED	187 DAYS	145 DAYS	124 DAYS
AVERAGE PER DAY WALKED	11.4 MILES	14.1 MILES	17.3 MILES
DAYS OFF	7 DAYS	32 DAYS	3 DAYS
MILES PER DAY INCL. DAYS OFF	10.9 MILES	11.2 MILES	16.8 MILES
TOTAL TIME OF TRIP	194 DAYS	177 DAYS	127 DAYS
BASED ON TOTAL LENGTH	2,123 MILES	2,046 MILES	2,140 MILES
YEAR	1980	1989	1990

planned, van-supported trip made up mainly of men and women much younger than Ray. Leader Doyle was on his seventh traverse of the trail. Except for the Smokies and Maine wilderness, the support arrangements permitted hiking with only a daypack. (Carrying significant pack weight is not considered a criterion for having truly thru-hiked; unloaded thru-hiking, known as "slackpacking" or "daypacking," is described in Chapter 17 under "Commitment and Attitudes: Rules of the Hike.") Note that they covered fewer than 10 miles on only four of 134 days on the trail and walked more than 20 miles in a day on 32 occasions. (For a list of other notable fast hikers, see Table 12-6, page 91.)

If these three thru-hikers' records seem unusual, that in itself reflects the nature of thru-hiking. Successful thru-hikers are a very idiosyncratic lot. They will leave the trail for a day, a week, or a month, not for sensible reasons such as rest, but because of some trifling promised amusement, such as a vacation on a beach, a TV sports event, or a visit to a friend. Given 24 miles to go, any sensible hiker would hike it about 12 miles per day. But thru-hikers as likely as not will go 24 miles in one day and sleep most of the next. Not only does an "average hiker" not seem to exist, but most trips seem to be characterized not by planning and organization, but by an attitude of excitement and adventure.

LENGTH OF DAY

Long-distance backpackers generally hike long hours, often pushing to the point of physical exhaustion. From the literature, one might suppose a six-hour day was typical, but our survey data show that on a basis of the starting and finishing times, hikers were on the trail an average of ten hours. But day length varied, and even the average for different people ranged from six to fourteen hours each day.

The typical hiker stopped for lunch and rested three to four times along the way. However, there was as much individual variety in stops as there was in techniques of hiking. An occasional hiker observed the classic pattern of a 5- to 10-minute break every hour. At the other extreme,

one hiker reported that she ate her lunch while walking and never stopped at all "except to go to the bathroom." Most hikers took off about half an hour for lunch and made three additional 10-minute stops. Thus, the typical hikers rested about one hour during the whole walking day for all purposes—lunch, rest, views, snacking, and visiting.

The usual thru-hiker in the survey started walking at 7:30 A.M. This pretty much required getting up with the first dim light of dawn. The figure may be slightly optimistic, as with hikers' guesstimates of how far they usually walk; comparison between the questionnaire estimate and entries in a number of journals indicates the actual departure time may be about three-quarters of an hour later than remembered. The recorded starting and stopping times from the detailed journals of four thru-hikers are listed in Table 12-3.

Almost no one hikes very often or very far without breakfast. And most hikers want hot coffee, tea, or cocoa at the start of the day. But for those willing to start with only a cold breakfast, the reward is an extra half hour of time on the trail each day. In the morning it takes surprisingly long to carefully pack the sleeping gear, clothing (sometimes wet), cooking equipment, and food. And woe befalls the hiker who dares to simply throw the stuff into the pack—it is possible to lose an essential item for a week or more by dropping it carelessly in some deep, dark corner of the pack. In the morning a few backpackers may take as little as an hour to prepare, but the average is closer to 2.5 hours. And should it be raining, only the most dedicated will resist the temptation to sleep an extra 40 winks and dawdle a while in the hope that it will let up. It often does. Although it rains and snows twice as much on the AT as down in the surrounding valleys, the mornings are the time of day when it is most likely to clear. By afternoon there is the distant rumbling of thunder. I have often just reached shelter in the late afternoon as darkening skies harkened rain. Nothing is cozier than to sit warm, comfy, and dry as the rain clatters on the metal roof of the shelter.

TABLE 12-3.
RECORD OF HIKING HOURS TAKEN FROM JOURNALS

HIKER	AVERAGE START	AVERAGE FINISH	AVERAGE HOURS PER DAY
OWEN ALLEN	7:37 A.M.	6:28 P.M.	10 HOURS 51 MINUTES
ED GARVEY	8:09 A.M.	4:47 P.M.	8 HOURS 38 MINUTES
MAC McCASLIN	8:48 A.M.	5:13 P.M.	8 HOURS 25 MINUTES
ROLAND MUESER	9:05 A.M.	5:00 P.M.	7 HOURS 55 MINUTES

The hours are severely constrained by darkness at either end of the day as the hikers conform to the customs of an earlier time in humankind's life on earth when schedule was determined by the sun. A quarter of those on the trail reported never walking in the dark; 50 percent did so less than three or four times; and a courageous 25 percent occasionally ventured along the trail at night but not often—between five and twelve times for the entire hike. Most reactions were like that of Bonnie Goulard, who reported getting caught out at 10 P.M.: "Night walking—couldn't see a thing!" Or they felt like Emilie Jeanneney, who hiked the Virginia portion of the trail in late December. Even equipped with a headlamp, she hated it. Blind hiker Bill Irwin also used a headlamp when hiking in the dark—so his dog Orient could see.

Only the raccoons, skunks, and four hikers in my total population of 136 showed much enthusiasm about being on the trail in the dark. John Heneghan and Noel DeCavalante quite often would stretch their days in this way, but only two hikers were genuine night owls who took to the trail for hiking on moonlit nights: Christian Lugo and Ted Murry Jones.

"Olympic" hiker Scott Grierson, who averaged 16 hours per day in 1991, reported that on one occasion he wandered off the trail at night, asleep but still walking. Even with a flashlight, getting lost or disoriented would certainly seem to be a predictable hazard of night hiking. Also, danger may be lurking in the form of snakes, as reported by Jim Adams, who hiked almost 300 miles after dark during his 1990 thru-hike, using a flashlight only rarely. He reported seeing rattlers on the trail every night, lying in wait for prey. (For more on rattlesnakes, see Chapter 15.)

HIKING THE WRONG WAY

Route-finding was one of the good reasons given for not hiking in the dark. But, personally, I did not have even that excuse in walking the wrong way. I was in Virginia, approaching Harpers Ferry through a dull and endless second growth. Toward noon I spotted a large, flat rock and opted to break for lunch. Then I took out my little radio earphones, fiddled with the tuning, and off I hiked—in the direction I had come from. Two miles later I came to a road. Funny, I thought to myself, there was no road on the map. Aha, but there was an AT sign—and it insisted that I was going south. I reached up and shook the sign. I figured some jokester had reversed it. But it was bolted firmly to a heavy post. Then I took out my compass, looked, sighed, and turned around.

I also walked the wrong way in Maine, but this time for a different reason. From my journal of September 28, 1989:

It was midafternoon, and although the distance to the Wadleigh Stream lean-to was only a few miles, the trail went over Nesuntabunt Mountain. This little 1,600-foot mountain was described by one thru-hiker as "the most ridiculous climb on the whole Appalachian Trail." Having been warned, I prepared for the worst. The path zigged and zagged, went north, south, east, and west, and finished steeply at the top where the view was largely obscured. On reaching the top, the most prominent object was a beautiful MATC (Maine Appalachian Trail Club) register. Fascinated by the fancy register and running around trying to find a view, I paid no attention to the AT itself. When ready to leave, I found two parallel trails leading downward. They seemed identical, and I had not the slightest idea which one I had climbed up. "Oh, the compass." But this was no help; both trails left the same point and seemingly wandered all over the mountain. So I carefully traveled down 100 yards of each to check landmarks for familiarity. Finally, I chose one because the other faced the register, and I had been so impressed by its beauty I figured I must have arrived by that trail. I traveled down about 15 minutes, going halfway down the steep part of the trail. But I was troubled by some familiar-looking landmarks: that square stone, that angled tree. Finally I took off my pack, set it on the trail, and scouted ahead to check for familiar sights. The trail followed a steep parapet—I surely would have noticed that—no, this was new. So I climbed back up, put on my pack, and continued on down. It was not to be. The path turned a sharp U and leveled off below a steep cliff. My heart sank, for this I did remember. I was at the beginning of the trail up the mountain. I cried my only tears of the whole trek as I climbed that damn mountain a second time.

All this misery had one saving grace: The adrenaline flowed, and I clambered up over those rocks in a rage. Back on top a second time, I now faced three more miles and oncoming darkness. I struggled down the other side, around ridiculous turns, rocks, gullies, and ravines. I was so tired. But the prospect of an impromptu night out in the leaves was so unpleasant that I did not stop. On and on and on. I considered looking for a flat spot, skipping dinner and making do with what water I had. But there ahead in the distance smoke was rising—smoke made by people inhabiting a shelter. I had arrived.

I wasn't the only one to hike the wrong way. Ed Garvey reported going in the wrong direction, and so did 37 others in my sampling of hikers. Bill Irwin, the blind thru-hiker, told me that he had gone the wrong way following a night on the trail. Orient, his seeing-eye dog, could readily locate the AT, but did not know north from south. After that experience Bill said he always carefully oriented his sleeping bag with his head facing the direction he was going.

In general, going the wrong way was due to confused blazing, a missed turn, trail relocation, or daydreaming. Perhaps this is what happened to Beverly Finnivan who wrote, "I haven't figured it out yet. I just ended up at a place where I had been."

How Fast Do They Hike?

We know the miles traveled and the hours spent on the trail, so it is easy to calculate how fast people are moving. This is "real speed," and more than any other characteristic, it is what shows when you see a person hiking. I ought to know. On some days I would arise quietly in the predawn darkness, stuffing my sleeping bag in the sack and heating my coffee around the corner of the shelter so as not to disturb those slumbering. I could then sneak away, glorying in my early start while the rest of the world was still fast asleep. Ahead were several hours of steady climbing. As the morning progressed, the contents of the shelter would pass me and zip up the mountain. I considered billing myself as the slowest human on the AT. My average speed for the whole day was about 1.3 miles per hour, only a little below average, but going uphill I would often drop below 1 mile per hour. Since my trail day was only about eight hours, this combination put me near the bottom in terms of speed, progressing only about 10 miles per day.

Road walkers speak casually of doing 3 miles per hour, and occasionally one hears about an AT hiker finishing 15 miles by noon. But, day in and day out, on the AT it was usual for the long-distance hikers to go at a slower pace, between 0.8 and 2.1 miles per hour. This includes all interruptions, so the calculated hiker's speed between any two points includes the time taken for all stops. Table 12-4 gives the breakdown of three categories of hiker speed.

Except for record attempts (noted in Table 12-6), almost all transits of the AT are done by hikers walking between 1 and 2 miles per hour. There are at least three reasons why walking speed is so much slower than for a typical walk in the streets, stroll in the park, or hike in the country: pack weight, mountainous terrain, and roughness of the walkway. To some extent each factor independently slows the walker. But the combination is clearly the prob-

TABLE 12-4.
HOW FAST DO TYPICAL THRU-HIKERS TRAVEL?

How Fast	Percent of All Hikers	Miles per Hour
Slow	20%	0.8 to 1.2
Average	70%	1.3 to 1.7
Fast	10%	1.8 to 2.1

lem. For example, there are many sections of the AT, especially along ridges, with large rocks. This is no problem if you can jump from rock to rock, staying along the top of the terrain. However, you can't do much jumping with a 50-pound pack. The heavily ladened backpacker is reduced to working his or her way carefully between and around the rocks, crawling over some, and using hands as well as feet—forced literally to a crawl.

The pack weight carried by hikers midway between provisions averages 45 pounds, but individuals deviate widely. In this survey, pack weight varied from less than 20 pounds to over 60. Some 82 hikers carried packs weighing more than 30 pounds. Their average progress was 14.5 miles per day. It seemed to make no statistical difference in distance covered whether they toted 31 pounds or 61 pounds. However, 19 hikers carried packs weighing *less* than 30 pounds. These hikers averaged 17 miles per day, or 2.5 miles per day more than those more heavily loaded. There is similar evidence from the pack weight of seven fast historical thru-hikes taking 99 days or less (averaging 81 days). Their average pack weight was 29.6 pounds. In her essay in James Hare's *Hiking the Appalachian Trail*, Dorothy Laker tells how she found, in walking the same section of trail with and without a heavy pack, that the pack cut her speed almost exactly in half.

The steepness of the AT is also a considerable factor. There are over 250 mountains to be climbed from Georgia to Maine. Thru-hikers are fond of pointing out that the trip is like climbing from sea level to the top of Mount Everest 16 times. There are many places where hiking is more like bouldering than walking. By comparison, the Pacific Crest Trail is graded from end to end so that livestock may use it, and traversing its 2,600 miles takes no longer than the shorter AT. (It has its own severe difficulties, however, including weather, altitude, and obtaining provisions.) My own problem on the AT was that on a steep climb I had to rest and catch my breath, sometimes every 50 feet. Conversely, those hikers with knee troubles had problems on the downgrade, particularly in New England. Tena Merritt

The author with Peter Mueser in the White Mountains (1960)

had painful knee troubles but "just bit my lip and kept on going." The significance of the mountain factor is recognized in an old formula used by the Appalachian Mountain Club, whose guidebook is the bible for the White Mountains: The calculated time for hiking in the White Mountains calls for 2 miles per hour plus 30 minutes for each 1,000 feet ascended. Assuming the AT hiker climbs 3,200 feet per day, the effect of mountains on a typical hiker will be to reduce mileage about 15 percent per day compared with hiking on the level. As thru-hiker Matt Cross put it, "I never got used to steep climbs, they hurt and drove me crazy."

Tina Seay and many others have commented on the trail roughness: "Pennsylvania rocks really got us down mentally and painfully. My feet throbbed. I wished I had my heavy leather boots." And in other states, too, rocks slowed hikers. There were also blowdowns, gloppy mud (especially in Maine), slippery roots everywhere, and places requiring the use of both hands and feet.

Practically everyone gets used to a pack, after a month or two. None of the Appalachian mountains requires technical skills; none of the rocky sections calls for more than a little balancing, good shoes, and patience. Blowdowns, roots, and mud are hardly insurmountable. It is the combination of heavy pack, steep mountains, and roughness of trail that makes the AT such a challenge—and leads to so many deciding they have had enough before coming to the other end.

HIKING SPEEDS THROUGH THE VARIOUS STATES

Hiking conditions doing the AT are, to say the least, variable. There are lovely graded paths, as in the Shenandoahs and the Great Smoky Mountains, that would please the family with a picnic basket and would suit the most finicky horse. And there are long stretches of loose rock in Pennsylvania and elsewhere that try the soul and also the soles. To amuse myself while walking, I devised a difficulty score from worst, "10" (Mahoosuc Notch and parts of Mount Katahdin) to best, "1" (smooth walking on level ground with soft pine needles underfoot). The average wasn't "5" but rather about "7." More often than not, the trail seemed filled with roots, rocks, steep sections, and mud, or was obscured so that I didn't know for sure where it was.

By studying hikers' journals, we can estimate how their miles-per-day averages varied as they progressed along the AT through the 14 states. Table 12-5 gives the averages for 13 hikers traveling from Springer to Katahdin and a rough estimate of a few who were going in the other direction.

As expected, thru-hikers started slowly, averaging only 10 miles per day in Georgia and 12 in North Carolina and Tennessee. It takes about a month to get to the Virginia state line, and in that month most hikers have built up their stamina. In Virginia they average about 15 miles per day. Note that hikers going in the opposite direction hike through these southern states at the same speed, 15 miles per day, as they do from New York through Virginia; this seems to bear out the argument that the true geographical difficulty of the 10 states south of Massachusetts is, on average, about the same. The four northern states, however, are a little different.

In Massachusetts and Vermont, rock and roughness are more frequent and mountains plentiful; average per-day mileage goes down to 14. In New Hampshire mileage drops precipitously to 12 miles per day, no surprise to any hiker who has crossed the White Mountains with their steep ascents and a thousand magnificent views. Finally, there is some evidence that thru-hikers slow down in Maine as they near their goal. Maine, the hiker's favorite state for its wilderness beauty, is also well equipped with obstacles. Hikers starting in Maine go a little faster than those finishing there, probably hurrying south through blackfly season to get away from the bugs.

TABLE 12-5.
AVERAGE MILES PER DAY OF HIKERS IN VARIOUS STATES

STATE	TRAVELING NORTH	TRAVELING SOUTH
GEORGIA	10 MILES	15 MILES
NORTH CAROLINA, TENNESSEE	12 MILES	15 MILES
VIRGINIA	15 MILES	15 MILES
WEST VIRGINIA, MARYLAND, PENNSYLVANIA	15 MILES	15 MILES
NEW JERSEY, NEW YORK, CONNECTICUT	15 MILES	15 MILES
MASSACHUSETTS	14 MILES	14 MILES
VERMONT	14 MILES	14 MILES
NEW HAMPSHIRE	12 MILES	12 MILES
MAINE	12 MILES	13 MILES
AVERAGE	13.2 MILES	14.2 MILES

WHAT MAKES A FAST HIKER

As we discussed in Chapters 4 and 5, hiking background, physical condition, and whether male or female seem to have no long-term effect on the performance of thru-hikers. Those who are not in such good shape initially, but who stick it out four to six weeks, eventually match those who were better prepared. Carrying a pack of less than 30 pounds helps. There is also an age factor: Older hikers walk more slowly and must plan their trip more carefully, perhaps starting earlier in the spring.

If average speed is measured by how far a person has walked in a day (about 15 miles) divided by the number of hours hiked (about 10 hours), the typical hiker walks about 1.5 miles per hour. But what about the many days when he or she goes faster or slower than average? It seemed logical that long days on the trail would be accompanied by walking more slowly. Not so. A comparison of hikers' speeds on their biggest day (meaning most miles) reveals that usually they walked faster than on a typical day. Thus, speed is not due to ideal terrain. Rather, fast walking is real performance based on hiking ability.

Thru-hiking provides an unusual endurance test of intrinsic athletic ability because of its long duration and the constancy of the challenge. Most of those thru-hikers who storm from end-to-end—that is, complete the trail in less than three months—are, in their own way, class athletes. Data shows that these fastest hikers make their remarkable time due to speed on the trail, not to longer hiking days.

Fast hiking, sometimes referred to as "power hiking," has always been very much part of the culture. According to Hare's *Hiking the Appalachian Trail,* Jim Shattuck wrote about it twenty-five years ago when crossing the Great Smoky Mountains: "The graded climb of Mount Cammerer was over five miles in length and was relentless. However, instead of people passing me—I found myself overtaking and passing others on the trail. Nothing is better for morale."

Table 12-6 (page 91) summarizes some notable thru-hiker trips, giving total transit times and an estimate of the hikers' speed for the days they were walking.

THE BIG DAY

Most AT thru-hikers in my sample had a fair idea of how fast they were moving. However, when it came to their one-day record (the runner calls it a "personal best"), everyone knew exactly. Greg and Tina Seay hiked a modest 13 miles per 9-hour day, but they once power-hiked 5 consecutive 20-plus miles per day and also did 25 miles in a 17-hour stint. Bill Gunderson usually racked up about 14 miles per day, but outside Damascus, Virginia, in the rain he did 32.7 miles and rubbed his toes raw.

Hikers in our survey were asked, "What was your best day?" Everybody knew what was meant, but some questioned the wording. Judy Gallant wrote, "Does this mean longest? I wouldn't call it best," and reported she had done 23 miles over some 16 hours. Most did over 25 miles, and about one in ten did over 30. When hikers decide they will do a "big day," they walk about twice as many miles that day. Going as far as you can in one day (or sometimes over several) is something of a tradition on the AT and good fireside chat material.

To pile up that long mileage, hikers started early, in one case at midnight, but mostly between five and six in the morning. The day usually was 15 to 16 hours, with the hike ending long after darkness and sometimes after midnight. While I was in Virginia I met a threesome nearing their goal of 75 miles in three days. They passed me one morning as I trudged up a long hill. It was not, however, a parting forever. A few hours later I pulled into a shelter for a late lunch, to find the 75-mile threesome fast asleep.

The longest day sometimes stretched out to 18 to 20 continuous hours, but two of the hikers in the sample did 24 straight hours and one 26. More than half a dozen hiked over 20 hours straight. Tracy Hill reported the farthest single day in the sample, a 43-mile record starting at 4 A.M. and lasting 18 hours—not bad for a hiker whose backpacking experience before this venture amounted only to four or five days each year. Although Bill Crawley's total hiking background was zero miles and his self-described physical condition at the start was "pitiful," this did not deter him from tramping 41 miles in a single stretch after an early start, ending up at 6 A.M., more than 24 hours later.

In 1991, short-time record holder Scott Grierson managed 50 miles in a single day in the flatlands of Pennsylvania near Boiling Springs. This Cumberland Valley area was a favorite spot for record mileage, presumably because of long, flat roads; it was relocated over more rugged land in the early 1990s. Dave Horton, running in the same area also in 1991, managed 52 miles in a day. But neither of these Olympic-style records qualifies as typical backpacking. Not only were the men superb athletes, but they carried almost no pack and each had a support team to make preparations ahead for eating and sleeping (see Table 12-6).

A number of groups and clubs sponsor long-distance "marathons" on a portion of the AT as a special event. One of the first such races dates from 1940 and called for crossing all of Maryland, now some 40 miles, in one day. The

TABLE 12-6.
NOTABLE THRU-HIKES, 1948–1991

HIKER	YEAR	NO. DAYS TRANSIT*	AVERAGE SPEED**	COMMENT
EARL SHAFFER	1948	124	1.7 MPH	FIRST THRU-HIKE; IN 1965 HE DID AT IN 99 DAYS
EMMA GATEWOOD	1955	146	1.4 MPH	FIRST WOMAN TO HIKE ALONE; 67 YEARS OLD
JIM SHATTUCK	1967	272	1.5 (?)	HIKED THRU WINTER, NORTH-SOUTH
ERIC RYBACK	1969	82	2.0 MPH	17-YEAR-OLD IN A HURRY
ED GARVEY	1970	187	1.4 MPH	FAMOUS AT HIKER AND AUTHOR OF MOST-READ TRIP ACCOUNT
BRANLEY OWEN	1970	71	1.9 MPH	RECORD-BREAKING TRIP. SPENT LAST NIGHT ON TOP KATAHDIN
WARREN DOYLE	1975	67	2.0 MPH	RECORD TRIP, SUPPORTED. HAS MADE 10 AT TRIPS AS OF 1996
JON AVERY	1978	65	2.0 MPH	BOSTON RUNNER, WITH SUPPORT
O.D. COYOTE	1980	263	1.4 MPH	ONE OF THE SLOWEST THRU-HIKES—"SLACK-PACKING"
SARAH GLASS	1989	165	1.5 MPH	TYPICAL HIKER IN 1989. TOOK OFF 20 DAYS. HIKED 10 HRS PER DAY
BILL IRWIN	1990	253	1.0 MPH	BLIND HIKER. HIKED 11 HRS PER DAY WITH SOME SUPPORT
WARD LEONARD	1991	61	2.8 MPH	RECORD TRIP, NO SUPPORT SYSTEM
SCOTT GRIERSON	1991	55	2.5 MPH	RECORD. WALKED OVER 16 HRS PER DAY, VAN SUPPORT
DAVID HORTON	1991	52	4.3 MPH	ULTRAMARATHONER, RAN ON LEVEL AND DOWN, VAN SUPPORT

*Total including days off the trail.

**For days actually hiked—not including days off the trail.

Hike descriptions, questionnaires, and journals were used in estimating the average number of hours walked each day and the number of days off the trail. Although the speeds given should be approximately correct, in most cases they are not based on detailed daily data.

1993 "dash" run by the Mountain Club of Maryland included 33 starters, but there was no report on finishers.

Jim Adams has reported going 52.4 miles in a day on the AT carrying a full pack, in his 1990 transit. Put to the challenge by several friends, he started at Dennis Cove campground in Tennessee at midnight and finished in Damascus, Virginia, at 7 P.M. some 19 hours later; he then rested in Damascus for several days. Not only was Adams carrying a regular pack, but perched on top was his cat Ziggy. Adams's feat illustrates the wonderfully idiosyncratic nature of the hike where one hiker's glory would be the end of the trail for another: In contrast to the slow and steady pace almost universally advocated by thru-hikers, Adams would storm ahead for two hours, and then rest for 30 minutes. And although he took a total of 177 days to go from end to end, he was off the trail 84 days, or almost half the time. He hiked over 40 miles on each of four days and over 30 miles on 17 days, for what must certainly be the most unusual hiking pattern of any thru-hiker.

The perfect swimming hole, northern Virginia

WATER: ITS JOYS AND PERILS

The question of safe drinking water and how to judge water quality will give pause to any investigator. And whether water is safe or unsafe is not the black-and-white situation commonly believed. *Standard Methods for Examination of Water and Wastewater,* published by the American Public Health Association, is 2½ inches thick and over 1,500 pages long. Another reference volume, the proceedings of a single conference on water quality, covers 1,089 pages.

There are hundred of pollutants, basic metals, and chemicals, as well as viruses

I've never found any drink that tastes as good as pure water from a spring or small brook in the woods.

—Albert Field

One drop of water from that crystal-clear stream can turn your trip-of-a-lifetime into a nightmare.

—advertisement for PUR water filters

and bacteria, that can poison water. However, the AT hiker is primarily concerned with viruses and especially bacteria infection. In recent years the presence of a specific microorganism, *Giardia lamblia*, has become a major concern. *Giardia* infection is debilitating and usually requires going to the doctor. This chapter restricts itself to gastrointestinal illness of a temporary nature, focusing on *Giardia* since this accounts for most of the most debilitating sickness suffered by AT long-distance hikers.

Notwithstanding the complexities involved, the long-distance hiker must make up his or her mind often several times per day: "Is it safe?" "What should I do before I drink?"

WATER ON THE TRAIL

I was in North Carolina, and, although it was only early May, it was hot. The leaves were just budding, and on the top of the ridge there was no shade from the sun. When I wanted to stop, I would wait for a big tree so I could rest on the shady side of its trunk. The trail here was not marked with signs directing the hiker to water; the secret was to follow a faintly blue-blazed intersecting side path. However, the *Data Book* warned that water was scarce, and I had not been able to find any blue blazes. I followed the dictum of never drinking more than half the water remaining in the canteen, and it was now down to a matter of a few swallows. I had seen no water for eight hours. The *Data Book* said there was a spring somewhere along here, and as the trail dipped down into a little gap I scrutinized every single tree for some sign of faint blue paint. There it was! Ten more minutes down the side trail brought me to a little pile of rocks and a tiny pool of water, no bigger than a cooking pot but clear, cool, and lovely. I filled my water bottles and settled myself against a big oak tree to eat half a candy bar and drink and drink and drink. Never has anything tasted so good.

We are only a generation away from the widely held belief that you could and should limit your water intake while hiking. There was a time when army sergeants and camp counselors strictly forbade more than just a few swallows while underway. It was even suggested that pebbles be rolled around the dry mouth with the tongue to help relieve thirst. Physical training, notably in northern Europe, included long marches without liquid intake. Those were truly the bad old days. Today it is recognized that although people vary widely, the problem is too little rather than too much water. So, drinking heartily is medically correct as well as deeply satisfying.

From the standpoint of getting enough to drink on the trail, 1989 was a good year on the AT. In previous years, when springs and streams dried up, some hikers were forced off the trail. Then, too, there is variability in the amount of water hikers need. A few can survive on as little as three or four liters for a whole day and night; others need two or three times as much. There are only a few hardy souls who can survive a "dry camp"—that is, a night with little or no water for drinking and cooking. If you watch the backpackers as they arrive at camp at the end of the day, you find the first priority after taking off their pack is to produce a two-gallon water bag and find water. Personally, I never felt secure until my bag, fat and full with sparkling, cool water, was hung on a nail at the shelter and I could have as much as I wished.

The ideal water source, a bubbling spring among the rocks, is not rare. Often a short piece of pipe has been inserted so that even if the flow is small, it can be captured free of dirt. On occasion I have waited half an hour for a dribble to fill my bottle.

Hikers who cover ground rapidly and have modest requirements for water are in the best situation—they can wait for the perfect source. I am, unfortunately, a slow hiker with great thirst and so I cannot always wait for the ideal water source. On one occasion we found the perfect camping spot in a deep glen just as darkness approached. All was perfect, except that the source of water was a dried-up muddy stream bottom. This was not a matter of being fussy about insufficient flow, it was a matter of squeezing out some drinkable fluid. Luckily, we were still carrying enough water to start supper. So we dug a hole in the mud, and in an hour or so it had filled up with water. We bailed it out once, refilled our water containers, and upon treating with iodine we were all set. It was wet, cool, safe, and if not sparkling or clear, still infinitely better than nothing.

Fifty or more years ago hikers drank freely from any clear-looking water, and although we like to think of that water as being pristine and safe, such is not the case. Accounts of pioneers and travelers contain their share of references to suspicious illnesses due to impure water. So, the long-distance hiker of today is well warned about dangers, in particular the *Giardia* protozoan. Indeed, as was noted in an article in *American Journal of Public Health* by J.E. Ongerth, et al., ". . . it is commonly considered a backpackers' illness." Ingesting a few protozoa can lead to a rapid multiplication in the stomach, with giardiasis symptoms appearing in a week or two. The resulting bloating, cramps, nausea, diarrhea, and fatigue must be treated with prescription drugs.

Giardiasis is not just a disease of the trail; according to an October 27, 1988, *New York Times* article by Jane Brody, it has been estimated that as many as 4 percent of all Americans may harbor *Giardia* in their intestines. In 1991, New York state had over 2,500 reported cases, and in Vermont it was the number-one reported disease. Small wonder the warning, "Never drink untreated surface water." There are a host of other organisms causing intestinal illness, such as *Campylobacter jejuni*, *Clostridium perfringens*, *Listeria moncytogenes*, and *Cryptosporidia* parasites. Most of them, fortunately, require no special treatment beyond ingesting fluids and a few days' patience. But *Giardia* infection is an exception. It requires diagnosis (based on stool sample) and treatment by a doctor. If the symptoms of gastrointestinal illness exceed several days in duration, the hiker should head out of the woods and obtain medical treatment.

Not only was there a lurking danger from polluted water in the wilds, but in the 1970s a new problem emerged, worse than any pathogen because it was completely unnecessary and manmade. Successful litigation directed at parks, clubs, property owners, and anyone seeking to aid the thirsty hiker raised the threat that putting up a sign directing the hiker to water made the good Samaritan responsible for that water being drinkable. Thus the legal profession precipitated a chain of events by which organizations tore down signs directing hikers to water. Needless to say, this added considerably to the burden of finding water. Just to be doubly safe, springs would be specifically marked unsafe and untested, or even the extreme "undrinkable, cannot be purified." Frightening though they were, such warnings did not have to be based on any biological evidence; indeed, because of variability over time and the costliness of the testing procedure (see "A Scenario," page 99), it seems unlikely that most of the warnings were based on reliable tests. Legal caution, rather than medical reality, had taken over. Fortunately, this litigious madness seems to have abated somewhat, and although nicely lettered signs directing the hiker to water are still not numerous, hundreds of bootleg markers—on stones, trees, written on old pieces of cardboard and scratched over other signs—have appeared.

Even if the area is demonstratively uncontaminated, something could happen tomorrow introducing pathogens and pollution—so there can be no guarantees, and no water source, short of its being completely self-contained and protected, can be recommended. As recently as 1994 the Appalachian Trail Conference adopted a government-recommended policy stressing "the need for ATC publications and Trail signs to state that water, even from pure appearing natural sources, is not protected and should be treated by boiling, filtering or chemicals before use by hikers." It is a scary way of looking at the woods and certainly sends large numbers of hikers to stores to buy chemicals and filters.

There have been outbreaks of giardiasis recorded in the West, with a higher proportion of cases among people who had visited the mountains. One such survey, described by R.A. Wright, et al., in the 1977 *American Journal of Epidemiology*, revealed that 3 percent of 22,743 stool examinations were positive for *Giardia lamblia*. The discussions in this chapter are restricted to life on the Appalachian Trail and may not be valid with respect to the problem outside that area.

OBTAINING SAFE WATER

When asked how they decided whether or not to purify, hikers most commonly depended on an examination of the source and consideration of the watershed feeding the

source. Thus, most hikers would not treat spring water flowing freely out of the rocks deep in the wilderness and high up on the ridge. One careful thru-hiker made his decision after examining "altitude, proximity to farms, temperature of water, nature of source, distance from source, proximity to privy and nearness to populated areas." Others considered trail talk, lack of taste or color, smell, and the advice of guidebooks.

Some backpackers endorsed the "camel approach," tanking up from safe sources and holding off until they were sure of another good spot. John Swanson espoused an engineer's carefully reasoned approach aimed at limiting exposure: "Ah, the question of water. Initially I would purify my water when it looked questionable, but I stopped that in 1984. Now I use the technique of selected usage. If you limit the number of water sources you drink from, your odds of drinking bad water decrease. I only drank from two sources a day. If you drink from preferred sources (i.e., springs or streams with small watersheds), your chances of drinking bad water are decreased even further."

One rule used by a hiker was to watch for water darters as a useful sign of purity. One experienced thru-hiker noted that she felt purity was assured if you collected the water dripping from moss. A good "gut feeling" was also recommended. But many simply followed the advice not to drink "if it looked iffy." The team of Spirek and Ensminger (trail names "Sweezel and Dweezel") followed the ultimate regimen, reporting that "In especially bad water like beaver ponds we added bleach, boiled, and filtered." But most hikers were moderate in their evaluations of purity and sometimes did and sometimes did not take special precautions. Table 13-1 illustrates the range of practice and on-the-spot judgment as to whether to purify the water.

There is no question as to what was conventional wisdom with respect to water and gastrointestinal illness: It focused on converting what was assumed to be the widely contaminated water along the AT to a safe drinking sub-

TABLE 13-1.
HOW FREQUENTLY DID HIKERS PURIFY THEIR WATER??

FREQUENCY	PERCENT OF HIKERS
ALWAYS	14%
USUALLY	27%
SOMETIMES	41%
NEVER	18%

stance by one or another means. Articles such as "Just Say 'No' to Untreated Waters" by Fred Bouwman, et al., provide detailed information on all aspects of the fluvial microorganisms with emphasis on elaborate and expensive ceramic filters. However, the evidence in this study is that the practice of purifying water is not accomplishing what the hiker believes it is.

METHODS OF PURIFICATION

Four methods of purifying suspicious water were used by the long-distance hikers: boiling, pumping through a ceramic filter, adding iodine, and adding bleach.

The classical method is, of course, boiling the water. In the days when a campfire was always made, a kettle of boiling water was routinely on the fire. However, now there is often no fire, and even when there is, it is seldom used for cooking. Who now carries a big, black kettle? The recommendation to make water safe requires up to 10 minutes or more of vigorous boiling. Besides requiring the gathering or carrying of fuel, boiling is time-consuming and hardly suitable for a spur-of-the moment quick drink. Boiling also deprives the hiker of one of the most sublime pleasures of the trail: taking deep drafts of cool, tasty water directly from the source.

Bleach and chlorine products have been used for years and will kill many organisms. They are not, however, effective against *Giardia*. Halazone is a chlorine-based chemical used in municipal water systems, but it is unstable and no longer recommended for the hiker. Iodine is the choice of the largest fraction of experienced backpackers but is not without its own special shortcomings.

Newest on the scene are ceramic filters. They have the capability of removing *Giardia* cysts, amoebas, bacteria, cocci, fungi, and all particles larger than about 0.5 micron. The filters are effective against almost all significant waterborne organisms.

Table 13-2 summarizes the methods long-distance hikers used to purify water. Most hikers depended on iodine. Iodine is also the preferred chemical method of disinfection by experts and is used in the U.S. Army. But several hikers complained about the bad taste, and a number covered it up by adding fruit-flavored powders, such as Kool-Aid. At least one person avoided iodine because of rumored danger to the kidneys from prolonged use, but the medical evidence does not support this fear. In *Backpacking, One Step at a Time*, Harvey Manning writes: "Contrary to warnings by misinformed laymen, iodine is not highly toxic. Individuals, even pregnant women, whose thyroid function is normal can consume water disinfected

TABLE 13-2.
METHODS OF WATER PURIFICATION USED BY HIKERS

METHOD	NUMBER OF HIKERS USING METHOD	PERCENT OF TOTAL
IODINE	57	43%
FILTERING	40	30%
BOILING	15	11%
CHLORINE	4	3%
NO TREATMENT	18	13%
TOTAL	134	100%

by 8 mg/liter for several months with no ill effects. Tablets containing tetraglycine hydroperiodide—or TGHP—are convenient and readily available. A single fresh tablet dissolved in a liter of water gives the required iodine concentration of 8 mg/liter."

I was introduced to the method of using saturated aqueous iodine solution when trekking in Nepal. It sounds technical but is really simple; I found it convenient and inexpensive. Manning describes it thus: "Iodine crystals (2–8 grams, USP grade, resublimed) are placed in a 30-cc (1-ounce) clear glass bottle with a paper-lined Bakelite cap. The bottle is filled with water and shaken vigorously for 30–60 seconds to produce a saturated solution. After the crystals have settled, one half of the solution (15 cc) is poured into 1 liter of water. If the water in the solution bottle is at 68 degrees F (20°C), the iodine concentration in the disinfected water is about 9 mg/liter. If 4 grams of iodine are placed in the small bottle initially, it can disinfect approximately 500 liters of water; so long as the crystals are visible in the bottom of the bottle, there is enough iodine to disinfect."

Thirty percent of the long-distance hikers used ceramic filters. There seems to be little question of their efficacy in removing the most common water organisms causing intestinal illness. (The exception is extremely small viruses, such as those responsible for hepatitis.) However, the very characteristic that makes filters effective, their fine pores, creates the problem. The experience in 1989 was that they were rather expensive, slow working, awkward to use, and prone to clogging. By far the most commonly used filter was the First Need, which cost about $48 in 1994. But about half of the First Need users complained; a typical lament was "The filter clogged in the first month and it stopped working." An engineer wrote, "A poorly designed device not worth the money or the effort." A number of hikers started the trip using a filter but sent it home after difficulties. And some users wrote, "more trouble than it is worth," "a pain in the butt," or simply "broke." A few hikers had equipped themselves with a Katahdyn filter, which was more expensive and heavier than the First Need but was reported to have worked well.

Many brands of ceramic filters are now on the market, and this is an area where some improvement is to be expected. In his 1994 column in the *Appalachian Trailway News*, Dr. Vernon C. Vernier, two-time thru-hiker, strongly recommends that all hikers carry filters.

In my survey, hikers were asked several questions about drinking water selection and purification, and also about illnesses, particularly gastrointestinal upsets ranging from diarrhea to giardiasis. They reported a total of 41 cases of what might be generally termed gastrointestinal illnesses. Table 13-3 summarizes the illnesses as a function of the type of water purification used. The first column of the table covers all 41 cases of gastrointestinal illness, including giardiasis; the second column breaks out the 8 cases of giardiasis.

According to the experience reported by the survey sample, it makes no difference how you purify your water or whether you treat it at all. That measures so conscientiously pursued by the backpacker, so logical, and so highly developed and tested should make absolutely no difference is among the more extraordinary surprises of the AT survey. Since only eight cases of giardiasis were reported, the tabulation in the second column is just a sampling and must be viewed with caution. However, for what it is worth, whether the treatment is iodine, filtering, or boiling, the infection rate is about the same as for no treatment. Note how different these practical hiking results are from laboratory tests. One series of such tests resulted in the measures of effectiveness shown in Table 13-4, as published by Ongerth, et al., in 1989.

INTERPRETING THE DATA

It is hard to make much sense comparing Table 13-4 and Table 13-3. This is one of the indications that the intrinsic effectiveness of various water treatments may be trivial compared with other factors on the trail.

One approach in interpreting the gastrointestinal illness data might be that it is not the method of purification but rather the *consistency* that is important. Polling the hikers indicates that two-thirds do not follow a rigorous rule of either always purifying or never doing so; these 92 hikers used their judgment and only purified under certain conditions. Table 13-5 (page 98) lists the gastrointestinal sickness rate as a function of how often the hiker bothered to purify water.

The findings of Table 13-5 (page 98) are confusing. It appears to reflect increasing incidence of gastrointestinal illness with decreasing water treatment, except that those who never purified water had the lowest illness rate. Apparently there is a "base rate" of about 20 percent illness due to some factor outside the usual purification cycle. Even the most cautious hikers who always purified their water suffered about 21 percent gastrointestinal sickness rate; those "usually" doing so had 28 percent, those "sometimes" had a substantially higher rate of 39 percent. It is intriguing that these two categories where some 92 hikers exercised the most judgment as to whether to purify had an infection rate

TABLE 13-3.
TYPE OF PURIFICATION METHOD VERSUS FREQUENCY OF GASTROINTESTINAL ILLNESSES EXPERIENCED ON THE TRAIL

PURIFICATION METHOD	PERCENTAGE OF USERS WHO BECAME ILL	GIARDIA ONLY
IODINE	26%	6%
FILTERING	30%	9%
BOILING	34%	3%
CHLORINE	75%	0%
NO TREATMENT	27%	3%
AVERAGE	30%	6%

Note: The number of chlorine users is only four, so the apparent frequency of illness is not statistically significant.

TABLE 13-4.
LABORATORY TESTS OF THE EFFECTIVENESS OF VARIOUS PURIFICATION METHODS

METHOD	EFFECTIVENESS
IODINE, 8 HOURS	99.9%
IODINE, 30 MINUTES	UP TO 90%
BEST FILTERS, NEW	100%
FILTERS AFTER 88 LITERS	ABOUT 75%
CHLORINE-BASED (HALOGEN)	LESS EFFECTIVE THAN IODINE
HEATING 70°C, 10 MINUTES	100%
HEATING 50–60°C, 10 MINUTES	95% TO 98%

Pennsylvania rocks are notoricus

TABLE 13-5.
FREQUENCY OF WATER PURIFICATION VERSUS INCIDENCE OF GASTROINTESTINAL ILLNESS

How Often Purified	Number of Hikers	Number Ill	Percent Ill
Always	19	4	21%
Usually	36	10	28%
Sometimes	56	22	39%
Never	25	5	20%

of almost 35 percent. In the two extreme areas, where some 44 hikers either "always" or "never" purified but simply followed a self-established rule, the infection rate was only about 20 percent. It is a strange circumstance in which no judgment appears superior to carefully reasoned decision.

The sample sizes in this study are small, and one is tempted to dismiss the results for this reason. But it should be noted that although the data are from a total of only about 136 people, we are measuring this phenomenon over an extended time—some 15,000 person-days of backpacking during which time the hikers sampled about 1,000 water sources, with each person typically "testing" several hundred sources in the course of the hike. This is no simple compilation of the sickness rate for a few friends backpacking over a weekend. The reported cases of sickness may only be 41, but the basic exposure and variety of sources are extensive.

These findings are not the first hint that how hikers purify their water and how often they do so may not be the critical factor in contracting a gastrointestinal illness. Byron Crouse and David Josephs conducted a medical survey of 180 AT backpackers, most of whom thru-hiked the AT in 1987–88. In a 1993 issue of *The Journal of Family Practice,* Crouse and Josephs reported that 63 percent of the hikers experienced diarrhea (compared to 30 percent in the survey of 1989 thru-hikers): "Only 7 percent drank exclusively from protected water during their travels, while the majority admitted consuming unprotected or untreated water approximately once a month. The majority used a form of treatment for their water supply such as filtering, boiling or chemical sterilization of the water. There were no significant differences in the frequency of diarrhea between those who drank untreated water and those who treated their water."

The authors appeared to doubt the negative finding that water treatment was not a key factor in gastrointesti-

nal illness: "The lack of correlation is likely because of the small size of the population in this study. Other possibilities for lack of correlation include incorrect use of filter or disinfectants by the hikers, resulting in a failure of purification methods."

In view of the similar results in this study and our sample, my own attention has been directed to an explanation that lies outside of the water purification process. The findings of both studies fail to bear out any consistent picture relating frequency of illness to water purification. Yet all together, the data reflect evidence of more than 300 hikers over a person-time sample exceeding 100 years of exposure. It seems probable that some systematic explanation for gastrointestinal illness beyond the simply water-purification process is likely.

What kind of scenario might explain such results? Using the figure of an estimated 4 percent of Americans harboring *Giardia*, one in 25 people might be a carrier. Under usual living conditions, the kinds and frequency of personal contact might not be sufficiently widespread to bring someone in contact with the carrier. But the AT is a different matter. At a workshop during the 13th meeting of ALDHA (Appalachian Long Distance Hikers Association) in October 1994, 17 long-distance hikers answered two key questions about food and drinks.

1. *Do you ever share a cup, plate, pot or bottle with fellow hikers?*

   Yes   16
   No   1

2. *If yes, how often?*

   Daily   4
   Several times a week   4
   Once a week   5
   Once a month   3
   Never   1

Anyone who has walked the Appalachian Trail knows that eating is often a community event. This raises the question of whether giardiasis and other infections come about in the mutual handling of food and water. To check this, questions relating to the likely sharing of food and drink were tabulated; these had to do with such factors as whether hikers were in groups, met friends, or were alone at night. An attempt was made to correlate such exposure factors with incidence of gastrointestinal illness. No significant correlation was found. That is, the higher contact level of some hikers with people was not matched by a higher incidence of illness.

There were also no differences between men and women, nor was there a lower infection rate for health-care professionals who might be considered to be especially careful. There was a difference between younger and older hikers; about 36 percent of the hikers under 35 contracted a gastrointestinal illness, whereas only 22 percent of those who were older got sick. This difference might be explained by greater caution or a greater natural resistance built up over the years. Another statistical finding is that the infection rate in the northern states was approximately twice as great as that in southern states.

A SCENARIO

A popular belief among hikers is that the woods are loaded with streams, lakes, and springs spewing forth contaminated water. It is a view supported by cautious advisors, the medical profession, and the many purveyors of purification chemicals and equipment. It is buttressed by the general philosophy "If in doubt, why take a chance?" and seemingly verified by high rates of illness. A small poll taken during the same ALDHA meeting revealed that the typical long-distance hiker estimated that at least one in every four water sources was polluted. Because a long-distance hike means exposure to hundreds of sources, practically every hiker on the trail would have to, on occasion, deal with bad water.

Yet, because multiple exposure is so pronounced, and because the increase in sickness with decreasing purification is confusing (Table 13-5), the actual infection rate of springs, lakes, and streams cannot be readily estimated. Since hikers had very high frequencies of exposure and yet infection trends are inconclusive suggests that the actual frequency of contamination in the water sources may be less than 1 percent. Only at such low levels could the apparent ineffectiveness of the usual purification cycle be explained. That is, if contamination were higher, purification would indeed make a difference. At this low level, the typical long-distance hiker would encounter few—perhaps three or four—infected sources, and there would be only a small chance of an infection due to direct consumption of a polluted water source. Such a scenario is compatible with the findings discussed in the previous section.

To guess the probability of ingesting a *Giardia* cyst at a single stop requires knowing not only the concentration of cysts in the water, but how much water the hiker will drink from that source. Cyst concentration has been measured, particularly for public water supplies where there is some evidence of infection. These tests typically are carried out over the better part of a year and involve many samples taken from hundreds of gallons of water. Conversations with Maine Bureau of Land and Water representatives and water testing laboratories help in understanding why we do not really know how widespread wilderness water pollution is. In the case of *Giardia*, it is not possible to get a meaningful answer by filling a little bottle and sending it off to the laboratory. For testing, minimum batches commonly are of 5 or 10 gallons and sometimes 100 gallons. A typical test program is so expensive that in Maine it is carried out only for public water supplies. An expert technician can process only 5 samples in a week, and the testing period can extend over many months.

Thus, with thousands of data points to consult and dozens of cases of gastrointestinal illness, I have only been able to glean confusing and largely negative results. But it does seem apparent that such exposure is not due to rampant infection of water along the AT. The odds are with you that you can go all six months without purifying the water and not get sick. But how, then, can the 41 cases of gastrointestinal illness reported in this study be explained?

That this type of illness can be readily passed from person to person does not require any discussion in this study. For example, in *Walking the Appalachian Trail*, Larry Luxenberg notes the fate of a group of hikers, reported by Jim Bodmer after he rejoined the group mid-hike in 1990: "Nine hikers got together near Damascus, including one who'd been married at Trail Days under a canopy of hiking sticks. The nine friends had several weeks of enjoyable hiking together—one called it the highlight of his trail experience—but then, one by one, five came down with serious cases of giardia. End of fun."

There is considerable evidence that in the general population there is fairly high frequency of *Giardia* infection. A one-year retrospective laboratory survey in Colorado, described by Wright, et al., revealed that 3 percent of some 22,743 stool examinations were positive for *Giardia lamblia*; this is close to the 4 percent estimate noted earlier. Using this 3 to 4 percent range for carriers in the general population, there would be a probability of about 30 percent that one of the nine hikers in Bodner's group was a *Giardia* carrier. The hiking and living together could have then led to passing around the infection.

The picture of innocent hikers being infected by the water supply may well be backward: It could be that the hikers are the source of contamination. According to a paper by T.J. Suk, et al., "Examination of surface streams in remote areas has shown that the frequency of cyst discovery is directly related to the intensity of human activity in the watershed."

It is now half a century since the great sanitation campaigns in America took place. In 1942, the health magazine *Hygia* told its readers to wash hands, avoid common drinking cups, and use only clean towels. Indeed, in *Chasing Dirt: The American Pursuit of Cleanliness,* Suellen Hoy reports that even before the turn of the century, health agencies developed educational techniques that included giving up "drinking from a common cup." Yet, on the AT, when gathering for meals and rest, it is common courtesy to pass around a water bottle, or allow each camper his or her turn at scraping out the pudding pot—a pleasant practice, but potentially the most efficient possible way to spread bacteria. As for cleaning utensils on the trail, water itself is often scarce and hot water a precious commodity. Many a dish goes days or weeks between being subjected to the ordeal of soap and hot water.

The hypothesis that frequent interchange of food and utensils is the problem seems reasonable but is unproven. Tests of the habits of campers in my survey failed to show that those hiking alone were less troubled by gastrointestinal ailments than those in groups. But the sample size is small, and other factors could readily obscure this one.

What, then, is left to explain the 41 sick hikers in this study? The most obvious untested danger lurks in the hiker's own mess kit, and perhaps in some way with other people on the trail. It could be the pot only partly scraped clean, the cup hardly more than rinsed, or the spoon dipped into the soup. Long-distance hikers almost never wash utensils in boiling water, and for many, scraping and wiping is the way of trail life. Cindy Ross notes a problem likely to escape the attention of all but the most meticulous: "Be careful to keep the threads clean on your bottle. Mold and bacteria can easily build up here, especially if you use your bottles for sugary drinks, making dysentery a possibility."

In October 1995, *Backpacker* magazine reported a study published in the journal *Wilderness and Environmental Medicine*, making the first public recognition that advice on water as the source of these ailments may be completely misdirected. "Most backpackers religiously treat water from alpine streams and lakes as though it were straight from the sewers of Calcutta, yet they routinely tolerate crusty cookware and body grime as part of the outdoor experience." And when the authors of the study surveyed health departments in all 50 states and scanned the medical literature for evidence that waterborne *Giardia* is a significant threat to backpackers, they found so little documentation that they compared the risk to that of a shark attack, "an extraordinary rare event to which the public and press have devoted inappropriate attention." *Giardia* and other intestinal bugs are for the most part spread "by direct fecal-oral or food-borne transmission, not by contaminated drinking water," they conclude.

Perhaps the time has come to move the focus of attention away from the beaver (who, according to one source, contracts giardiasis from humans rather than vice versa), away from elaborate, expensive, time-consuming purification methods, and toward those possibly contaminated dishes, the unrefrigerated food, dirty fingernails, and unclean pots. Cleaning utensils with hot water and not sharing utensils among companions may be more effective measures against gastrointestinal problems. The time spent in care and cleanliness may be no greater than that presently expended on filtering, boiling, and other purification steps.

OTHER SICKNESS

Most other health problems were similar to the minor illnesses of the outside world. Despite isolation, almost a dozen hikers complained of getting a head cold or the flu. Only two cases of heat exhaustion were recorded; but an eye infection, an abscessed tooth, an intestinal blockage, hemorrhoids, and appendicitis temporarily forced hikers off the trail. In addition to the 41 cases noted above of intestinal trouble, hikers noted about a half dozen examples of food poisoning, eliciting such comments as "Ate fast food in Gorham—Blahhh."

Despite dire warnings and the fact that long-distance hikers were in short pants 95 percent of the time, no case of Lyme disease was recorded in this survey. However, informal reports indicate there have been cases since 1989. With the Appalachian Trail largely confined to higher elevations, ticks infected with the spirochetes responsible for Lyme disease do not seem to be common (see Chapter 16).

All together, about 40 percent of the hikers in the sample had to put up with some kind of illness during their hike. About three-quarters of the cases were gastrointestinal, the other quarter being the usual miscellaneous maladies. In a very few cases sickness required interrupting the trip for a week or more; but even under circumstances that appear disabling, hikers took off only a few days, and most of the time the backpacker gamely held on. For example, one brave hiker replied to the question of intestinal illness: "Yes, frequent watery stools and gas. One day I was so weak I hiked 1 mile, pitched my tent, and slept for three hours. Woke up and trudged for 6 more miles without eating."

The problem of diarrhea, whatever its cause, can certainly ruin your fun hiking. The drug Lomotil (available by doctor's prescription) is highly effective in stopping diarrhea symptoms, but for a better overall treatment many doctors recommend Pepto-Bismol (bismuth subsalicylate), an over-the-counter product good for upset stomach and diarrhea.

Although the difference is not very great, the men on the trail appeared slightly more susceptible to illness than did the women. About 43 percent of the male hikers reported some sort of illness, compared to 31 percent for females.

WOODS HABITS

One evening, while sitting at a campfire, a middle-aged hiker told me that he was going to have to leave the trail tomorrow, even though his vacation was not yet over. On asking why, I received a one-word answer: "Constipation." He claimed that this problem was so serious that it restricted the length of time he could spend in the woods to four or five days. It was not the first time I had heard such a complaint, and I had noticed some on-the-trail practices aimed at this problem, such as eating a lot of dried fruit or drinking much coffee. Being away from conventional toilet facilities, combined with the absence of fresh fruit and vegetables, can have a disastrous effect, especially in the initial days in the woods. The solution (as initially suggested by a proctologist) is simple and effective: Include in the diet the soluble husk fiber of psyllium. Psyllium is available over the counter at pharmacies and many grocery stores and is a nonchemical powder usually taken once a day. Metamucil is a common brand, although many similar products are available. It is a natural preparation and highly effective. Contributing to this problem of "woods constipation" is having to squat in unstable, unfamiliar terrain. Initially, it may be uncomfortable, to say the least, but it is quite sanitary and once the hiker gets over the novelty, squatting can actually prove helpful in elimination. Surprisingly, the best arrangement is to face downhill.

Most AT shelters and campsites have outhouses. However, this is not always the case, particularly in the South and on less heavily traveled trails. Under such circumstances, the hiker must go off into the distant woods; fortunately, there is lots of woodland around the AT. Where there is frequent use of campsites and limited disposal areas, all human wastes, including the toilet paper, must be carried out. A few meticulous people advocate this as a general practice, but I have never found someone who actually followed it on the AT. Conventional wisdom calls for digging a "cat hole" far removed (at least 200 feet) from water sources, trails, and campsites. No one questions the wisdom of getting far away. Go over the hill! Find a spot where the quiet, the view, and the surroundings are pleasant. Indeed, I have known several long-distance hikers who live out in the country and who, after years of backpacking, feel uncomfortable in the confines of a toilet booth. At home they regularly disappear to the remote corners of their property.

Although the 200-foot rule appears thoroughly justified when it comes to deep burial, many backpackers do not conform to this practice. Rather than follow the usual advice of digging a 6-inch hole in the soil, they deposit the waste on the ground and cover it securely with porous material, such as leaves, twigs, and sticks, and add stones to prevent scattering. Besides convenience, this practice is based on the notion that air and water permeate the disposal area and a high level of bacterial action composts the feces much more rapidly than when they are buried.

A final warning should be raised with respect to wandering off from the campsite in the dark of night without a flashlight. Ed Garvey once had to spend the night covered with leaves when darkness overcame him on a search for water. Taking off into the blackness to get to a remote location or outhouse can be easier than finding your way back. If a campfire is blazing and others are at the site there is no problem, but if you are alone or it is late and everyone else is asleep, be cautious.

Dinner for two in Georgia

FOOD, CALORIES, AND WEIGHT

Carol Moore, a 1989 thru-hiker, prepared a printed postcard, "A.T. Diet," for long-distance hikers to send home:

~ A.T. DIET ~

— ON THE TRAIL —

BREAKFAST: OATMEAL

SNACK: GORP

LUNCH: PEANUT BUTTER ON MOLDY BAGEL

SNACK: SNICKERS

DINNER: UPTON NOODLES
(DELUXE: ADD CAN TUNA)

DESSERT: DRIED FRUIT

— IN TOWN —

BREAKFAST: LEFT HALF OF MENU

SNACK: CHOC. MILKSHAKE
ANY PIE ALA MODE

LUNCH: SALAD BAR (3 TRIPS)

SNACK: PINT BEN & JERRY'S
LITER SOFT DRINK
½ CASE CHEAP BEER

LUNCH II: PIZZA (LG. W/ EVERY THING)

SNACK: PINT B&J'S
(DIFFERENT FLAVOR)

→ NAP ← (OPTIONAL)

DINNER: FRIED CHICKEN, FRENCH
FRIES, VEGGIES, BREAD

DRINKS: H₂O, MILK, COFFEE, WINE, BEER

DESSERT: CHOC. PUDDING — NOT!

Carol's summary of the backpacker's diet is not too different from the answers I received from polling the 136 hikers. Despite the conventional wisdom of planning a sensible, well-balanced diet, only about half the hikers did so. Few long-distance hikers could afford the weight of fresh fruits, vegetables, salads, and meats that would be part of the usual well-balanced diet. Considerations of weight, availability, need, appetite, spoilage, and calorie content result in a trail food selection that is somewhat limited but adequate to satisfy the hungry traveler. To meet the required 4,000 calories per day, sugar, fats, and carbohydrates weigh in heavily.

Although hikers had ravenous appetites and typically lost 10 to 20 pounds, most got enough nourishment to keep going. The overall consumption of peanut butter, Snickers bars, and macaroni-and-cheese is so enormous that the hiker does usually get enough of the essentials to make it over the last mountain.

FOOD FOR THE TRAIL

Thru-hikers laugh when a tourist asks, "Do you carry the food for the whole trip?" Actually, the weight of food carried by long-distance hikers averaged 2.15 pounds per day in our sample; that amounts to about 300 pounds for the whole trip. On average, they go off the trail about every six days to pick up 13 pounds of food, reprovisioning at local markets or stopping at post offices for packages forwarded from home.

When queried, 70 percent of the long-distance hikers said they planned specifically for food stops, including enough extra for one or two days. Only 22 percent admitted to simply packing a standard load and then hiking until they ran out. A hiker writes: "At the post office we would check our mail first for goodies. Then check the food supply . . . then buy what we needed to get to the next supply point."

Notwithstanding the claimed degree of food planning, there is evidence of a somewhat more casual attitude. If food plans depended on the number of days before the next replenishment, you might expect that the person planning an eight-day absence would load up with twice as much food as the backpacker on a four-day cycle, but the records show no significant difference. In practice they may decide to stop in three days, or stretch the supply out to ten. And they may pick up as little as 5 pounds or as much as 25 pounds. They do not usually have the next

> What hikers think about . . . 94 percent of the time.
>
> —"The Lagunaflic," Carol Moore

food replenishing stop clearly in mind except when it is a post office to which they have mailed a package.

Living off the land is an intriguing idea but not really an option. Resourceful and hungry thru-hikers have eaten ramps (wild onions), mushrooms, frogs' legs, partridge, and rattlesnakes. Berries—blackberries, blueberries, raspberries, and strawberries—are an absolute delight and can be shared with the local bears from Georgia to Maine. But these are mere snacks or a special-occasion treat and cannot even approach the hiker's requirements for a daily fare of thousands of calories.

A few experts who have spent years in the wild, such as Catherine Eich, know enough about the vegetation along the trail so they might survive by gathering. But there is the problem of time: Digging ramps, collecting fiddleheads, picking blackberries, and chasing frogs are time- and energy-consuming—and such food is not available in unlimited quantities. In a letter to *Backpacker* magazine, Bob Brooks reported his experience in living off the land: "After setting up camp, I realized my carefully planned, labeled, and neatly packed dinner was sitting on my kitchen counter. This, I thought, would be the ideal chance to exercise my Rambo-like survival skills—tempered with the knowledge of Euell Gibbons, the wilderness sensitivities of John Muir, and the hunger pangs of the Donner party. Lacking an edible traveling companion, I decided to let Mother Nature provide the buffet. The morning brought the sun, slugs, and the promise of wilderness fare of epicurean proportions. Dandelions, stinging nettle, three nightcrawlers, and two sluggish grasshoppers rounded out the worst meal in recent memory. All things considered, I'd rather have cold, stale pizza."

Long-distance hikers buy a little more than half of all their trail food at local stores, bringing or mailing the balance from home. In addition, they scrounge a few meals and in a very few cases cache the food ahead of time.

BUYING FOOD ALONG THE WAY

The availability of freeze-dried food from convenience markets and remote country stores has made it possible to buy all the food for the trail along the way. A few such places are located right at intersections of roads and the AT. Most of the time, by making use of the *Data Book* and hitching a short ride, the hiker can find such a store within a few miles. Almost one-quarter of the hikers obtained *all* their food by buying it along the way, and another quarter depended *primarily* on this source. Almost everyone occasionally bought trail food locally.

Depending on locally bought food saves much preparation and packaging effort, but the most important advantage is flexibility. It is difficult to predict how many days it will take to cover a distance ahead. Not only does it depend on weather and terrain, but meeting friends, taking advantage of scenes and sights, and listening to one's own body can drastically alter how far one travels in a day. Supplying oneself at predetermined fixed points can result in having to stop while still carrying 10 pounds of food, or even worse, running out prematurely. Because of this, almost everyone occasionally buys some provisions along the way. Besides, it is difficult to predict your tastes, desires, and needs while sitting at home the previous winter.

Quite a few hikers gave up on commercially prepared freeze-dried dinners. And such items as pasta, noodles, rice, beans, and raw grains were sometimes in surplus. But I never saw a hiker with extra peanut butter, cookies, Pop Tarts, Snickers, or M&Ms.

SENT FROM HOME

The other major option is packages prepared ahead of time and forwarded to post offices along the trail. Almost half the thru-hikers dried and prepared food, often bought in bulk, and packaged it for mailing to themselves along the AT. An obvious advantage is economy, although mailing costs can add up (see Table 17-5, page 136). A comparison of thru-hikers who mostly bought food along the way with hikers who mainly sent food from home indicates that the "care package" scheme saves a thru-hiker about $350. Preparing and packaging five months' worth of food is time-consuming, and couples write of spending the winter before the hike buying, drying, and packaging food parcels. But this saves much time on the trip that might otherwise be spent planning and shopping for provisions. And the home-prepared food can be delightfully varied and interesting, with such concoctions as wheat spaghetti with dried peas and spices, pesto with noodles, and home-dried vegetarian cashew chili. There is also pemmican, dried papaya and other unusual fruits, and even homemade oatmeal bars. And nothing can match a surprise box of chocolate-chip cookies from a loved one. In my own case, my son Kim regularly baked and shipped delicious packages of brownies, enough for an allowance of one or two each day. I always saved them for dessert in the evening or times of despondency, which usually came when it appeared that the next shelter had been swallowed up and would never appear.

THE CACHE

Trappers, hunters, and woodsmen have historically cached food in the wilderness for later use. In Hare's *Hiking the Appalachian Trail,* early thru-hiker Howard Basset describes burying 28 caches of food in preparation for his 1968 thru-hike: "Dehydrated foods and other supplies were packed in glass and plastic gallon jars with screw tops sealed with paraffin. All this preparation took many hours at home but paid off splendidly. The idea was to make a cache, with food sufficient for one week, at predetermined points along the trail. This would save the time and effort needed to walk to stores that were often many miles from the trail." For his 1969 trip, Jeffrey M. Hancock buried 30 caches, although he noted that it took a great deal of planning, a lot of advanced automobile travel, and was expensive.

Of the 136 hikers in the survey, only six made use of caches and then only to supply for a few days. More often than not this would be a special circumstance, such as some bottles of wine for a celebration. The only exception was David Meyerson, who is tackling the AT piecemeal (having started in 1966) and who has cached 90 percent of his food on his various jaunts.

FOOD FROM OTHERS

Overloaded weekenders, hikers cutting short a proposed outing, overfed car campers, and friendly tourists can supply an unexpected food bonanza; some 40 of our 136 hikers reported these categories as a delightful, but unreliable, source of nourishment. Thru-hikers themselves are not stingy but must be careful with their food supplies; they are continually hungry, and running out can force a long detour at an inconvenient place. But weekend hikers are a blessing: They often lug more fresh food, meat, goodies, and drinks than they can consume. They are the ones who leave the extra supplies in shelters and are often generous in sharing with the famished long-distance hiker.

There is an unusual phenomenon surrounding long-distance hikers that can never be predicted but can result in some unexpected nourishment. Where the AT crosses tourist paths in national or state parks such as Shenandoah, the Blue Ridge Parkway, the Great Smoky Mountains, or campgrounds along the way, tourists will stop the heavily loaded hiker and ask questions. The atmosphere of immediate friendship (and the half-starved appearance of the thru-hiker) sets the stage for offerings of food ranging from a banana to a full family meal. One time I was walking a short stretch of country road near Windsor Furnace, and a car slowed down as the outstretched arm of a young woman held forth a large apple. No word was exchanged, but the apple was delicious and the sense of being cared about was wonderful. Another time, when hitchhiking in Vermont, I was picked up by a retired banker who immediately invited me to have dinner and spend the night.

Thru-hikers have named this sort of incident after Yogi Bear, who perfected the "Yogiing" technique with picnic baskets in Jellystone Park. The very image of having walked such an enormous distance, the hiker's gaunt appearance, and the bare legs in short pants all provide a gallant, but also pitiful picture to melt the heart of the sympathetic tourist. These Good Samaritans are sometimes glad to feed, and even take home, this unwashed symbol of a great adventure.

FOOD OFF THE TRAIL—THE PIG-OUT

The average long-distance hiker takes a day off every six days to pick up mail, reprovision, and clean self and clothing. This day off in town fills another deep need—that seemingly endless desire for fresh food. The typical thru-hiker loses 10 to 20 pounds during the trek, generally burning more calories in daily hiking than he or she can make up in meals on the trail (see the following section and the later "Weight Loss and Nutrition"). Taking into account the total number of days on and off the trail, the average hiker runs at a daily deficit of about 400 calories. Thus, he or she comes off the trail hungry as a bear and eager to make up as much of the deficiency as the pocketbook, or the goodwill of the proprietor of an AYCE (All You Can Eat) restaurant, will allow.

When Jan Curran found himself in the Tennessee Hills Motel with no food nearby, he did not hesitate to pay $5 for a four-mile ride to the local Pizza Hut: "I was starved for fresh food and made two trips to the salad bar, heaping my plate each time; then I ate a medium Pizza Supreme plus a spaghetti dinner and washed it all down with a pitcher of beer. The waitress was astonished."

What food does the long-distance hiker crave when stuck out of town, facing a freeze-dried mac-and-cheese dinner? The items most noted in the survey are listed in Table 14-1.

Noting the typical weight loss of thru-hikers and the difficulty of carrying and eating enough food on the trail, the weekly day off, with its glorious hours of ice cream, pizza, milk, and beer, acquires an importance beyond mere rest and cleanliness. The "pig-out" is part of trail lore.

MEALS HOT AND COLD

The average thru-hiker is propelling a total load of about 200 pounds (his or her body weight plus pack weight) al-

TABLE 14-1.
FOOD CRAVINGS

OFF-TRAIL FOOD	TIMES MENTIONED
ICE CREAM	53
BEER	39
PIZZA	38
MILK AND SHAKES	35
SOFT DRINKS	30
SALAD	23
FRESH FRUIT AND VEGGIES	23
FRUIT JUICE	14
BURGERS	13
STEAK AND MEAT	10
A LOT OF EVERYTHING	3

most 15 miles per day with a total climb of over 3,000 feet. This results in a food requirement of 4,000 to 6,000 calories per day, compared with only 2,300 to 2,400 calories per day for the general population. With trail life demanding about *twice* the calories as normal activities, it is not surprising that food dominates the thinking of most thru-hikers.

More than half the hikers in our sample will take the trouble to prepare a hot breakfast such as hot cereal and coffee, tea, or cocoa—many even in summer. The rest will usually eat cold cereal and a wide variety of foods and not bother lighting the stove. The cold-breakfast payoff comes in an early start, about half an hour ahead of those enjoying their hot food and coffee; this extra time is generally spent walking an extra mile or so each day.

Relatively few hikers light their stoves for lunch; when they do, it's usually to make some hot soup. Dinner, however, is quite another matter. Few hikers will forgo a hot dinner—and when they do, it is for a special reason, such as a stove breakdown or very hot weather, or during power hiking, when they wish to dedicate little time to meal preparation. Only one person in the survey traveled the AT planning to eat only cold food. In general, the dinner hikers prepared was hot more than 90 percent of the time.

Until about 50 years ago, wilderness meals were almost always cooked over a wood fire. Mountaineers and explorers used alcohol and kerosene stoves, but it was not until after World War II that inexpensive, lightweight stoves were used by backpackers, and only in the last few decades that they have become the popular choice (see Chapter 8). Hikers commonly carried an ax or hatchet, and chopping firewood was as much a part of the long-distance experience as walking. If you study the 1920s plaque at Springer Mountain, you will notice a hatchet carried on the hiker's belt. Earl Shaffer, the first AT thru-hiker, carried a hand ax on his pioneer trip in 1948 and still brought along a hatchet when he rehiked the trail in 1965. Although Gene Espy, the second thru-hiker, carried a Primus cookstove, he also carried a hatchet. By 1989 the only people I spotted on the AT carrying ax or hatchet were teenage weekenders.

Fifty years ago the White Mountain huts of the Appalachian Mountain Club and Randolf Mountain Club were delightfully warm and cozy on cold winter nights as the fire roared in a stove. My wife and I joined the crowd at Craig Camp on Columbus Day 1953, and I remember the 5 P.M. call for volunteers to cut firewood. It was an era where mountain courtesy required never leaving a shelter or hut without stowing a pile of dry kindling and logs inside for the next hiker—and wood was a seemingly unlimited commodity. However, the picture was changing. There were more hikers, and around huts and cabins in the north there was an ever-widening circle where the forest had been cleared for firewood. What had once been a way of life (like a bed made of soft hemlock boughs) became forbidden practice. Thus, although early thru-hikers cooked on wood fires, those days are gone. In our sample only 5 out of 136 long-distance hikers counted on a wood fire for cooking, and only one of those was a thru-hiker. Thru-hikers reported cooking over a fire on the average of once a month and 60 percent never did. Other long-distance hikers out for extended periods, but not attempting to complete the AT in one year, were much more likely to take the time to cook over an open fire.

There are many reasons for the popularity of stove cooking. Stove plus fuel for a week weighs a manageable 2 to 4 pounds. Freeze-dried, precooked, concentrated, or home-dried food is readily available, often inexpensive, and sometimes good tasting. Its preparation in the woods requires almost no cooking—just add hot water and stir, blend, and wait. A double-sized dinner for a hungry thru-hiker can be prepared in 5 to 10 minutes. A careful cook can make a pint of fuel (1 pound, with container) last a week. The pot stays easy to clean—and saves a dish, since most thru-hikers eat right out of the pot. In addition to speed and convenience, the hiker is spared the hassle of wood collection, fire regulations, blazing-hot handles, blackened cookpots, dumped food, and, most of all, the exhausting challenge of breathing life into a pile of wet twigs that have been soaking along the trail in a week-long rain.

If all this makes the reader sigh forlornly for the cozy warmth of a campfire, do not despair. Even though most thru-hikers are exhausted and will fall into sleeping bags at the first hint of dusk, the lure of the wood-fire flames remains. When hikers congregate and tell their stories of trails going straight up the mountainside, curious skunks, pack-eating mice, fabulous views, and 30-mile days—there must be a fire. And the larger the crowd, the more certain that there will be at least one fire buff willing to take on the job. Even though the most that will get cooked is a marshmallow, it is the perfect ambiance for an evening with friends.

BREAKFAST

Practically everyone on the trail wants breakfast. The most popular item for breakfast, as noted by hiker Gregory Seay, is "oatmeal, cold cereal, oatmeal, pancakes, and oatmeal"—sometimes two, three, or even four packages at one time. Other cereals and breakfast foods reported by our sample are listed in Table 14-2. Undoubtedly the most unusual breakfast is listed in the diary of the "Biker-Hiker": Apple Jacks and Captain Crunch. But for most hikers it was "pretty much oatmeal until I got sick of it."

Although no hiker carried bacon, a dozen sometimes took the trouble to make pancakes, and almost as many occasionally made eggs (usually fresh but some freeze-dried). Among the individualists, one soaked raw oats overnight, two had cheese, three carried fresh fruit, four could not keep out of the peanut butter jar, and one loved macaroni-and-cheese so much he also had it mornings. Finally, one ate leftover dinners, and a single holdout never wanted breakfast.

LUNCH

Almost all the hikers stopped and rested to enjoy a real lunch. The usual meal was based on various sandwich breads or crackers, rounded out with sweet and salty snacks.

Some 25 also added jelly, and a few carried honey or marshmallows. Peanut butter is the omnipresent food on the trail, and it seems to have been so for many years. A few drank Kool-Aid, Gatorade, lemonade, and Tang. About 10 percent fired up a stove for the real thing: soup, noodles, even mashed potatoes. At least one hiker lunched on dinner leftovers, and one took the trouble to make instant pudding.

TABLE 14-2.
BREAKFAST FAVORITES

FOOD	TIMES MENTIONED
HOT CEREAL	
OATMEAL	81
CREAM OF WHEAT	11
GRITS	6
OTHER	7
COLD CEREAL	
ANY	44
GRANOLA	14
GRAPENUTS	6
RAISIN BRAN	4
MUESLIX	3
SPECIAL K	3
BEVERAGES	
COCOA/HOT CHOCOLATE	17
COFFEE	14
TEA	13
INSTANT BREAKFAST	6
TANG (SOMETIMES HOT)	5
BREAD, BARS, AND TOPPINGS	
POP TARTS	27
RAISINS AND NUTS	18
GRANOLA AND BREAKFAST BARS	12
BAGELS, BUNS, AND MUFFINS	7
CANDY	5
BROWN SUGAR	3
GORP	2

TABLE 14-3.
LUNCH FAVORITES

FOOD	TIMES MENTIONED
SANDWICH SPREADS	
PEANUT BUTTER	77
CHEESE	54
CANNED MEAT, FISH	31
HONEY	9
SALAMI, PEPPERONI	7
SWEET AND SALTY SNACKS	
CANDY BARS	35
GRANOLA	13
NUTS	11
COOKIES	10
DRIED FRUIT	6
CHIPS	4
JERKY	4

TABLE 14-4.
TRAIL SNACKS

FOOD	TIMES MENTIONED
GORP AND TRAIL MIXES	59
CANDY BARS (VARIOUS)	52
SNICKERS BARS	19
DRIED FRUIT AND RAISINS	18
COOKIES	13
M&Ms	11
LITTLE DEBBIE'S CAKES	8
GRANOLA BARS	7
CHEESE	7
FRESH FRUIT	6
HONEY, BY THE SPOONFUL	2

SNACKS

For many, on-the-trail eating is more or less continuous. Sharon Rise ate three lunches per day. Adam Ticknor did not eat any real lunch, but his snacking was like six small meals. I found I could go three or four hours in the morning after a good breakfast, but as the day stretched out the intervals between food breaks became shorter. If I was on the trail longer than seven or eight hours, I found I had to stop and eat something every hour.

Snack time is when long-distance hikers turn heavily to sweets. Gorp is the favorite. The traditional gorp mix-ture is equal parts nuts, raisins, and chocolate chips. George Ziegenfuss reported, "Gorp—I must have eaten 30 pounds of it." Like peanut butter, and unlike oatmeal and freeze-dried foods, no one ever said they got tired of it.

Berries picked along the way were a delight and some-times saved to eat with breakfast cereal. Many hikers had a favorite snack food, such as Oreos, Fig Newtons, corn chips, oatmeal cream cookies, soy milk packets, fireballs, pretzels, sugar wafers, beef jerky, dried papaya.

The long-distance hikers' favorite candy clearly was Snickers. Bob Schroeder wrote that he ate "Snickers with a normal civilian strength of 290 calories or industrial strength of 510 calories, for professional use only." But no one can match Tena Merritt's indulgence: "Snickers bars dipped in peanut butter."

DINNER

On my own trip from Georgia to Maine, I quickly lost my taste for commercial freeze-dried dinners. (And I didn't like macaroni-and-cheese even before starting.) As I learned what was available at convenience stores, I found I could assemble a delicious dinner with so many interesting variations that I was still experimenting in Maine. My basic dinner recipe was:

> A small (3-ounce) can of tuna, salmon, chicken, or turkey
>
> Instant mashed potatoes or rice, double portion
>
> Instant gravy, whole envelope (many different kinds are available)

Make the gravy first. Where whole milk or cream is called for, use powdered milk plus non dairy-creamer for richness. When it is ready, pour the hot gravy into a 12-ounce thermal cup, and cover; it will stay good and hot while you cook the other items. Cook the rice or potatoes in the just-emptied pot, and add fish or meat. Cover with hot gravy. Eat out of pot, adding hot gravy from time to time. Do not stir the potatoes (or rice) with the meat or gravy; allow the separate flavors to retain their differences. After eating, clean the pot by adding a little water and soap, heat if possible, and stir and scrape with a spoon while sitting around the fire swapping stories.

No matter my own lack of enthusiasm; the traditional AT thru-hiker dinner is "mac-and-cheese," with a small can of tuna added if available. Few, however, could hope to equal Gonzo's feat the night he tented by a farmer's pond encircled by croaking frogs, when dinner consisted of "mac-and-cheese with tuna, besides frogs' legs and sautéed chanterelle mushrooms."

As one hiker put it, "Freeze-dried—never again." Nevertheless, the typical dinner on the trail for long-distance hikers is either commercially freeze-dried or home dehydrated. The favorites are listed in Table 14-5.

As for brands, the three-to-one trail favorite was Lipton's, undoubtedly due at least partly to its universal avail-

TABLE 14-5.
DINNER FAVORITES

FOOD	TIMES MENTIONED
MACARONI-AND-CHEESE	44
RICE (USUALLY INSTANT)	44
NOODLE DINNERS	40
MISC. DEHYDRATED DINNERS	33
CANNED TUNA, CHICKEN	28
PASTA	25
INSTANT CUP OF SOUP	25
INSTANT MASHED POTATOES	12
LENTILS	9
PUDDING	9
ADDED CHEESE	8
BEEF STROGANOFF	4
VEGGIES	4
BEANS	4

ability even at the most remote country store. Such brands as Richmore, Mountain House, Kraft, Alpine Aire, and Backpacker's Pantry turned up only rarely.

Hunger drives a certain lack of discrimination, and Namie Bacile wrote that he would eat "anything that had cooled enough not to burn my mouth before I shoved it down my gullet." Others offered to eat the bark off trees or simply anything they could chew and get down. Robie Hensley put it, "I could have eaten the east end of a westbound mule."

Amid the freeze-dried and dehydrated food, there were a few circumstances that allowed for a more elaborate dinner. Many hikers would carry in a special meal for the first night on the trail after leaving town: David Walp cooked steak, baked potatoes, and corn-on-the-cob. Wally Stae and Sally Ford had refried beans, flour tortillas, onions, and tomatoes. And the Finnivans packed chicken, baked beans, and wine for their first night out of town.

On the whole, dinner for Appalachian Trail thru-hikers has been characterized as "oodles of noodles" (everything from pasta to Ramen oriental noodles), but even on the AT one can find the spirit of the gourmet. Frank Spirak and Diane Ensminger going northward "carried a Silverstone frying pan, extra mess kit, and a spice kit for elaborate meals" until Vermont, at which time they succumbed to the necessities of cold weather and "sent home all above items to lighten packs and make room for extra cold-weather clothes."

It seems that the women tended to have more imaginative menus. Julie Elman-Roche describes her dinner menus as "mac-and-cheese, wheat or spinach spaghetti, dried vegetables (corn, peas, carrots, spinach), English muffins, fresh vegetables (zucchini, carrots), and chocolate pudding." Catherine Eich was one of very few thru-hikers who knew enough about edible plants, berries, nuts, and mushrooms to significantly supplement her diet. Emilie Jeanneny would occasionally vary her freeze-dried dinners with "stir-fried veggies or potatoes and onions," and Joyce Vorbeau's favorite dinner was "home-dried vegetarian cashew chili." But no one could outdo Robie Hensley, whose dinners included "wild plants, mushrooms, ramps, fish caught in streams, rattlesnakes, frogs, and clams." (To top it off, he is the only hiker who had a dinner—pizza and chicken—air-dropped on the AT from an airplane.)

In general, however, long-distance hiking focuses on miles, not dinners. Gourmet cooking requires fancy pots, and although I have seen a reflector oven, wok, and even an iron frying pan dangling from a pack, they were not being carried by thru-hikers. The fresh food weighs more. Most critical, though, is the creative energy required; most long-distance hikers are not up to making a fancy meal at the end of a 15-mile day.

WEIGHT LOSS AND NUTRITION

The average body weight for long-distance hikers at starting time was 140 pounds for women and 166 pounds for men. Table 14-6 summarizes the survey sample, including

TABLE 14-6.
WEIGHT OF LONG-DISTANCE HIKERS

MEN	AT START	AT FINISH
LIGHTEST	115 LBS	110 LBS
AVERAGE	166 LBS	150 LBS
HEAVIEST	250 LBS	200 LBS
WOMEN	AT START	AT FINISH
LIGHTEST	110 LBS	101 LBS
AVERAGE	140 LBS	130 LBS
HEAVIEST	190 LBS	180 LBS

Note: Sample sizes vary somewhat with the number of completed answers on the questionnaire. For men, the total numbers were in the range of 72–96. For women, the range was 21–25.

the heaviest and the lightest. The range is not unusual, but clearly some weight is lost along the trail.

It is no secret that long-distance hiking is an excellent prescription for weight loss. Accompanying this, and notwithstanding sore knees, ankles, hips, and backs, most hikers at the end of this trek have a marvelous sensation of having achieved a kind of ultimate physical fitness. I can remember awakening one morning after months of hiking 50 hours a week, week in and week out, and feeling, "This is what the body is built for, not the stop and go, psychic stress, the competition and battle. The body is truly happy with this simple, strenuous, physical life."

Women do not lose as much weight as men, even in proportion to their smaller body size, as shown by Table 14.7, page 111.

Although most hikers lost quite a bit of weight, a few did not, and four in the sample actually gained a few pounds. Statistically, 13 percent of the men and 12 percent of the women did not lose weight.

In Karen L. Lutz's 1982 study of the diet and nutrition of six AT thru-hikers, five men had an average pre-hike weight of 194 pounds. During the hike they lost an average of 20 pounds, or about 10 percent of body weight. The sixth person was a 142-pound woman who lost 10 pounds, or about 7 percent of her body weight, Lutz's study included careful before-and-after anthropometric measurements to separate lean body mass from fat. For the men, most of the weight lost was fat, an average loss of 13 pounds of fat; however, they also lost about 7 pounds of lean body tissue, probably in the upper body. This is in sharp contrast with the lone woman in the study, who lost 10 pounds, but whose skinfold measurements indicated a loss of fat equal to 15 pounds. Lutz explains, "The discrepancy is explained by an interesting phenomenon not seen in any of the male subjects. [She] indeed gained [over 5 pounds] of lean body mass. As she became more physically conditioned, she was gaining muscle mass which is, of course, denser than adipose tissue."

Lutz also studied the hikers' diet adequacy from the standpoint of recommended allowances for protein, calcium, iron, vitamin A, vitamin C, and thiamin. Although intake of calcium and vitamin A was below optimal levels, she concluded that the hikers consumed an overall adequate diet.

The results of Lutz's in-depth study complement findings from our own larger sample. Not surprisingly, weight loss depended on how long the hiker walked. Those out for only a matter of a few weeks lost about 10 pounds;

Hikers near the end, at Antlers Camp, Maine

TABLE 14-7.
WEIGHT LOSS FOR MEN AND WOMEN

SIZE	TYPICAL STARTING WEIGHT	MEN WEIGHT LOSS	WOMEN WEIGHT LOSS
SMALL	120 LBS	11 LBS (9%)	6 LBS (5%)
MEDIUM	155 LBS	11 LBS (7%)	9 LBS (6%)
LARGE	175 LBS	23 LBS (13%)	—
EXTRA-LARGE	200 LBS	31 LBS (16%)	—

those doing a long stretch, or the whole AT, lost over 16 pounds. This agrees with the finding that even for hikes lasting many months, two-thirds of all the weight loss occurs in the first 30 days.

Lutz found her six thru-hikers consumed between 3,076 and 6,137 calories per trail day, an average of 4,306. In addition, these hikers were all losing weight. We can assume they spent around 20 days off the trail, eating large quantities of food, so a good, round figure for total thru-hiker calories burned per trail day would probably be close to 5,000 calories. This caloric requirement is not far different from that reported for other sustained long-distance foot travel over rough surfaces and carrying a full load. Antarctic explorer Randulph Fiennes wrote in *Mind Over Matter* that on a basis of 16 years of polar journeys, he calculated daily need at 5,200 calories. A 1993 study of 10 climbers on Mount Everest revealed that they burned an average of 5,100 calories per day.

Weight loss was not a problem for 90 percent of the hikers in our sample. Several women even said they did not lose enough. John Swanson lost only 3 pounds but reported a big change, a large reduction of body fat after the hike. Most hikers reacted similarly, noting that they felt good, strong, and self-satisfied, albeit many commented that they did look rather seedy and haggard.

Several hikers invoked heroic measures when their waistbands got loose, purposely eating more and seeking high-calorie foods. Bill Gunderson credited "Squeeze Parkay, tuna, and Ben & Jerry's" with arresting his weight loss. Understandably, Joan Felthousen complained that her 42-pound pack got heavy as her body weight sank from 130 to 110 pounds. Fourteen hikers experienced some problems: Karl Kraus took off 20 pounds and noted that he had "lost extensive muscle mass on arms and upper body." Charles Hydeck had serious troubles with malnutrition and ended up by having to take a one-week break mid-hike to fatten up. These hikers lost an average of 27 pounds, almost 19 percent of body weight and about twice that of the usual AT hiker. But these were the exceptions. Most hikers felt like Buddy Newell, who said, "I looked a little *too* thin, but I felt strong." And many echoed Bill Harrison, who wrote, "Wish I could keep it off."

Entering the Smokies

ANIMALS ON THE TRAIL

This chapter looks at animals encountered by the thru-hikers in order of size, beginning with moose and bear. The trip through Maine was widely regarded as incomplete without actually viewing these large inhabitants of the north woods.

THE MOOSE

Moose, wags say when waxing witty,
are deer designed by a committee.
This isn't true. God made the Moose—
From blueprints drawn by Dr. Seuss.

—Peter Farrow

The largest animal to greet the AT hiker is the enormous moose, a thrilling sight usually reserved as a grand finale in Maine. Most commonly the moose will be standing knee deep in a nearby pond dredging up savory vegetable mat-

ter with hardly a slurp. But sometimes the backpacker turns a corner suddenly to find this horse-sized beast blocking the trail. Usually the meeting is peaceful enough, for despite its majesty, the moose in temperament resembles the domestic cow more than a truly wild creature. Indeed, to call bagging this amicable animal "hunting" seems a misnomer. Moose are considered dangerous when being bothered by flies, when rutting or pregnant, or when protecting their young. In *What Use are Moose?*, Peter Farrow notes that there is at least one instance of a moose falling in love with a domestic cow.

> *I suggested we sit and chat for a while.*
>
> —thru-hiker George Ziegenfuss, on meeting a bear in Maine

BEAR

This peaceful herbivore (in the words of one hiker) was usually sighted only once or twice on a thru-hike. A significant number of people, much to their disappointment, never even glimpsed a scurrying distant patch of fur. Besides a curt "met bear," there were few good bear stories for 1989. An exception was related to me on the trail by a lone woman hiker. She turned a bend in blackberry country, coming face to face with a munching bear. Neither party moved. Finally the woman stomped her hiking staff down hard on the path and said "Shoo." The bear turned and left the scene.

My favorite bear story is related in a letter by 1989 thru-hiker George Ziegenfuss: "I had spent the night at Sabbathday Pond lean-to in Maine. My supplies were running kind of low, so I decided to hike out to Route 4 and hitch a ride into Rangeley. It had been raining for what seemed like weeks, but this morning the sun broke through. The trail was easy as it wandered through this section of beautiful woods already showing the fall colors. Some of the leaves had fallen and lay in the trail. My spirits were high, and as I walked along I broke into my favorite song: 'All things bright and beautiful / All creatures great and small / All things wise and wonderful / The Lord God made them all.'

"At one point the trail made a sharp bend to the left around a magnificent oak that obscured the trail in front of me. As I rounded the bend going north, so did a bear coming south. We met; this black form appeared all too suddenly before my eyes. My immediate thought was, 'Someone's dog,' and at the same moment I glimpsed the long claws at the end of the animal, almost at my feet now. With that, the bear reared up on its hind legs, towered over me for the briefest instant, then threw itself to my right and ran off the trail. It stopped about 20 feet from me and just shook its head, then looked at me and shook its head again as if to clear the morning cobwebs. I made a feeble attempt at apologizing for having evidently frightened the creature and suggested we sit and chat for a while. But after shaking its head several more times, the bear finally meandered off into the woods, leaving me alone.

"To this day, I cannot understand how that bear could have failed to hear me. I had been singing, I had been making noise walking in the leaves, and besides, I had not had a bath for two weeks. Oh well! I am happy for the experience and the memory. But I am still sorry to have scared it so, and that it would have none of my conversation."

The hiker's fascination with black bears seems endless. The explanation may lie in similarities discussed by Philip Johnson in the July/August 1994 issue of *AMC Outdoors*, the membership magazine of the Appalachian Mountain Club.

"It's easy enough to find the human side of animals, but in the case of bears this exercise borders on self-reflection: It's easy to see the bears within us. People are the most bear-esque of animals, intelligent, curious omnivores, with a nasty sweet tooth and a propensity to oversleep. Our shared cosmopolitan habits have made us competitors in the past, and could be the key to our coexistence in the future.

"A human is uniquely endowed as a bear's alter ego, a sort of skinny, naked runt of the litter with a penchant for straight lines and flush toilets. Besides this subtle divergence, we are from the same mold. We snore in our sleep; we spank our children; we have an inordinate fondness for back-scratching and a tendency toward idle contemplation; we can be moody or taciturn; we eat garbage; and we love picnics, just like bears. We can only imagine what our hirsute cousins find in common with us. But our similarities have ideally suited bears for the veneration and denigration they have received throughout human history."

Finally, it must be noted the intrusion of bears into the hiker's world is not merely an AT phenomenon. As loosely translated from the Stockholm newspaper *Svenska Dagbladet* (August 4, 1996): "The possibility of meeting a bear in the Swedish woods has become so high that advice is called for as to how people should act when meeting the 'King of the Woods.' Bears do not like the clatter of metals as from bells, and they dislike loud human talk. Instead, the quiet conversational approach is recommended. What subject of conversation would interest a bear mother out picking berries with her cubs? It may be difficult to start a dialogue. Politics is definitely out. In the tricky situation where you find yourself caught between the mother and her cubs, there are two good conversational possibilities. One of them is, of course, 'What are the children's names?' The cubs' names can be praised and gone over again and again. And when that is done, you can try, 'How are the blueberries this year?' One should be warned, however, that in addition to avoiding politics it is not advisable to start talking about the weather; there is a risk that this may make her angry."

In general, then, bells and clatter are disliked, and the Ziegenfuss conversational approach would seem to be internationally recommended. But stay away from politics and the weather.

DEER, RACCOONS, SKUNKS, AND THEIR FRIENDS

Along the ridge tops there are few deer, but the AT has many miles of trail through meadows and deep woods, and here the hiker finds grazing, graceful, and occasionally snorting deer. No hiker I know has kept track of the number of deer sighted, but it would typically seem to be in the hundreds. To see deer along the way is a universal pleasure, and to have a doe and fawn sniff at the edge of your tent is exciting and a little flattering. But in this era when the deer have invaded all but the most urban neighborhoods, they are so common as to be like the trees, rocks, and plants—a part of the experience but not generally newsworthy.

Other medium-sized animals prowl the woods trails, steal hikers' food, wake them at night, and in the case of skunks and porcupines get treated with considerable deference. The raccoon, which has been an abundant resident of suburbia from Georgia to Maine, will usually move into a camper's kitchen after dark. However, recent events have cast an ominous shadow over this night prowler: Diana Schemo reported in the August 20, 1994, *New York Times* that a rabies epidemic in raccoons, which started in 1979 in West Virginia, has spread so that by the summer of 1993 the infected animals ranged from the northern border of North Carolina to southern New Hampshire. While I was hiking in 1989, we got word via the grapevine of a strange-acting raccoon on the trail. Sure enough, we soon came upon a large raccoon sitting right in the middle of the trail, looking sick and unhappy. All hikers were beating a path around the animal with far more room left than if it had been a bear or a rattlesnake.

Skunks have stripes in the north and spots in the south. I have heard firsthand of several occasions where skunks entered tents and shelters and wandered around as if they had paid the month's rent. The only way to handle this situation seems to be to wait calmly for the intruder to exit at his own discretion. The wrong way is related in a story of the hiker who was disturbed at night in his closed tent by a weight pressing in from the outside. He punched the offending bulge and found he had to bury his tent.

DOGS—PETS AND OTHERWISE

No animal on the trail is as widely discussed, as much loved, and as genuinely feared as our best friend, the domestic dog. In responses to the questionnaire there were many more comments about dogs than all other animals combined. Dogs are encountered on the AT in a wide variety of circumstances.

In 1989 there were two occasions noted where hikers encountered packs of wild dogs menacing and circling a shelter attempting to get at the food. In both cases the dogs were beaten off and disappeared into the woods seeking more placid game.

A different kind of experience was to meet a lone, hungry dog and build a meaningful trail friendship. When it happened to me, I was hiking alone and initially noticed that a dog was following me. Every time I stopped, she stopped, always staying a respectful 100 feet back. Over the course of four hours the friendship grew, and at

lunchtime I showed her where the water was. I was regrettably out of food, and amidst peanut butter, jelly, Tang, and instant coffee there was only a bag of potato chips. She ate them, but not with much relish. I ascertained an owner from the collar and was going to take her with me and try to locate him. But as we approached the town that evening I guess she decided in favor of life in the woods, even if it were to be based on potato chips. And she was gone.

Bill O'Brien, who hiked the trail in 1969, described a similar experience, reprinted in James Hare's *Hiking the Appalachian Trail*: "I had a dog visitor with a tag reading *Mr. Price, Dahlonega, GA,* on her collar. The town was quite a few miles away, so she shared supper with me. After eating she bedded down in leaves, and I covered her a bit because it was turning cold. Soon after I got into my sleeping bag I heard a scratching on the tent. I opened the front and said 'OK, come in where it's warmer.' She did, right down into the sleeping bag headfirst, with her tail in my face. I turned her end for end, and she shut her eyes happily and fell off to sleep at once. 'What the heck,' I thought. 'She doesn't have bad breath and I don't think she has fleas.' So I went to sleep, too."

Many of the hikers felt very warmly about dogs on the AT, reporting that people with dogs were "friendly and courteous" and that "most of the dogs seemed happy." There was a feeling that dogs were "fun to have around," and several hikers echoed Christian Lugo's wish that "I could have had a dog with me." All in all, about a quarter of the hikers expressed unquestioned satisfaction with their experiences with dogs on their trek. An ultimate tribute was paid by Karl Kraus, who shared his trip with a woman named Sue and a dog. Karl wrote, "Dog and woman were both outstanding."

About the same portion of backpackers, one-quarter, had mixed feelings about dogs on the trail. Another 10 percent of the comments expressed specific concern. A thru-hiker and veterinarian, Eric Muller, commented on two dogs he had met on the trail: "The dogs had sore feet, were losing weight, and not enough food was being provided for their higher metabolic rates. One dog was so hungry he would try to steal your food while you were cooking it. They are good companions for short hikes, but on a long hike and thru-hiking they should be left at home." Bill Irwin, who had to have his seeing eye dog Orient with him every step of the way, hiked an average of about 10 miles each day. Thus, although Orient experienced a very long trip, it was not necessary for him to travel as far each day as did the average thru-hiker. Irwin was extraordinarily sensitive to Orient's needs and condition, and on occasion he even ended up carrying Orient's food.

The only circumstance I have ever run across where dogs actually served as pack animals is in northern Canada. In the early part of the 20th century the dogs used to pull sleds in winter were sometimes used as pack dogs during the summer. A typical dog weighed about 110 pounds and would carry about 25 pounds, or about 23 percent of body weight. This compares with about 25 percent for thru-hikers on the AT. However, on the AT, the human animal more often carried some of the dog food than vice versa. In a few cases they also carried the dog.

In late August 1993, Bill Irwin and Ken Wadress, both thru-hikers from an earlier period, teamed up to do the 100-mile Maine wilderness together. And, of course, Bill's guide dog Orient was part of the expedition. Bill Irwin, the perennial optimist, decided they would move fast and thus require only about five days' rations. On the first day, after 20 miles of rough mountain travel, they reached the top of Mount Nesuntabunt, no mean feat even for the strongest, experienced hikers. But Orient, a dog that had walked the entire Appalachian Trail, could go no farther. The three of them spent the next several days camping on the top of Mount Nesuntabunt where Ken gathered water from a drip partway down the mountain. After three days they worked their way down and out to a lumbering road where eventually they were trucked to Millinocket, Maine.

Several thru-hiker accounts mention having to take time off to rest an accompanying dog. Karl Godshall wrote in the July/August 1992 *Appalachian Trailway News* about a trip to Sunfish Pond in New Jersey with a family and its dog. When they reached the pond, the dog would budge no further, and upon examination it was found that the dog's pads "bore a strong resemblance to raw hamburger." The dog was eventually rescued by a park ranger with an all-terrain vehicle who said, "Do you all have any idea how many dogs we take off this trail each year?"

About 40 percent of the long-distance hikers on the AT had serious reservations about dogs along the way. In some cases this grew out of direct confrontation, such as the hiker who was bitten by two different dogs on his trip. Thru-hiker Greg Phegley "had to wait for a ride in the back of a pickup truck to get around two Doberman Pinschers at a house on the Pennsylvania road walk. The only couple of hundred feet I did not hike." Adam Ticknor advises dog owners to "leave dogs home or your dog will be your only friend. I walked an extra 10 miles one day to avoid spending a second night with one of their dogs. While other hikers may act civil to the face of a hiking dog owner,

they are downright brutal behind the owner's back." As if confirming Ticknor, one backpacker who *did* travel with a dog commented that he "constantly felt people were unhappy with our dog."

The issue of sharing a shelter with dogs cannot be avoided on a long hike. And although I have seen a dog owner move the dog out of the shelter when room was needed for later arrivals, that was the exception. Unfortunately, many dog owners honestly think more highly of their dog's comfort than of the comfort of some stranger arriving after them. On one occasion we were approaching a partially filled shelter when we were greeted by growls and unfriendly barking. The owner of a large German shepherd explained that since her dog had arrived first he was protecting his territory, and there was nothing she could do about it. Although there were places for at least two hikers, we were afraid to come any closer. We and other later arrivals ended up tenting.

It was not unusual to be squeezed in and have to share tight accommodations with someone's dog. The questionnaire responses contain many comments like "dogs were my biggest problem," "got attacked by a mean one," and "Dogs do not belong on the trail! They scare wildlife; in shelters are wet, muddy, and smelly; get into food; and are a pain to thru-hikers."

As for bringing a dog along as company for a thru-hike, it is clear that most people on the trail will be outwardly tolerant, and some will downright enjoy the four-legged participants. However, a large number of hikers will feel they are being taken advantage of and will not enjoy the experience. The decision about bringing a dog, therefore, involves weighing the owner's increased enjoyment against imposing on the comfort and pleasure of many others. A final twist is apparent in the comment made by one person, but echoed by about a half dozen others: "I had a hard time caring for myself. Caring for a dog might be too much." Regardless, from the standpoint of the majority on the trail, a dog will be an imposition, and although the hikers will put up with it they will not enjoy the experience.

CATS AS TRAIL COMPANIONS

"Surely you jest," the reader must be thinking. But 1990 thru-hiker Jim Adams hiked the AT with his cat Ziggy perched on top of his pack. Ziggy earned his keep; see the section "Mice" later in this chapter.

SNAKES

Hikers report that in the South, when they descend into the valley and gaps, the most common question asked by

Keith Walker providing a few days' company on the AT in Vermont

local inhabitants was, "Did you see any snakes?" The gravest warning issued was always about hordes of dangerous, poisonous reptiles. I did not see any snakes for the first several weeks of my trip. When I responded negatively to questions from locals and tourists, they were visibly disappointed. I hated to disillusion them and so appropriated a hair-raising tale of a fellow hiker who had almost stepped on a rattler.

Later I was able to substitute my own account of a tête-à-tête with a very large rattlesnake. It was a hot, short-pants day in Virginia, and Mike White, a friend of my son Peter, had joined me for a couple days of the trip. We had been climbing for an hour to reach the ridge crest, and my head was bent over as the drops of perspiration dripped onto the trail. I awoke from my daze because of an unexpected sound. The first thing that came to my mind was, "How extraordinary—crickets in the middle of the day." And then I looked slightly to my left, and there, curled in the dry leaves, looking like a coiled fire hose, was the biggest rattler I had ever seen. Probably, Mike had first alerted the snake. Stories of striking rattlesnakes indicate it is not the first, but often the second or third member of the party most likely to be struck. His (or was it her?) tail was stuck straight up and buzzing furiously, but his head was still sleepily resting on the coils and the general attitude was more one of nonchalance than threat. I stayed a respectful couple of feet away and we discussed the heat of the day, before I moved on and left my polite friend alone guarding the trail.

Only two poisonous snakes are likely to be met on the AT, the copperhead and the rattlesnake. Up until the mid-1970s, long-distance hikers made a point of killing every rattler and copperhead they met. Hikers truly believed they were thus making the trail safe for others. George Outerbridge, who hiked the trail in the 1930s, mentions killing half-a-dozen rattlers on various early trips. Gene Espy, who in 1951 was the second AT thru-hiker, reflected the ethos of the period, claiming he had killed 15 to 20 rattlesnakes and five copperheads on his journey north to Katahdin. In the same year, Elmer Onstott reports that groups at Dismal Mountain had a competitive hunt, killing a total of 104 rattlesnakes. In a few cases, fat rattlesnakes were eaten—tasting delicious, about halfway between fish and chicken.

But times were changing. Dorothy Laker seems to be one of the first hikers to espouse a new sensitivity to wildlife. In 1964 she joined pioneer hiker Earl Shaffer for a few days walking northward to Damascus. Her report appears in James Hare's *Hiking the Appalachian Trail*: "All too soon we were descending through a fine forest to a road that led into Damascus. It had been wonderful hiking with Earl, and I hated to see it end. Earl stopped so suddenly that I almost ran over him. He had spotted a rattler on the trail ahead. While I was still wondering whether there was enough light for a picture, Earl stunned me by saying he had to kill the snake because it was too close to town and people. And he did kill it, and cut off the rattles. Inwardly I was numb, and all the way to Damascus I kept thinking that if I hadn't happened along when I did, Earl would have traveled with a different timetable and would never have seen the snake, and now there would be one more wild creature helping to maintain the balance of nature, instead of a sad trophy in a hiker's pocket."

Within another decade the feeling about sharing the trail with snakes had radically changed, and hikers no longer viewed the rattlesnake as a lurking enemy. They now gave way to the rattler when they met, and avoided lurid battles. And over the years aggressive snake killers had sharply reduced the prevalence of poisonous snakes so that sighting one was more of an exciting event than a dangerous encounter. Most hikers in my sample of 136 saw only one or two rattlesnakes. The highest number reported was five, and a considerable number of disappointed thru-hikers never saw one. However, when one hiker spotted a water snake in the pool in which she had swum the night before, she was not enthusiastic.

Jim Adams, who did quite a bit of hiking after dark on his 1991 transit (see Chapter 12, "Length of Day"), reported that although he had seen two rattlesnakes by day, the situation at night was very different: The rattlers were lying along the trail awaiting some unsuspecting mouse to come along. He suspended night walking from Pennsylvania through Massachusetts because of this danger.

Snakebites are extremely rare on the AT, and in the 1989 sample population 70 percent of the hikers did not carry a snakebite kit. However, Tom Carroll, who was thru-hiking just ahead of me, had an unusual encounter. Camped under a bridge, he rolled over during the night in his sleeping bag and felt a sting on his arm. Since he had seen wasp nests under the bridge, he assumed that he had been stung by one of them. However, in the morning he woke up with a swollen arm. Carroll wrote in the Harpers Ferry register: "A copperhead snake decided I was entitled to a two-week vacation, so off he/she sent me with my backpack to the Roanoke Memorial Hospital for three days' AYCE (all you can eat), and then a Greyhound trek to Baltimore for 10 days of rest and relaxation. . . . Before I could go he/she puckered up and gave me a big fangtooth venom-packed kiss on the arm. Now I am back feeling fine and headed north."

Carroll's experience was one of the very few snakebite encounters on the trail. Fortunately, the copperhead bite is rarely fatal (only to small children, the sick, or the very old). Although the rattlesnake bite is more dangerous, and despite dozens of close calls where hikers report "nearly stepping on one," the rattlesnake/hiker relationship is now one of mutual respect. As Greg Knoettner put it, "Saw a few rattlers, but they were friendly." Greg's laid-back view of snakes is shared by other hikers today. Eighty percent of the long-distance hikers regarded snakes as being no problem, and only one in a hundred considered snakes something to really worry about.

IF A SNAKE BITES YOU

I've never seen a reference to a rattlesnake bite on the AT, and attacks on hikers are generally rare, according to snake expert Laurence Klauber's monumental 1982 study, *Rattlesnakes.* He notes, "In the past twenty years there has been only one report of a backpacker in the Sierras of California bitten by a rattlesnake, and he was bitten while changing a tire at the end of his hike."

The reason for including this section is because of the confusing and changing advice on what a hiker should do if bitten, particularly when in a remote area. The situation is not helped by 440 years of myths about the rattlesnake, almost all of which are in error or are misleading. With respect to trusting such advice, new and old, Klauber notes, "A folklore remedy for rattlesnake bite is dangerous folly." Indeed, some of the most widely applied remedies, such as incising and the application of a tourniquet, when performed by amateurs, are more likely to endanger life and limb than be of help.

The universally prescribed remedy for what to do on being bitten is to stay calm, keep the patient immobile, and get him or her as quickly as possible to a hospital. There are cases on record of fatalities and near fatalities due to panic when someone wrongly believed that he or she had been bitten by a rattler. Thus, positive identification is useful—but only if it does not take time away from attending the patient. Bob Myers, Director of the Rattlesnake Museum in Albuquerque, New Mexico, explains, "The actual snake does not have to be brought in for identification, as many believe. A polyvalent antivenin (made for North American pit viper venom) is used for all rattlesnake, copperhead, and water moccasin bites." He points out that snakebite fatalities in the general population are rare, and "as hikers are in very good condition, I

would estimate the chance of survival after a poisonous snakebite to be even higher."

The situation faced by an AT hiker, however, is very different from the usual circumstances. Klauber reports that of 200 snakebite cases treated by physicians, the average time from bite to hospital was less than an hour. Not so on the AT. Here, the backpacker's problem is that professional medical help is often a long hike away.

The best advice is to find shelter and warmth, and expect to be sick. A poisonous snakebite can be very painful. There may be swelling, nausea, and shortness of breath. Be calm. Tough it out. Send for help if possible. The odds are heavily with you, and the chances are extremely high that you will survive. Maynard Cox, director of the North Florida Snakebite Treatment Center, notes that of about 8,000 poisonous snakebites reported each year, there are only about five deaths. If the swelling and nausea are not extreme and there is a chance of getting to a hospital, walk out very slowly, taking time to rest every three to five minutes.

According to Cindy Ross and Todd Gladfelter in *A Hiker's Companion,* the key thing is to prevent shock, which can kill the patient within 30 minutes of the bite. "Victims go into shock because of terror and pain. A burning, fiery pain accompanies a bite, and when it is located on a main artery or nerve trunk, the pain is greatly intensified. If the face is pale, raise the tail. If the face is red, raise the head." Maynard Cox says not to allow the victim to get hot or cold. Get him or her to a hospital to get antivenin.

MICE

Many little animals, such as squirrels, chipmunks, rabbits, and the like, enliven the evenings at sites and shelters. But only one has settled into these locations in massive numbers. Mice are surely the most ubiquitous and most unpopular animal encountered on the AT. About 10 percent of the hikers found mice a serious nuisance—twice as many as complained of dogs, and five to ten times more than those bothered by bears and snakes. Reactions were often strong against the "pain-in-the-ass moochers."

When one is tenting out in the open woods, mice are seldom a problem. With a host of natural enemies, mice are only occasionally seen on the trail. However, the mouse population has taken the word "shelter" to heart, and whole villages of the rodents have sprung up at these locations. Hikers complained of holes in their socks, bags, and packs. Stuart Wilson lamented, "They ate my authentic Akubatra Bushman's hat." Craig Mayer suffered the ultimate depredation one night when he "lost a Snickers bar to the buggers. Now, that's what I call serious." George Schindler awoke one morning to find that a mouse had removed the entire wool lining from the inside of his leather gloves. A good many hikers objected to the gnawing noise and mice running over their faces and sleeping bags. One only felt safe when sleeping with his face completely covered. Finding feces in the food and dishes was not only unappetizing but raised the question of disease.

In 1994, a hiker from Australia contracted a rare but deadly lung infection called hantavirus while hiking the AT in Virginia. The disease is serious enough that Forest Service workers wearing protective clothing and face masks trapped mice at the Wapiti shelter so blood and organ samples could be studied at the Centers for Disease Control and Prevention in Atlanta. The advice is that hikers should avoid touching or sleeping on top of mice feces or stirring up dust in an enclosed, infected area—easier said than done! Although hardly a widespread danger, hantavirus is yet another reason for disliking sharing shelters with mice. Besides hanging up packs and food with mouse guards, a number of hikers (including myself) took to carrying and setting mousetraps. One man claimed to have caught five mice before going to sleep. Another always carried two traps, setting one on top and one underneath his pack. He always caught two mice, and his pack was never disturbed. (Experienced hikers never zip packs at night so mice who wish entry can run right in; otherwise, they will gnaw their way in.)

The most successful antimouse device was carried by Jim Adams at the top of his pack. It was there that Ziggy the cat rode from Georgia to Maine in 1990. Since Ziggy rested all day as Jim walked, he was in fresh condition to handle the mouse problems at night. It is worth noting that Jim was not blind to proper trail courtesy and always checked with other shelter occupants to make sure no one minded Ziggy's being on the loose; no one objected. Ziggy's record night was at the mouse-infested stone hut on top of Blood Mountain, Georgia, where he finished off 11 mice in one night. Ziggy was not only a scourge for the mouse population but would not hesitate to take on dogs and raccoons and had to be restrained from chasing a skunk.

Wholesale mouse extermination is now carried out by the section-hiking group known (for other reasons; see Chapter 6) by the trail name "Three Blind Mice." In 1994 they were in New York state hiking northward and cleaning out shelters on the way. They found boiling water poured in the mouse holes highly effective.

In all fairness, it appears that even mice have some friends. There were a few hikers who took a pro-life stand on these creatures, making such comments as "They were fun," "Gotta love those little guys." On several occasions, in deference to such gentle feelings, I avoided setting my mousetrap for the night.

WOMEN, MEN, AND ANIMALS

Our questionnaire asked about hikers' feelings toward animals on the trail. The unpopularity contest for four types of animals came out as below.

TABLE 15-1.
ANIMAL POPULARITY AMONG THRU-HIKERS

THE CRITTERS	"SERIOUS PROBLEM"	"NO PROBLEM"
MICE	10%	40%
DOGS	5%	63%
BEAR	2%	95%
SNAKES	1%	80%

The survey data reveal a surprise: In the case of mice, dogs, and snakes, about three times the percentage of males had some reservations as did females. In facing wildlife it would appear the female is less afraid and more tolerant of others in the woods than is the male. As for bears, there were too few responses to reach any conclusion.

Finally, it should be noted that there is a plethora of turtles, toads, frogs, salamanders, and other little friends to be seen at the bend in the trail, the brook, forest floor, and bottom of the spring. They are part of the environment, a reward especially for the lone and silent hiker.

BIRDS

Some birdwatchers who have hiked the AT are attuned to the sounds and sights of a thousand birds. For James Wolf, who hiked the AT in 1971 carrying his 9 X 35 binoculars, the woods were full of redwinged blackbirds, crows, robins, nuthatches, warblers, bluebirds, chickadees, juncos, and even a male hairy woodpecker and great horned owl. However, for the untrained, the birds appear only from time to time when the woods are quiet and they can recognize a feathered friend.

No one hiking in the South in springtime fails to hear the distant drumming of the ruffed grouse. This thumping lasts for a number of seconds, is utterly unbirdlike, and can be heard on a quiet night miles away. Sometime later in the season many hikers report a scenario that stars the mother grouse. She may be spotted on the trail dragging a wing pitifully and wholly distracting you until you are well clear of the nest of chicks nearby.

Animal experiences come suddenly. Once while hiking the ridge in a sunny spot I was startled when struck by a great but silent shadow as a hawk glided by six feet above my head; Hawk Mountain, in Pennsylvania, is a favorite lookout for birdwatchers. Throughout the South I often heard a strange, distant barking at night, but the call turned out to be not the four-footed animal I thought it was. My friends identified it as the barred owl calling out into the distant darkness. Nighttime is also when you'll hear the echoing calls of the loons in the North, as this amazing flying submarine makes known its exclusive territory to other loons.

The bird most widely noted by hikers is usually heard after dark. The whippoorwill does its calling at night, and even the most exhausted hiker will awaken should a pair open a duet in the neighborhood of the shelter. Elmer Onstot, a 1968 thru-hiker, reported: "If you have ever heard a whippoorwill in the moonlight or twilight hours, you have probably wondered how many times he repeats his name. A total of 1,507 calls were counted by the well-known naturalist August Derleth during a period of 33 minutes. And another persistent singer did 1,088 in unbroken succession for John Burroughs."

Although one hiker described the whippoorwill who woke him as a "rude bird," having a nighttime interlude with a pair of these birds is like meeting a bear or being invited to dinner by a stranger. It is part of that wonderful Appalachian Trail magic.

Passing through the home of many others

INSECTS AND REPELLING THEM

Five hundred years ago, man and woman's battle against biting bugs became more desperate when Europeans, leaving the largely bug-free Continent, invaded the New World with its endless swamps and wilderness. Only along the northern fringes of Europe and Asia were there such vicious insects as seemed to overwhelm much of North America. To combat this adversary, the new Americans invented a succession of protective concoctions, based on two theories: No bug would alight on a really sticky surface; and, the stronger the smell, the more effective the repellent.

Hiking and camping covered with goo was unendurably messy, however, so hope and faith turned to citronella—that greatest of all hoaxes, a volatile, sharp-smelling oil from the South Asiatic grass *Cymbopogon nardus citronella.* To this day, candles mixed with the stuff are sold to gullible hosts and hostesses for outdoor dining after dark. And, though it's hard to believe, it is still sold sometimes as an insect repellent. As a boy growing up amid the swamps of New Jersey, I was already inoculated with the adventure of spending a summer night outside down by the lake, accompanied by one or two friends, under the friendly starry skies, supposedly protected by citronella. However, citronella was not strong enough to thwart the mosquitoes; every time we attempted sleeping out, we ended up back in the house.

> *Terrible and pitiless enemies.*
>
> —M.F. Sweetser,
> *White Mountains*

A third defense against insects, smoke, probably has been made use of as a protective screen ever since humans learned to use fire. Although the warmth and friendly flicker of a fire are its primary attraction, it has historically been the last line of defense against the onslaught of biting bugs. Smarting eyes, polluted air, and stinking clothes are all more endurable than stings and bites. But a fire is only possible when the traveler has time to make camp and gather fuel.

And so it has been through the ages. Over 100 years ago, the most widely circulated book on New England's wilderness, M.F. Sweetser's *White Mountains,* succinctly discussed the problem of blackflies and mosquitoes: "The traveler among the deep forests and uninhabited glens is apt to meet terrible and pitiless enemies in the form of black flies and mosquitoes, especially during May, June, and July. They come in such vast numbers, and with such unappeasable hunger, that it is almost impossible to keep them away for a moment and their stings are so sharp and empoisoned as to well nigh madden their unfortunate victims. Various preparations of tar and oil, and other ingredients, are used to anoint the hands, face, and neck, to keep off these ferocious insects. But their feeling and odor are unpleasant, and it is the height of discomfort to march through a warm morning, perspiring freely, and with the face smeared with these abominable compounds." In her article "Biting Back," Annie Getchell tells us that half a century earlier, Henry David Thoreau had come to the same conclusion about the favorite mixture of sweet-oil, oil of turpentine, spearmint, and camphor—that is, the remedy was worse than the disease.

The situation today is considerably better, yet about 10 percent of the AT hikers still complained about bugs—a larger number than were bothered by snakes, bears, and dogs combined. Serious stings were rare, but there were some: Emilie Jeanneney was forced off the trail for six days with swollen hands from 15 "bee" (probably yellow jacket, hornet, or wasp) stings. Craig Phegley had to resort to a medical clinic and antibiotics to clear up a sore due to the bite of a brown recluse spider. However, bugs were usually more of a source of misery and madness than debilitating injury.

The literature on biting insects offers plenty of gratuitous advice on how to dress to avoid being bitten. In the July 1975 issue of *Scientific American*, R.H. Wright advises: "Swaddle yourself. Tuck long pants into long socks. Wear gloves and a turtleneck. Top off this stylish outfit with a mesh head net." But I have yet to meet a long-distance hiker so outfitted.

A special situation faces hikers heading south from Mount Katahdin. The weather usually prevents a Maine start earlier than May or June—and by that time, that most monstrous of all insect cycles, the invasion of the New England blackfly, is underway. Most southbound hikers endured stoically but reported it as a miserable experience. As Emilie Jeanneney put it, "Blackflies in Maine (June and July) were *hell*. I had a very bloody and swollen face." The Maine blackfly encounter was considered the worst experience of the whole trip by a number of hikers. Their comments ranged from "they drove me crazy" to "nasty bugs from New Jersey to Maine—*arrgh.*"

Wearing a head net does not appear to be a satisfactory solution for the hikers in the sample. Although I have known a number of thru-hikers to have carried head nets, including myself, I know of no hiker who actually admitted to using one. Perhaps with so much other exposed flesh, protecting a limited area is just not worthwhile. Or perhaps, like kissing someone through a screen door, the barrier detracts too much from the experience.

Besides flies and mosquitoes, hikers were occasionally bothered by spiders, wasps, yellow jackets, ticks, deerflies, and especially no-see-ums. But unlike sore feet, aching backs, rain, and rocks, insect problems on the trail were occasional rather than constant—due largely to a single marvelous modern development, DEET.

DEET

Though covering the body with clothes or sticky potions proved unsatisfactory armament in the war against bugs, the idea of surrounding yourself with a powerful wall of odor seemed promising. Besides citronella, other aromatic oils—anise, basil, catnip, eucalyptus, pennyroyal, and, of course, garlic—have been tried. (Western civilization seems to have a small but dedicated cult following the dictum "When all else fails, use garlic.") However, there was no scientific study of repelling biting insects until World War II, when finding an effective repellent became a war objective to help protect soldiers in tropical areas. More than 25,000 organic compounds were screened in various government and military research programs. The most effective repellent was N, N-diethyl-m-toluamide, or DEET. To achieve the same protection as DEET, citronella would have to be 1,000 times more effective than it is. As noted by researcher R.H. Wright in *Scientific American,* it was not a case of DEET being a substance which the mosquito somehow finds distasteful. Rather, "It jams the mosquito's sensors so that it is not able to follow the warm and moist currents given off by a warm-blooded animal."

After World War II, DEET emerged as the insect repellent of choice. Additional review by the U.S. Environmental Protection Agency and the U.S. Department of Agriculture in the 1950s confirmed both DEET's effectiveness and its safety. Many other substances were tested and some marketed, but DEET was clearly the winner. Today it forms the active ingredient in most commercial insect repellents. DEET is not only highly effective against mosquitoes, but is recommended for use against ticks, gnats, fleas, and chiggers.

Despite the extensive research, the public is almost completely ignorant of the way DEET works. Articles have credited the "oily surface where insects fear to tread" or a "masking of body odor" or that it "creates a smell." DEET works for one reason only: Normally the insect's "attack program" is triggered when a rise in the level of carbon dioxide alerts it to the approach of a living, breathing host. DEET's huge molecules in the air clog the insect's sensing mechanism on which its homing ability is based. Thus the insect cannot follow the warm, moist air currents to pursue its prey. The repellent only fails when the insect accidentally intercepts the victim in random flight.

Perhaps a mosquito does not like her feet sticky, but she won't usually be able to find you if the air is filled with those big molecules. This also explains why DEET works if you spray it just on your hair and clothes, but not your skin. Unfortunately, DEET attacks certain synthetic fabrics (including some waterproof tent fabrics) and can be harmful to such materials as watch crystals. Inside use is not recommended because of DEET's unfriendliness to certain painted and polished objects. But shelters and trails pose no problems. If you're wearing wool, cotton, nylon, rubberized fabric, or one of many common materials, spray away your problems. If you are unsure, rub a little repellent on a hidden corner of the material. If you're leery of getting DEET on your skin, apply it on other surfaces such as shoes, clothing, and packs.

Be advised that DEET is a powerful creation of the chemist's laboratory, and although there is a long history of its safe use, it can still be harmful, particularly when used on children carelessly or for extended periods. (The American Academy of Pediatrics recommends concentrations of 10 percent DEET or less for children.) In addition, there can be allergic reactions, particularly when strong concentrations are applied directly to the skin.

My grandfather always took twice the doctor-prescribed dose of medicine, reasoning that if the prescription was good for the ailment, doubling it would fix you up twice as fast. The late 1980s and early 1990s has seen a modern application of this belief to repellents. Concentrations of from 7 to 30 percent DEET appear to work well and have been used for decades. DEET is now sold in "more powerful" concentrations up to 100 percent. Some tests suggest that the higher concentrations work no better, and concerned authorities (including several state health departments) have issued warnings about the highly concentrated dosage. There may be some increase in the number of hours of most effective protection when using higher concentrations; 30-percent mixtures last several hours, compared to only an hour or so for 15-percent DEET. Ken Wadness, who walked southward through Maine in June and July, says the only effective protection he was able to get was a preparation of 100-percent DEET. For general use, however, the high-powered DEET is probably not necessary unless you are using it as a furniture polish remover.

I am one of those unfortunate human beings with a high heat or moisture gradient, such that bugs find it easy to home in on me. Like most AT hikers, I would sometimes find myself walking in the middle of a cloud of buzzing and biting insects maddening enough to make even the most determined thru-hiker consider the comforts of home. I found a good application of DEET-based repellent—sprayed on shoes, socks, pants, shirts, even my hair—vanquished all the small flying objects and usually left me free for several hours.

At home in New Jersey, I devised a controlled experiment and carried it out in the nearby woods and swamps during blackfly season: I ran a 4-mile course through the woods wearing DEET repellent on alternate days, and tallied the number of bites (ugh!) sustained during each run. It tested 95 percent effective against the blackflies when applied just before the run.

Other suggested remedies include Avon Skin-So-Soft and various "natural" mixtures that have captured the public fancy as insect repellents, usually containing an exotic combination of oils such as eucalyptus, lemongrass, and, of course, the old favorite citronella. They are attractive because they are nontoxic; unfortunately, they are ineffective as well. But at this point we come to the end of scientific reporting and must note that a small but absolutely convinced group pursues a favorite personal remedy that "really does work." It is a measure of the highly subjective nature of bug troubles that a strong belief in a substance may influence its perceived effectiveness. Is this the "placebo effect"—or, could it be that if you truly believe in the bug-juice you use, your body temperature becomes cooler, your sweating decreases, or your carbon dioxide gradient become shallower? Regardless, the objective evidence from thousands of tests and decades of use is overwhelming. According to Michael Hodgson's October 1992 *Backpacker* article "Much Ado About DEET," no other repellent comes close to the effectiveness of DEET.

OTHER INSECTS

As noted, the AT insect world runs the gamut from big southern spiders to no-see-ums. Victoria Logue, in a recent book, *Backpacking in the '90s*, has prepared a compendium of the hiker's insect world, ranging from anaphylactic shock to red bugs. The large flying insects are often

Woods hiking in Maine

lumped together as "bees," but are more likely to be hornets, wasps, and the very aggressive yellow jackets. These do not home in on gaseous gradients and so are unaffected by DEET; as are spiders, usually found in the dark corners of places like barns, outhouses, and shelters, which makes it wise to look carefully before you reach in or sit down.

There is a tendency to call any large buzzing and threatening insect a "bee," but most stings are from yellow jackets. Yellow jackets usually have their nests underground and are apt to assault any who pass nearby. Bees are more inclined to a tolerant, mind-your-own-business attitude; they will not usually attack unless you disturb their hive or squash them. Beekeepers sometimes work entirely without protection and can be literally covered by hundreds of crawling bees without receiving a bite. But bees must be treated gently. They like light-colored clothing and abhor loud noises. Note, however, that if you are bitten once, other bees will become alarmed and a chain reaction is possible. One of the hiking guides advises that in this circumstance you should "move on quickly"—a good idea. Actually, if you are being attacked, the best escape is to plunge into some thick underbrush or bushes. Bees and their like will not follow you into a thicket. If none is available, "move on quickly."

Most hikers occasionally experience finding a large dog tick or wood tick (about the size of a pencil eraser) on their skin. If the tick has been there for some time, it may be disgustingly bloated with your blood. But in most cases the bite is not dangerous. It is the tiny deer tick—only the size of a pencil point until engorged, when it is about the size of a match head—that may carry the dreaded Lyme disease. Lyme disease is not only a serious disease with many after-effects, but is also difficult to diagnose. In some areas this combination has led to an irrational fear. Along a local highway near my home in northern New Jersey there is a full-sized outdoor billboard advertising the name of doctors to treat your Lyme disease.

The conventional warnings are to wear long pants and shirts, all carefully tucked in, and to spray cuffs and clothing with a strong preparation of DEET. In practice, few hikers feel that such precautions are worth the discomfort and trouble. For thru-hikers, infection with Lyme disease is actually fairly rare, possibly because the AT usually follows high along the ridge and is somewhat removed from the most thickly infested areas. The deer tick is usually picked up at the extremities, the arms and legs, but prefers the warmer, darker torso regions of the body and will spend several hours making the journey before biting. Thus, there is time to inspect, brush over, or wash limbs to eliminate the tick before it digs in. If an infected tick does bite, about 70 percent of the time a large red area or bull's-eye results; that is a good time to seek competent medical help. Repellents against ticks are available, but according to the July 1987 *Consumer Reports,* DEET products are said to deter ticks only 75 to 87 percent of the time.

Lyme disease falls in a category with a number of other dangers on the AT: It is rare, but not totally unknown. It is serious, but can be successfully and reliably treated. The likelihood of getting it is small for any single traveler (and can be reduced by examining those bare limbs, particularly after passing through long grass or weedy areas). Rocky Mountain spotted fever, caused by a bacteria that hitches a ride on wood and dog ticks, is another unlikely—but possible—danger of the trail. It can be treated with antibiotics; left untreated it runs its course in about two weeks. In the end, these risks, along with a number of others, are small compared to the rewards of the journey.

Balds are a pleasant change from trail darkness along the southern AT

ALONG THE TRAIL

The Appalachian Trail was first opened as a continuous 2,000-mile thru-path in 1937. However, more than half the miles of trail were located on private lands. With the rapid expansion of suburbs and development of highways, the next 25 years saw more than 200 miles of path forced off the mountain ridges and onto roads. The trail was saved by the National Trails System Act of 1968, leading to federal land acquisitions in the 1970s and later. In 1994, after decades of enlightened management and land purchases by the Appalachian Trail Conference, its supporting clubs, and especially government agencies, all but a few tens of miles of the trail were safely tucked away among the mountains and ridges,

> *The trail is what it is. If it goes up, over, under—there is the choice to follow it or not. As for weather, it will be what it will be. One cannot choose conditions, only to hike or not.*
>
> —George Ziegenfuss, 1989 thru-hiker

with a minimum woods-and-space corridor 1,000 feet wide along the footpath.

The Appalachian Trail Conference thus manages a 100,000-acre strip park crossing 14 states. And in an extraordinary arrangement carried out largely by the 32 affiliated local clubs, every mile is maintained by volunteers whose effort is valued at over $2,000,000 annually. However, finding an alternate wilderness route has added 150 miles to the AT length. Thus, the end-to-end trip is ever longer, and with relocations along the ridge, it is ever more mountainous.

No matter how the trail is relocated, nor how circuitous or steep it may be, the distance as the crow flies from Springer north and east to Katahdin is fixed at a mere 1,117 miles. No thru-hiker will be surprised to hear that for every mile closer to the goal, he or she must walk two.

It is not just length that creates the challenge for the thru-hiker. In addition to carrying a pack, trail roughness, rain, and snow, the greatest difficulty for many is the mountains to be climbed. As

Tom Pappas put it, "So many up and downs, up and downs, up and downs. . . ." As noted by Jean Cashin in the March/April 1993 *Appalachian Trailway News,* Don Desrosiers has calculated that the AT thru-hiker must climb 471,151 feet on the entire trip, over the tops of about 270 mountains and climbing an average of 3,000 feet every day. A more vivid picture is to realize that it is like climbing Mount Everest 16 times from sea level to its peak.

"HOW TO HIKE"

In the 1970s, while visiting the Northwest, I planned to climb Mount Rainier with my son Ted leading the rope. Although I had previously done some technical climbing, I had no experience with glaciers, and Ted urged me to take the self-arrest course taught by the local mountain climbing school. So off I went on a beautiful sunny morning with a dozen other hopefuls. Most of the class was going to take the school's guided climb the next day and were being critically scrutinized. We were carefully attendant to our instructor, a young man, tanned and muscular, who exuded total self-confidence. Before we were allowed to hike up the mountain to the glacier, we were subjected to a lecture on "How to Hike," specifying the correct placement of the foot, weighting, lifting, stepping, balancing, and length of stride. And if you could not keep up with the instructor, you were doing it wrong.

Such advice is nonsense. There are as many ways to hike as there are people. Given the opportunity for experience, each person will optimize his or her style. Nowhere is this more obvious than among thru-hikers, each of whom must find his or her own best way to adapt to hiking 2,100 miles. For example, in the average 10-hour day, two-thirds of the hikers in my survey made two, three, or four stops to take off their packs and perhaps eat a meal or snack. But a few durable men and women took only a single break all day. At the other end of the scale was the "break for five or ten minutes once each hour" school. Since all these folks were experienced hikers, all kept going for a long distance, and each happily pursued his or her own style, they are themselves the best response to the myth of "how to hike."

Anyone in reasonable health can hike from Georgia to Maine simply by putting one foot ahead of the other and perfecting the sequence at his or her leisure. The best way to hike is what you find most comfortable for yourself.

COMMITMENT

As we have seen in Chapter 2, if there were to be any single word to define those who successfully complete the thru-hike, that word would be *committed.* Of the long-distance hikers in the survey, 77 percent said they had a strong commitment to complete the entire length; 18 percent had serious intentions to finish; only 5 percent had no specific plan as to how far they would go. Thus, 95 percent of the successful hikers reported that they were committed to going the whole length from the very beginning.

These statistics give an insight into the intentions of hikers, but what were the rules of the game? There is no subject more topical, but less openly addressed, than the personal rules for following the AT; this is not a topic that is always freely and honestly discussed in a friendly give-and-take around the fire. Initially, most thru-hikers clearly intend to go every foot of the trail, and a few report that their commitment increased as they progressed. But it was more usual as the miles, mountains, and months rolled by for thru-hikers to become more relaxed in interpreting their hike rules. As senior thru-hiker Buddy Newell put it, "After two months I realized it was *my* hike and didn't feel badly about a blue-blaze" (an alternate route, off the AT).

PURISTS, MODERATES, AND LIBERALS

Extremes in interpreting what was "correct" seem to have become hardened as the endless trail unwound. Those of a more compulsive nature and with strong personal feelings became more committed. But for many, the long struggle, the endless variations of the trail, and the month after month of daily hiking, bred an attitude best summarized by the saying, "There is enough trail for everybody." It is interesting to note that tourists, friends at home, and the media covering a trip are fascinated by the goal of walking every single step of the way. They are often noticeably disappointed if the hiker admits having missed even the shortest section of the trail. But the duration and variability of the challenge makes the AT different from almost any other sporting event. It is not over in a few minutes, a few hours, or even a few months. It is a test of endurance that brings out sharply different responses. And there are many easy ways to "cheat," if that is what you choose to call it.

The most common alternative to following every single white blaze is to "blue-blaze." This is to follow an alternative route around a mountain, down a farm road, through a little town, or along the original shorter AT, now blazed in blue over the white. Before relocation, the AT route was usually more direct and sometimes less strenuous, so the temptation to blue-blaze occurs frequently.

Hitchhiking a stretch, sometimes called "yellow-blazing," is a less acceptable but faster way to get ahead. Many is the hiker who, having passed a person on the trail, suddenly discovers that person's name in trail registers *ahead*. This raises hackles, as well as philosophical questions as to why the hiker is there and what his or her objectives might be. Challenging the transgressor is usually considered to be in as bad taste as the yellow-blazing itself, so the event is often passed over. In all fairness, yellow-blazing is often done so the hiker can make up for lost time (delays due to injury, going into town, etc.) and catch up with friends who couldn't afford to wait and had moved on. The friends know what has happened and do not criticize. In one case a woman reported the only way she could shake a too-persistent admirer was to hitchhike ahead. The hiker often intends to hike the skipped section at a later date, and sometimes does so.

Since thru-hiking the trail is not an organized sporting event, it leads to no important trophies, does not improve the hiker's means of livelihood, and has traditionally been monitored as a do-it-yourself thing. There are many answers. To probe this, I asked questions about the hiker's own objectives, and also how he or she viewed the way *others* chose to follow, or not to follow the AT. Table 17-1 records these questions and how the thru-hikers responded.

TABLE 17-1.
HOW THRU-HIKERS
SAID THEY HIKED THE AT

I ATTEMPTED TO FOLLOW EVERY BIT OF THE AT MISSING NO SIGNIFICANT PORTION, PEAK, ROAD, RELO (RELOCATION), OR ANYTHING ELSE.	33%
I WALKED EVERY FOOT OF THE WAY, BUT ON VERY FEW OCCASIONS I WOULD NOT FOLLOW THE LATEST RELO, EXACT STREET, ETC.	18%
I WALKED THE DISTANCE BUT OFTEN TOOK A BLUE-BLAZE, ALTERNATE ROUTE, ROAD, ETC.	7%
I TRIED TO DO IT ALL BUT MAY HAVE MISSED A FEW MILES BECAUSE OF BAD WEATHER OR IN TOWNS AND WHEN HITCHING BACK AND FORTH TO THE TRAIL.	5%
I WALKED THE TRAIL BUT SKIPPED SOME PAVED ROADS AND A SHORT SECTION HERE OR THERE FOR PRACTICAL REASONS LIKE TAKING A BREAK, MAKING MONEY, CATCHING UP WITH FRIENDS, ETC.	5%
I EARNED THAT 2,000-MILE ROCKER (BADGE)!	15%
I WALKED MAJOR SECTIONS OF THE TRAIL IN ALL STATES.	3%
I WALKED BECAUSE IT WAS FUN AND DID NOT CONCERN MYSELF WITH MORE THAN GETTING A REAL FEELING OF THE WHOLE TRAIL—WHICH I GOT.	14%

We can see from these answers that there is a wide range of intentions and interpretation of what might be called the rules of walking the AT. The attitudes can be divided into the following three categories.

Purists. These hikers (51 percent of the total) maintain they walked very close to every foot of the current marked trail—"every single blaze." Many felt strongly about observing a personal code that would not accept any non-AT substitution. As one hiker put it, "I walked every step of the AT following the white blazes all the way. I was one of the very few who did it that way. If you're going to be out there, why skip portions—blue-blazing, wimp, slackpacker. The rocker stands for 2,138.1 [the published mileage as of 1989], not 2,000. . . . That's okay, but don't call yourself a thru-hiker."

Moderates. These hikers (17 percent of the total) admit to deviations but draw the line at walking versus taking any other transportation. The major difference is the freedom they exercise in going on alternate routes. They may also skip a few miles now and then. For Taro Narahashi, "Walking from Georgia to Maine is good enough for me, white or blue." Eric Muller said, "I walked the trail for myself. I was out to enjoy the countryside. I took old blue-blazed sections of the AT when it would be more interesting." Bob Schroeder admitted that he "missed 26 miles" (about 1 percent of the total distance).

Liberals. These hikers (32 percent) have "tasted" the whole trail but missed some. Most of them completed at least 2,000 miles. For the liberals, total mileage was of secondary importance: They didn't hike "to walk every step of the trail"; instead, "the trail was what we made of it." Liberal hikers were satisfied applying a different measuring stick. As Sharon Rice said, "Despite skipping some, I feel like a thru-hiker—I didn't do all 2,138.1 miles, but I did enough. I don't care if people did more or less. It's their hike."

Practically all hikers, including purists, will occasionally hike short distances without a full pack. (The amount you carry is not considered one of the requirements for having truly thru-hiked.) This usually occurs when it is possible to send the pack its own way, courtesy of a friend with wheels, and meet it a little farther down the trail.

Traditionally, such hiking with a daypack, fanny pack, or no pack has been called "slackpacking." However, in 1994, O.d. Coyote published in *Chained Dogs and Songbirds* a plea to reserve the term "slackpacking" for an imaginative, unhurried style of hiking—that is, letting the circumstances of each day determine progress while staying on the trail for an extended period. As for other

George Schindler, a brief partner on the trail in New York

words to replace the old definition, the most promising substitute seems to be "daypacking," a term that is more specifically descriptive of unloaded backpacking and is already in use.

At any rate, regardless of O.d.'s success in modifying established vocabulary, his proposal has received widespread notice, because the idea of an unhurried, gracious trip focusing on trail life rather than destination fills an important niche. There really are very few O.d.-style slackpackers on the AT (from my questionnaires, they seem to be limited to less than 5 percent of the long-distance hikers); it is more common for thru-hikers to respond to the challenge and push themselves to the very limit of their physical endurance. But it is the slack hiking style that in many ways comes closest to meeting the ideals of being submerged in a long wilderness journey—the utopian, back-to-nature approach favored by the person who conceived the AT, Benton MacKaye (as described in Chapter 1, "The Concept of Thru-Hiking").

For many years the Appalachian Trail Conference appointed a committee to certify 2,000-mile awards. Recently a more relaxed attitude has resulted in eliminating elaborate requirements and proofs before dispensing the highly valued certificate and 2,000-mile "rocker," a diminutive patch to sew on your sleeve. The ATC requires some kind of a written account of the journey, which allows for simple recordkeeping and a dignified recognition. Since the AT was originally only a trifle over 2,000 miles in length, the figure was quite accurate as well as a suitable round number. In 1997, with the actual length creeping up toward 2,200, it provides a good basic argument for the moderates' and liberals' interpretation of "doing the trail"—that is, approximating the distance rather than specifying it exactly or dictating how it must be done. Backpackers not wishing to get involved in the problems of what exactly constitutes a thru-hike may simply describe their journey as "Georgia to Maine." Another widely used term is simply "end-to-ender."

An unusual twist on the views hikers have is that they are more rigorous in the standards they set for themselves than the standards they use to judge others. To explore this, I asked: "How do you feel about others who hiked fewer, or more, miles than you did?" When it came down to advocating how *others* should hike, our sample is much more tolerant than the standard they set for themselves. About one-quarter are still inclined to be purists, one-quarter are moderate in their approach, and half of the responses are liberal. One purist commented: "We believe 'thru-hiker' has only one definition. . . . It irks me when

people lie about the miles they did. . . ." A moderate wrote, "I don't think less of them, but I am glad I did all of it. . . . I'm proud to say I'm a 'white-blazer'! I don't concern myself with negative attitudes toward people who are not." And a liberal: "The trail has no rules. It doesn't make them a greater hiker or less of a hiker by how they hiked the trail. Everyone's trip is different, so you can't pass judgment. . . . Let each do it his own way."

TRAIL DIFFICULTIES

Hikers were asked, "All things considered, how difficult was it for you to hike the trail?" On a six-point scale, the average difficulty was rated by 112 hikers as follows:

TABLE 17-2.
HOW DIFFICULT IS THE AT?

	MEN	WOMEN
NOT DIFFICULT	13%	2%
NOT TOO DIFFICULT	31%	21%
SOMEWHAT DIFFICULT	27%	39%
FAIRLY DIFFICULT	20%	21%
VERY DIFFICULT	9%	17%

Note how differently male and female hikers evaluate trail difficulty. More than 10 percent of the men did not find it difficult at all—easy hiking. But only 2 percent of the women found it easy. At the other extreme, 9 percent of the men found it very difficult, but twice as many women rated it so. Women clearly found the trail harder to hike than did men. This also bears out a consistent finding that great difficulty on the trail, though real, does not appear to present an overwhelming block to success.

Table 17-3, page 131, lists the environmental circumstances and conditions which hikers said were serious problems during their hike.

Trail conditions bothered women more than they did men, particularly steep and rocky sections, finding water, and following the trail; however, women hikers were no more squeamish than men about slogging through mud. Other than mice, animals did not constitute a very significant problem. In this respect, the men were more bothered than women by mice, dogs, and snakes.

Interestingly, in contrast to the actual difficulties reported, the hikers perceived animals and trail/physical/environmental hazards as being less of a threat than troublesome people; see "People Problems" later in this chapter.

TABLE 17-3.
SERIOUS ENVIRONMENTAL PROBLEMS

Condition	Percent Reporting Problem
Snow/Cold Weather	30%
Rain	20%
Steep Trails	11%
Rocky Trails	10%
Muddy Trails	10%
Hot Weather	8%
Finding Water	8%
Following the Trail	7%
Animals	
Mice	10%
Dogs	5%
Bears	2%
Snakes	1%

COGNITIVE DISSONANCE

When you compare what thru-hikers have written during and after their hikes, there is a surprise in store: There is no correlation between how hikers felt while doing the AT and how they feel afterwards. I had expected that strong and tough individuals who experienced little difficulty would afterward describe their experiences as great. And I thought that others who barely scratched their way to the top of Mount Katahdin would be somewhat reserved about their adventure. Although this was sometimes true, the opposite was just as common. Many hikers who reported at times having a thoroughly miserable life on the trail described the whole experience in the most glowing terms.

This "inverse" phenomenon is well known among social psychologists as the Theory of Cognitive Dissonance. One of the early investigators, Leon Festinger, wrote: "Rats and people come to love the things for which they have suffered." And commitment, an attitude that is a major factor in completing a thru-hike, is essential for cognitive dissonance. In their book *Theories in Social Psychology*, sociologists Deutsch and Krauss note that although dissonance theory has solved no problems, "It has stimulated research which suggests that there may be less objectivity and more partiality and bias in the way a person views and evaluates alternatives *after* he makes his decision than *before* he makes it." Thus the concept of cognitive dissonance helps interpret long-distance hikers' varying reactions to the experience, particularly in comparing how they felt along the trail and how they felt after finishing.

TRAIL RELOCATIONS

In the last several decades there has been a major effort to relocate the AT away from roads and off privately owned property. The movement has been forced on the trail supporters and agencies by encroachment of developments and the construction of roads. Until the mid-20th century, the privately owned back land along the Appalachian ridge was of little use except for hunting, fishing, and cutting timber at intervals of 50 to 100 years. Since the AT route was intentionally remote, travelers along it disturbed no one and easements to allow passage of the AT were readily obtained. Those who followed the trail (and there were only a few) were welcomed by the backcountry farmers, sometimes fed and often bedded down in the barn or farmhouse. Hikers saw more local people along the way, there were fewer hills to climb, and the route was a little shorter—but it was also haphazardly marked, so getting off trail was a constant problem.

With civilization encroaching, land values skyrocketed and the wilderness disappeared. The solution has been to buy the land or, as has often been necessary, acquire land nearby onto which the threatened AT could be relocated. Although widely praised and supported, relocation has received mixed press by long-distance hikers. This is because the thru-hiker really has a very different view of the trail than those who make shorter trips.

Trail relocations are typically carried out by a cooperative effort between the government (most of the money), the Appalachian Trail Conference (coordination, management, and sometimes money), and local affiliated clubs (the actual work). From the standpoint of the local expert on the trail, the most important objectives have been to preserve or to improve the remoteness so as to make that portion of the trail as interesting and enjoyable as possible. This may include running it over several successive peaks, out to scenic views, over scree and rocks, or through a swamp. For the hiker out for the day, this makes a wonderful trip. However, this is not always the trail the long-distance hiker would vote for. Some would gladly trade a mountain peak for a smooth dirt road. To those with a far-off destination, there is something intrinsically irritating to have climbed over a peak for several hours and end up just around the back side of the mountain, only a 15-minute walk from the starting point.

Grandma Gatewood, the second woman to thru-hike the AT and the first person to complete the trip three times, described the trail in words echoed many times by later thru-hikers. Her essay on hiking the trail appears in James Hare's *Hiking the Appalachian Trail*. She found it "lovely" and "wanted the satisfaction of doing something I wanted to do," but at one point she wrote, "This is no trail. This is a nightmare. For some fool reason they always lead you right up over the biggest rock to the top of the biggest mountain they can find. I would never have started this trip if I had known how tough it was."

About half the long-distance hikers surveyed gave unqualified support to relocation even when it made the trip longer or steeper. They wrote, "Great, keep the AT in the wilderness" and "The farther away from civilization, the better." They expressed strong feeling "for the best possible scenic trail which can be created." As writer/hiker Cindy Ross put it, "Good . . . thinking of our children."

About 35 percent of the hikers basically approved of "relos" but raised a number of objections. After days of isolation in the mountains, long-distance hikers look forward to a "day on the town." They also enjoy local color and getting to know the inhabitants. This all comes about easily when the trail passes right through towns such as Hot Springs, North Carolina, or Damascus, Virginia. Such towns require no hitchhike, and often there develops a warm relationship between hikers and locals. While no one enjoys hiking along paved roads bearing heavy traffic, a few miles along a country road or fire lane through the forest can provide a pleasant change from rocks, peaks, mud, and tangles. About 15 percent of the hikers, mainly thru-hikers, note they "would rather walk on roads for a change," or "I enjoyed much of the road walks—some were scenic, and even the long Cumberland Valley [Pennsylvania] crossing offered a challenge/change." (Since 1989, the Cumberland Valley walk has been completely relocated.)

A recent relocation placing Monson, Maine (where Shaw's famous boarding home is located), several miles away was described as "a bummer." The Atkins, Virginia, relo was called "worse than the road." One respondent commented, "Great for weekenders but sucks for thru-hikers." Feelings like this bred a dark suspicion traded around campfires in the South: Relocations were in the hands of clubs that were in competition to create the most difficult, rocky, and miserable detour so that a club's own section of the AT would be remembered. Pond Mountain, Tennessee, was for years avoided by many thru-hikers as a long and dreary detour. It was improved in 1994. Farther north, from New Jersey to Connecticut, hikers said that the trail had been relocated "off the land owned by the wealthy onto swamps with mosquitoes."

On the whole, however, what the long-distance hikers missed most were the towns and people. Thru-hiker Keith Cornell wrote: "I believe the road walks, through farms in Virginia, Pennsylvania, and New Jersey, added to the experience, and it is a mistake to push the trail completely into the woods. The locals were great . . . in fact, that is how I met my girlfriend."

It is clear that most hikers would like a complete wilderness trail, more remote, and longer if necessary. But many thru-hikers feel that towns "break the monotony and provide a window to the local culture . . . this is where you meet America."

LIGHTNING

Hikers following the AT through the southern Appalachians cannot escape the thunderstorms that roll down the valleys and over the mountains, usually in the late afternoon. I can remember one time hearing the first distant rumbles as a storm approached and hoping it would follow some other valley; then when it didn't, I gave up and crouched away from tall trees as the water poured over me. That night, in a Smoky Mountains shelter, everyone talked lightning. Because I was the only one who had much experience in the subject, I talked and temporarily acquired the trail name "The Professor."

Lightning kills about 100 Americans each year. In the Rocky Mountains, where mountaintops are open to the skies, the hiker on the ridge or near the summit is indeed in danger. And, no one who has had his or her hair literally stand on end in the atmosphere of an approaching electrical storm needs urging to get out and down from high open peaks. But the Appalachians, on the whole, are different. With the exception of a few bald peaks in the South and in New England, hikers are immersed in a deep forest (the "long green tunnel"), and as long as they avoid being close to isolated trees, particularly a dominating tree that is higher than the surrounding forest, they will be safe, even if wet.

The Appendix of the National Fire Protection Code (1992 edition) advises staying away from hilltops, open fields, bodies of water, wire fences, and isolated trees. The Code suggests seeking depressed areas, dense woods, and shelters not standing alone at high points. Although hikers have been killed in an exposed high shelter in the West, most AT shelters are deeply buried in the woods and would appear to be reasonably safe.

According to the Code, "If you are hopelessly isolated in an exposed area and you feel your hair stand on end, indicating that lightning is about to strike, drop to your knees and bend forward, putting your hands on your knees. Do not lie flat on the ground or place your hands on the ground." It is tiring kneeling with a pack on your back, so it may be more comfortable to remove it. However, there seems no scientific reason to state, as one recent publication did, "External-frame packers, you have a lightning rod on your back." Since the heart is the most vulnerable part of the body to electrical surges and resulting ventricular fibrillation, an electrical path bypassing the heart area would appear to, if anything, decrease the danger. Since the pack parallels the body, and is probably also wet, theoretically it would seem to protect rather than endanger the hiker.

PEOPLE PROBLEMS

Three-quarters of the thru-hikers traveled the 2,000-plus miles without a single unpleasant experience involving other people. In general, human kindness, warmth, generosity, and interest emerges as among the pleasant surprises of the journey.

The most common people problem during the trip, the few times there was one, involved drunkenness, usually at hostels or bars, sometimes on the part of the hikers themselves. There were two reported instances of problems involving drugs, and a few complaints about two abusive individuals on the trail who criticized the hiking techniques of others. Two or three hikers had run-ins with local inhabitants, and some reported uncomfortable hitchhiking incidents. More seriously, two hikers were threatened with guns, and there was one (not officially reported) attempted rape. None of the above was brought to the attention of the police.

There were a few instances of theft, the one area involving clear-cut criminal activity. One hiker had $7,000 loss and damage to a truck left at a Tennessee trailhead. Another backpacker had his pack stolen as he slept in a roadside camp, one lost $50 at a B&B, and one had clothing disappear at a hostel. There were also a few close calls: When crossing from Maryland to Pennsylvania I leaned my pack against the AT sign on the highway to check the trail. I was barely into the underbrush when a truck pulled up across the street and the door began to open. I hurried back to my pack. The truck drove off.

When one considers that we are dealing with the experiences of 136 people over three to six months, the unpleasant occurrences were relatively few.

In dealing with strangers in their travels along the trail, experienced hikers universally agree on how to act: The hiker must never advertise that he or she is alone. Because spread-out groups are the rule on the trail, the word to strangers is always that your group is just a few minutes behind you. The general rule is, "Always be cautious, but very polite, with strangers," or "Just use your common sense."

The other generally proffered piece of advice is to shy away from public campgrounds and never to camp at a trailhead or, if possible, even within sight of automobiles. Pack theft is rare in the deep woods, where you commonly see unguarded packs and camps. Thefts occur where there is ready vehicle accessibility. Similarly, a tent or camp within beer-can–throwing distance of cars is a temptation not to be offered late-evening revelers. Some 65 percent of the hikers reported that during their whole trip they had stayed at public campgrounds no more than two nights—and quite a few of these nights were at Baxter State Park, where park officials are in close attendance. More than a dozen of the respondents said they *never* stopped at a public campground, much preferring "to camp well inside the forest."

When asked what they considered the major hazards on the trail about which they might wish to warn new hikers, responses boiled down to three categories, as summarized in Table 17-4.

According to the incidents reported by the hikers in our sample, it turns out that although on rare occasions one meets a stranger who is kind of scary, except for minor threats and unpleasantness people were seldom the cause of serious trouble. Yet, compared to difficulties encountered with trail and weather conditions and problems with animals (detailed in Table 17-3), it was people that seemed to pose the greatest potential threat. In general, fears have been heightened by several much-publicized cases of violent crime that have occurred on the AT in recent years.

TABLE 17-4.
SOURCES OF TROUBLE

TROUBLES	NUMBER OF TIMES NOTED
PEOPLE (DRUNKS, THEFT, VIOLENCE, "REDNECKS AND LOCALS," HITCHHIKING, PEOPLE WITH GUNS)	23
TRAIL/ENVIRONMENTAL HAZARDS (HYPOTHERMIA, COLD, LIGHTNING, FALLS, INJURIES, CARRYING TOO MUCH WEIGHT, GOING TOO FAST, POISON IVY)	19
ANIMALS (DOGS, SNAKES, MICE, BEARS, SKUNKS, TICKS)	14

MURDER ON THE AT

America has the unfortunate reputation of harboring the most violent society of any of the developed nations of the world. Coupled with this there is a fascination, fanned by accounts on TV and elaborated in movies and the press, with brutal personal assaults—particularly against innocent victims. And if the setting is a deep and peaceful forest, and the attack is against defenseless persons, interest is even greater. Note, for example, the success of the book and movie *Deliverance,* a bone-chilling account of a sexually motivated attack and murder deep in the peaceful southern Appalachians.

Unfortunately, there has also been violence on the AT. Some of it was described in the "nonfiction novel" *Murder on the Appalachian Trail,* based on a murder that took place on the AT in Virginia in 1981. Then in 1988 two women hiking together were shot and one killed in Pennsylvania, a tragedy documented in a 1995 book by Claudia Brenner, *Eight Bullets.* And in 1990, there was a double murder of a man and a woman in Pennsylvania, quite similar to the highly publicized 1981 murder in Virginia. In late May 1996, two women were murdered in Virginia's Shenandoah National Park; the tragic circumstances had certain similarities to the events described in Brenner's book. In all the cases except the recent Shenandoah killings, which took place shortly before this writing, the murderer was found and convicted. There were two other homicides on the AT prior to 1981, making a total of nine homicides.

Almost all the murder victims were women traveling with one male or female companion. No group larger than two has ever been attacked. More surprising, although about half the long-distance hikers of both sexes are usually alone on the AT, in only one incident did a homicide involve someone hiking alone.

Unfortunately, these murders under the peaceful skies and idyllic surroundings of the deep woods have commanded wide media attention. In addition to many sensible and thoughtful reviews of these tragic events, there has also been a spate of scare articles playing on the possible fears of hikers, with such titles as "A Fright in the Woods," "The End of Innocence," "New Fears on an Old Trail," "Trail Dangers—Precautions for Hikers Essential," and "Footpath Shadowed by Crime."

Shocking though they have been, the events have elicited a confident, intelligent response by the hiking community. Inquiring minds have studied whether certain steps could be instituted to reduce the danger. Hundreds of letters and editorials have blanketed the subject. Such measures as trail telephones, ID cards, registration, patrols, and carrying mace or a gun for protection have been proposed. Some changes have actually been tried, particularly increased monitoring personnel along the trail. It is not clear what can and should be done. Unfortunately, many of the measures have the tendency to nullify the very charms and features that make the Appalachian Trail so attractive.

Carrying guns is almost universally damned as resulting in a significantly increased hazard. And a review of the circumstances of the nine murders reveals that possessing a gun would not have altered the outcomes because the victims were taken by surprise. In all the cases, the perpetrators were non-hikers described as "psychopaths" and "drifters."

Prompted by the 1990 tragedy, many hikers have voiced their opinions, and in some cases tried to evaluate the danger on the trail—for example, how does it compare to those dangers faced in everyday life? Some of these comments cast an interesting light on the reasons for backpacking and why the hikers really are in the woods.

John Viehman, executive editor of *Backpacker* magazine, noted in "Leave the Guns at Home" in the February 1992 issue: "Readers arguing against guns in the wilderness cite statistics that show you're much safer in the wilderness than walking city streets. On the Appalachian Trail, for instance, there is one crime for every 800,000 users, and there have been only seven people killed while backpacking there in the past 50 years. So statistically speaking, you're 190 times more likely to die in an accident while driving to the trail head than from a violent act in the wilderness."

The Appalachian Trail Conference staff cited its poll on security measures in the March/April 1993 issue of *Appalachian Trailway News,* noting the importance of the matter but nevertheless emphasizing, "The Appalachian Trail is statistically safer than the highways, safer than your home."

In general, hikers avoid discussing the safety issue and prefer an unspoken stand somewhere between being reasonably careful, basically optimistic, and somewhat philosophical. A familiar kind of "what will be will be" is evident in Julie Elman-Roche's comment on dangers after finishing her 1989 thru-hike: "I guess it's a matter of being in the wrong place at the wrong time. Anything can happen to anyone—there's no way to predict anything."

The possibility of carrying a gun as the ultimate deterrent against attack comes up again and again. Gary "Lawman" Serra, a police officer for many years, like most others elucidates a variety of reasons for strongly opposing firearms on the AT. However, in a letter in the May/June

1992 *Appalachian Trailway News,* Serra also touches on a significant point on the general problem of safety, which many others report as a deep-down feeling: ". . . like many hikers who escape to the trail, I too, leave the cruel reality of our world and walk into a world of peace and contentment. While hiking I free my mind and take in all the natural beauty around me. When the day comes that I am forced to carry my service revolver on the Appalachian Trail, it will be the day that I sell my backpack and find another mode of escape."

To which one might add a delightful story as told by Isabella Bird, who traveled alone by horseback in the Rocky Mountains in 1872. In a letter to her sister (which later appeared in her book *A Lady's Life in the Rocky Mountains*), Isabella wrote about spending a night in a strange hut with a number of men: "I never told you that once I gave an unwary promise that I would not travel alone in Colorado unarmed and that in consequence I left Estes Park with a Sharpe revolver loaded with ball cartridge in my pocket, which has been the plague of my life. Its bright ominous barrel peeped out in quiet Denver shops, children pulled it out to play with, or when my riding dress hung up with it in the pocket, pulled the whole from the peg to the floor, and I cannot conceive of any circumstance in which I would feel right to make any use of it, and in which it would do me any possible good. Last night, however, I took it out, cleaned it and oiled it, and put it under my pillow, resolving to keep awake all night. I slept as soon as I lay down, and never woke till the bright morning sun shone through the roof, making me ridicule my own fears and abjure pistols for ever!"

For better or for worse, most of the extreme measures such as guns, policing, and communication nets are alien to a true wilderness experience. The AT hiker does not feel threatened by prevalent danger and rejects the need for constant awareness and surveillance. As David Franklin put it in a letter printed in the April 1994 issue of *Backpacker* magazine: "After reading 'Playing It Safe (Everyday Wisdom),' I wondered if you were writing about hiking in New York City instead of a national forest. I have never felt a martial-arts course was required before going out hiking—maybe a fly-fishing course. I've hiked solo for years and have never had to hide behind a tree when I saw someone approaching. If you don't feel comfortable on a certain trail, go somewhere else. There are lots of trails out there. I do agree that guns have no place on our trails. I carry a knife. I might need it to clean some fish if I get lucky."

Ultimate safety from all danger, like an ultimate escape, lies beyond the promises that can be fulfilled on the AT. As Julie Elman-Roche noted, "anything can happen." Nevertheless, the probabilities are on your side. "Trail magic," rather than serious danger, is the most likely companion for a trip on the Appalachian Trail.

"A DOLLAR A MILE"

Except for food, almost everything on the trail itself is free, so you don't have to be rich to hike it. For many years hikers were charged 5 cents, then 10 cents to cross the Bear Mountain bridge—which outraged not a few, including Ed Garvey, who noted that it was the only toll on the whole AT. Now the bridge is free.

One dollar per mile is the widely used figure for how much it will cost to thru-hike the AT. Some frugal thru-hikers have undertaken the whole trip spending less than $1,000 for food, travel, equipment, and beer. The tally in my study of about 100 hikers is in close agreement for the strictly on-the-trail costs—about $2,200 for the trip. This does not, however, cover the cost of preparation. The expenses for new equipment, food prepared at home, postage, guidebooks, maps, transportation, and the like bring the average real cost for doing the whole trail to about $3,200, or about $1.50 per mile.

The money spent on the trip does not vary significantly with the age of the hiker; it averages out to be the same for those in their 20s as for the middle-aged and those in their 60s, men and women alike. These are, however, averages; the range of actual amounts spent is broad. Over 10 percent spent less than $2,000 in all, and about the same number spent over $5,000. The cheapest trip cost only $800, and several other trips were estimated at a little over $1,000. On the other end of the scale, the most spent was $8,000, with several other trips reported as having cost $6,000 or more.

In their comments, a number of hikers complained of money problems, and about 10 percent of those who dropped out early said a shortage of funds was the reason. Several hikers emphasized that being short of funds was a "bummer." "Running out of money—a feeling of despair." And although it sounds feasible to stretch the dollar by working en route, short-term jobs like chopping wood, gardening, washing dishes, and the like seldom worked out in practice. Among other reasons, thru-hiking leaves little spare energy for physical labor. In a few cases, however, hikers stopped for a matter of weeks or months, worked and saved, and then returned to finish the trail.

The breakdown of an average trip's costs, based on the hiker survey, is shown in Table 17-5.

TABLE 17-5.
HOW HIKERS SPENT THEIR MONEY

1. PREPARATIONS BEFORE STARTING	$1,000	30%
2. FOOD ON THE TRAIL	$825	26%
3. RESTAURANT MEALS	$275	9%
4. TRAVEL, PHONE, MAIL	$275	9%
5. EQUIPMENT ALONG THE WAY	$250	8%
6. HOTELS AND BOARDING	$225	7%
7. BEER AND FUN	$225	7%
8. HOSTELS, CAMPS, AND SHOWERS	$125	4%
TOTAL	**$3,200**	**100%**

Item 1 in the table covers not only equipment and clothing purchased in advance, but also the cost of preparing food drops. Because almost half of the food consumed on the trail was sent from home, about $400 of the $1,000 "preparations" costs might accurately be included in item 2. Thus, the non-food "preparation" cost would be about $600, or 19 percent of the total budget. This results in the not-very-surprising revelation that on-the-trail food costs were the largest single item, averaging about $1,225 or 38 percent of the total budget. Adding restaurant meals (item 3) brings the average cost for hiker food to $1,500 or almost half of all expenditures. This does not really seem too much to feed a body in return for five or six months spent walking some 2,000 miles and climbing mountains with a pack on the back.

More than half the establishments en route—restaurants, motels, and stores—honor credit cards. Therefore, it is well worthwhile to reduce cash requirements by obtaining and using a popular credit card such as Visa or MasterCard. A fair number of places that do not take credit cards will nevertheless accept a personal check. Despite the itinerant nature of backpackers, they fortunately enjoy a pretty good reputation for honesty with local inhabitants. However, this still leaves the requirement for between $500 and $1,000 in cash for the whole trip.

Most hikers carry traveler's checks, rely on money sent to their post drops, and use the not-always-plentiful ATMs. But they still must carry some cash. It is most convenient if the hiker can have several hundred dollars, for it saves a lot of fuss and bother waiting for and cashing checks. The choice becomes whether to carry the money on your person or in the pack. The pack is better when in the deep woods where there is no need for money and the pack is relatively safe from theft. But in towns and on stops it is a nuisance to have to dig out money from the pack, and the backpacker is often separated from the pack just at the time the money is needed. So the money gets shifted back and forth. I always carried the bulk of cash in a money belt, and so as long as I kept my pants on I knew where my wealth was. However, this works only if you are wearing pants that are held up by a belt—not skimpy nylon shorts.

THE BIGGEST BARGAIN

The best bargain of the trip is unquestionably the trail itself. Here is a wonderfully blazed continuous pathway maintained by hundreds of volunteers. There are scenic views, deep forests, rocky mountain peaks, and, not the least, about 250 shelters being continuously improved and supplemented. There is nothing else like it in the world. As Julie Elman-Roche put it, "Walking the AT is *free*. . . . I'm glad I didn't have to pay to walk, climb mountains, breathe fresh air, make friends, see animals in the wild, pick berries, and sleep in shelters." To which one hiker added, "All these experiences and joys for so little money." Another wrote, "God expects no rent."

There are also many other real bargains. The couple-dozen free, or almost-free, hostels along the trail have been described in Chapter 9. All-you-can-eat restaurants were targeted miles in advance and regarded as a hard-to-believe bonanza. In general, southern eating places offered wonderful food often at bargain prices.

POOR BARGAINS

In response to the survey question about complaints, quite a few long-distance hikers insisted there were none. Considering the duration and circumstances, it is remarkable that there should be anyone whose entire trip was unclouded by a single "ripoff."

Regrettably, one experience irked enough thru-hikers to be mentioned by about a quarter of the questionnaire respondents. This was the perceived treatment received by thru-hikers at the White Mountain Appalachian Mountain Club huts. Often referred to by these hikers as the "Appalachian Money Club," the problem stems from the fact that the usual backpacker staying at a hut is not a thru-hiker but a casual hiker who, before visiting the White Mountains, has carefully reserved his or her space and time, often months in advance, gladly paying $40 to $60 a night for dinner, a bunk, and breakfast. This places the thru-hiker at a disadvantage in the competition for affordable accommodations.

The thru-hiker runs afoul of the AMC hut system in three ways. First, it is difficult to make a reservation for a night at the hut: Not only is it tricky to know how far one will go when facing unknown terrain and the possibility of sudden bad weather, but there is seldom a convenient telephone from which to call giving the information. Second, thru-hikers typically have traveled over 1,800 miles at this point without having been faced with mandatory overnight charges; as a group, they are much more accustomed to hostels that cost only a few dollars. Finally, the usual alternatives are blocked: Long-standing AMC practice forbids camping within a half mile of any hut so as to discourage the use of hut facilities without sharing the cost, but the rugged White Mountain terrain sometimes makes it impossible to camp within several miles. All of this frustrates the long-distance hiker, who is used to eating and sleeping any place where there is water and a few square yards of flat ground—and if necessary, right on the trail itself.

There is a historical reason for this perceived lack of hospitality. Until recent years, the total number of thru-hikers in a season would be a dozen or two, and the huts would seldom see more than one or two thru-hikers a night. In these circumstances, the thru-hiker was fêted as a visiting guru, and it would be considered a treat to have him or her give a talk after dinner about the trip. Thru-hikers were heroes and often invited to be non-paying guests.

Today, due to the huts' popularity with reserved weekend backpackers, there is no longer much room available to thru-hikers on the first-come, first-served basis that characterizes the rest of the other accommodations on the trail. In August and September it is not unusual for a half dozen northbound thru-hikers to descend for the night upon an already crowded hut. They are hungrier, dirtier, poorer, and much more filled with their great adventure than the casual visitor at the hut. In some cases, the hard-won battle over the mountains and ridges has infused not only considerable self-confidence but a degree of hubris as well.

The AMC has attempted to accommodate thru-hikers by offering them room and board at the huts in exchange for two to four hours of cleaning tasks. This works out to a payment of about $15 per hour, so it would seem that the AMC has gone more than halfway to ease the financial burden. Some hikers recognize this and gratefully pitch in. However, there is a fly in the ointment: The work tasks to pay for room and board are nominally available for only one or two persons per night; and the AMC hut system has become immensely popular in recent years, with reserved customers gladly paying their way. Thus, work opportunity is minimal.

Not only is sleeping space often severely limited, but the thru-hiker is also likely to be one of the last to arrive at the hut, either just before the 6:00 P.M. dinner, or even after dinner—at which time he or she would be most grateful if the crew would allow a bite in the kitchen. The huts usually observe the wilderness tradition and never turn anyone out—no matter what the crowd. However, under these circumstances, the thru-hiker is likely to find that he or she must sleep on a dining room table, on the floor, or in some out-of-the-way corner. (At the popular Lakes of the Clouds hut, a ground-level room has been equipped with space for about six thru-hikers, and the hut crew has been known to look the other way when the incumbents cook supper on the rocks outside their room.) However, such accommodations are sometimes viewed as the treatment of thru-hikers as charity cases. And although thru-hikers have often slept in much less elegant quarters, here they are separated from their admiring public. To each other they refer to the special accommodations as "The Dungeon."

Most of the effort, then, has been put out by the AMC. In a circular "To the AT-Hiker Community" in the summer of 1993, the tone is conciliatory, but the rather severe limitations are nevertheless clear. The initial paragraph states: "The Appalachian Mountain Club has a long tradition of providing room and board to A.T. thru-hikers in exchange for work at our facilities in the White Mountains of New Hampshire. This arrangement has worked well for many years, with AMC crews appreciating the extra help and thru-hikers enjoying a soft bed and somebody else's cooking. . . . The AMC wishes to encourage thru-hikers to visit our backcountry facilities. Feel free to stop in at any and all of our huts for a glass of lemonade, home-baked desserts, and conversation. Please do not be offended, however, if no room and board is available. The White Mountains are popular, and we are busy all summer. See you on the Trail!"

The AMC is a highly organized and successful outing club, with the seven huts being the jewels in the crown of the system. The huts are designed to provide young and old with a genuine wilderness experience. The AMC's making available bunk and board allows the thru-hiker to reduce his or her backpack load to only a few pounds. The service as offered is expensive. The general hiking public perceives it as a reasonable value.

The thru-hiker, by virtue of the long trek, has become a modified species. The end-to-enders are used to being admired for carrying out a feat that many hikers would emulate. If there is a touch of arrogance in some, that is also true in sports in which the apprenticeship is no more severe. Meanwhile, the rules of the game are clear, and it behooves the thru-hiker to be aware that this is another test of ability to overcome all trail obstacles.

Besides the AMC brouhaha, the only other stop-off receiving several bad notices was the Rainbow Springs area, the first commercial campsite after leaving Springer Mountain, Georgia. A number of hikers objected to prices, facilities, and personnel, although others were satisfied. A smattering of hotels and B&Bs also distinguished themselves in their notoriety, particularly in Kent, Connecticut, where 1989 motel stays were billed at from $90 to $100 per night. Shenandoah National Park and its lodges, Fontana Dam Village, and isolated instances usually associated with tourist areas completed the list of bum buys. It would seem that if the only grump about the trip was that of the hiker who "was overcharged for a hotdog at the top of Mount Killington," the ripoff list is indeed limited.

THE BEST AND THE WORST

The happiest moments of the whole trip were most often enjoyed in the company of trail friends, family, and loved ones. "Lounging by the campfire, chatting, and sharing," "the sunshine of camaraderie," "just being silly at the shelters," or simply meeting old friends. Family was often important—a son coming along for a few days, or having mother waiting as a hiker comes down from Mount Katahdin. Some special kindness from strangers moved hikers, as in this account by Adam Ticknor: "While at the Fontana Hilton I met a couple who had driven up from Atlanta to prepare a wonderful steak-and-mushroom dinner for all the hikers who happened to be at the shelter when they arrived."

There are touching accounts of the surprise and happiness of meeting or being with a loved one: "Meeting Lou and sharing two months with her" or simply "fell in love."

The studies in Chapter 2 of this book conclude that the most common reasons for hiking the AT are challenge and the sense of adventure. Thus, it is not surprising that satisfying these is a high point for many. For some it is the final day, reaching Baxter Peak on Mount Katahdin. Or it may be overcoming a difficult stretch like topping Mount Washington in a 77-mile-per-hour gale. Many also found it exciting at the very beginning to at last have a dream come true and be started on the trail—there was a thrill just in the first night out on the wilderness trek.

Nature lovers wrote about "seeing the different wild-flowers, mushrooms, trees, and snakes," "the fantastic beauty everywhere." And despite the importance of friends, there was also beauty in solitude: ". . . three hours on top of Mount Moosilauke in calm and quiet," "the peacefulness of walking and reaching your goal every day," "the serenity of camping alone on a mountain peak," or simply "feeling the presence of God."

In any thru-hiker popularity contest as to which was their favorite state, Maine wins, with the White Mountains and New Hampshire a close second; these two states garner three-quarters of the votes. The Smokies, Vermont, and Virginia get honorable mention, but there was a commonly voiced feeling that the trail is fun, interesting, and different in every state. As veteran Bob Sparks put it, "Each section has its own charm."

Because of its remarkable collection of loose but sharp rocks and some rather bedraggled barrens, Pennsylvania is the winner as the section of trail thru-hikers would be most willing not to hike. But there is almost a tie with my own state, New Jersey. I would insist that some of the prettiest lakes and waterfalls on the whole AT are in New Jersey; but alas, the crowds, litter, and second-rate overnight facilities do us in. The state of New York comes in third with a Bronx cheer.

About a third of the worst trail experiences involved storms: heavy rain, wind, cold, and especially the problems of pitching camp under such circumstances. Many hikers noted how afraid they were of lightning, despite the fact that unlike the exposed peaks in the Rockies, the danger on the AT is small. But as one hiker puts it, "I think thunderstorms with the high winds and lightning are the only things I truly *fear* while on the trail." Hikers also were sometimes worried about hypothermia; but although there were some close calls, no serious cases were reported.

Even experienced hikers got lost, and when a pair jointly carrying equipment got separated for the night, it proved a miserable experience. Hikers got lost on mountaintops unable to find blazes in the snow, got lost at crossroads, and got lost at night. One woman separated from her partner wrote ". . . forced to face myself with all my strength and weakness, alone."

Hikers are only human, and sometimes trail conditions became insufferable. There were poorly maintained sections of trail, bugs, crowded shelters, lonely times, hot days and nights, a few bad people, numerous personal conflicts, and the sadness of friends dropping off along the way. But as Alex Kopista, a dedicated hiker if there ever was one, put it: "Sadness and reflection lent validity to the whole experience. It's these extremes that give you the entire picture."

FATIGUE, BOREDOM, LONELINESS, AND SOLITUDE

Hiking more than 2,000 miles over hundreds of mountains is a tiring task. For one backpacker, the thing to do when tired was to take "a nap in the sun, on a rock—it did wonders." But it was more common just to take a 15-minute break and eat something. If a hiker was really tired, the answer was to take a day off, preferably in town. Many reported becoming more fatigued toward the end of the trip—"I was getting ready to finish. My body was tired. Melancholy."

Hikers were used to pushing just as far as mind, body and darkness would permit. I found that if I wished to hike day in, day out, I would have to keep down to about eight hours per day on the trail. More was possible, but after several long days I would find myself hating the drudgery and considering quitting; that wonderful refreshed feeling greeting me every morning was gone. Others, particularly younger men and women, regularly hiked 10 hours per day, and a few did 12 and up to 14. Most hikers slept nine hours per night—the thru-hiking fraternity does not thrive on a short night's sleep, and one hiker complained, "I never slept enough." Dave Bally had the right approach for long-distance hiking: "I know I will make it. Just take your time. Hike your own hike."

For many, the mountains, and getting over them, became the major natural barrier to completing a thru-hike. As Bob Rzewnicki put it, "I got very tired of up and down and would have enjoyed more flat trail. Mountains are fine, but as a constant?" Many agreed that it was 20 percent physical and 80 percent in the mind—a matter of keeping a positive attitude. One hiker found too much information a hindrance: "I stopped looking at the profile map in advance."

Boredom was not a usual problem for hikers, because the trail itself was ever-changing with beauty, something new just around the next corner. To relieve boredom, hikers gave speeches, recited poetry, thought up stories, listened to their headsets, and sang. In camp a few read or wrote in their journals, but it was mostly small talk about hiking, their fastest day on the trail, or the good time in town discussed with shelter mates. People were the most valuable source of trail information, and this was always passed along around the campfire and in the register.

Julie Elman-Roche wrote the following about coping: "I never was at a loss as to what to think about. I liked being alone and then greatly appreciated joining up with people after a long day of hiking. . . . My body was tired the last 300 miles, but my mind won out—mental strength helped me the rest of the way . . . If I was having a particularly bad, exhausting day, I tried to talk to myself into changing my thought patterns from negative to positive. I tried to think about upcoming pleasures like a roof over my head or ice cream. I focused by singing 'Mac the Knife' when fording the Kennebec."

Christian Lugo had an unusual coping strategy: "Throughout the trip I had several problems that I was trying to work out and come to grips with. Some of these problems I used to my advantage while working them out. A couple of my problems would make me very angry whenever I thought about them. What I would do was to bring those thoughts to mind whenever I came to a long climb. I could channel that anger into energy; put my head to the ground and *hike like an animal or madman*. It was very effective. Instead of the hills being a struggle, and searching for the energy and motivation to press on, I found it effortless. I could out-hike anyone on the trail, even those people who were much taller and would walk off and leave me on the flats."

One hiker wrote, "The challenge was an inner need to complete the AT despite all the pain and loneliness. I knew I couldn't fight the path or the mountain. I would have to accept them as inevitable."

Lonely hikers often talked: with themselves, other people, animals, and "neat-looking trees." And they listened to the forest when they found themselves all alone for an evening. A few were comforted by prayer, others wrote home, and most called home when they were in town. But although loneliness could be a problem (Emilie Jeanneney, hiking late season, suffered nine days without seeing another person); others welcomed the solitude. Tena Merritt wrote, "I could always entertain myself. I treasured the moments when I walked alone. It allowed for great reflection."

People in small groups or hiking with a partner sometimes complained that they needed more privacy: "I had to get away from my hiking partners for about five days." And even when the partnership was the single positive factor in keeping going, one hiker noted, "I could have used a break from my brother during the day. He got on my nerves sometimes."

HITCHHIKING

Except for the few who are backpacking with car support, it is practically impossible to thru-hike the AT without hitchhiking. Although some hostels, post offices, motels, and stores are near the trail, more often they are miles away—and nobody is eager to add road miles to their day's quota. Early hikers sometimes sequestered their packs deep in the woods, which made it much easier to walk into town. The practice is less common today, especially since a hiker without a pack invites the question, "Where is the pack?" Even well-hidden packs have been located and stolen.

Although I had not hitchhiked for 45 years, it was not hard to learn. And although fitting a pack into a car can be a hassle, actually the pack is your salvation. Many people who will not pick up anyone else on the road will stop and offer the AT hiker a lift. And, as noted by several thru-hikers, the hitchhiking can be an adventure all on its own. Drivers usually want to know where you're from, where you've been, and from where you come and where you're going. They are incredulous upon hearing the foot travel distance. Some wistfully say, "I'd like to do that." On the other hand, if you are a good listener, they are eager to tell about their own lives. Often a driver would go out of the way (in a few cases, traveling 20 to 30 miles) to drop me off at my destination. Only once out of some 40 rides did a driver allow me to buy gasoline, and she had a battered old car, six children in it, and drove far out of her way to accommodate me.

Particularly in the South, drivers often had never heard of the Appalachian Trail and were quite doubtful about climbing over "them mountains." But they would pick you up anyhow because it was the hospitable thing to do. In the South the most common ride would be in the back of a pickup truck, which at 75 miles per hour on an interstate is an experience unto itself.

When seeking a ride I would smile hopefully and try to look alert (or at least interesting and nonthreatening). Possibly because of my age, even women picked me up. The drivers were almost always local folk. For some odd reason, whether in the North or South, tourists never seem to offer a ride.

When rides are tough to get, it pays to walk to a nearby gas station or diner—if one can be found. There you can usually find someone already stopped who you can interest in your trip. After failing to hitch a ride along the Blue Ridge Parkway for half an hour, I ducked into a men's room at a restaurant. The young man I met there was one of the most interesting friends I made on the whole trip. We shared accommodations for the night and hiked together all the next day visiting local sights.

In general, motorists are most comfortable picking up a young couple. Threesomes or more seem not to work and often must break up. The neater you can look, the better your chances—although, coming out of the woods, only a limited degree of "neatness" is feasible. Single women reported that hitchhiking was one of the few situations where being alone could be a problem. They would usually join up in advance with a male friend for the ride into town.

I kept track of my rides and can report on the statistics: In about 40 attempts to hitch a ride, the time to get picked up ranged from instantly to one-and-a-half hours. The wait averaged 20 minutes. Several times the first passing car stopped, but once I had to wait for 118 cars. My quickest pickup was when a driver spotted me coming out of the woods and pulled up at the trail crossing waiting for me to get in. Only once did I fail completely. I had to travel about 12 miles to the nearest town, and over the course of three hours, three rides only advanced me five miles. In this case, a farm wife permitted me to call town, and I took a taxi. Returning to the trail was usually easier. Often a motel employee or a newly made friend will be glad to take you to the trailhead.

Hitchhiking reflects the warmth and curiosity of the drivers who pick you up. They are almost always friendly and helpful, and this is your free ticket to the customs and lifestyles of the local area.

LEAVING THE TRAIL EARLY

An experience on the AT cannot really be measured by miles or by whether the original plan was followed. Although it was always satisfying to reach a dreamed-of goal like the top of Mount Katahdin, some of the most interesting stories and published journals of hiking the AT are about incomplete trips. In a number of cases they cover less than half the end-to-end distance. But although about 85 percent of the starters normally do not complete a planned thru-hike, there are also a few who have no intention of going the whole way but get the bug and do so.

Of the surveyed hikers who did not continue, 35 percent left the trail for various personal reasons, from missing loved ones to simply losing interest. Eric Muller wrote, "Homesick, I especially missed my wife. During periods of bad weather I would think 'What am I doing this for? I would rather go home.' By mid-trip, with all the bad weather, I felt I was on a self-imposed prison sentence. . . ." Another hiker said simply, "lovesickness trail problems." It was not always a piece of cake. Shane Angus, coming all the way from England, at times was "Bored, tired, lonely, and not knowing what I was doing here."

Outer-world obligations forced 25 percent to get on with job or school. Bonnie Goulard started hiking the trail after being let go from her job; several months later a court action reversed the decision. Reluctantly, she gave up her trek and returned to "the normal world." Some hikers were offered jobs, ran out of their allotted time, or headed back for the next semester.

Sickness and injury (see Chapter 5) accounted for 17 percent of those departing—a rather surprisingly small fraction in view of the fact that half the hikers struggled with such problems and one out of every two thru-hikers considered quitting at one time or another. Physical discomfort was something that hikers were prepared for; thus it had to be serious to drive them permanently off the trail.

Some 13 percent left because of bad weather—often a single hiker giving up as the New England winter approached and he or she faced ice, cold, and snow alone. Finally, a few ran out of money, although there is a sense that many others were short but stretched and borrowed enough money to finish.

Thoughts of quitting lurked in the minds of many who nevertheless kept going. Judy Gallant wrote that despite such thoughts, "Usually when I felt really low and considering getting off the AT, something good would happen— the sun would come out, a hiker would make a cup of hot chocolate for me, I'd get a nice letter from home." Greg Knoettner said, "This may sound strange, but I often compared the thought of quitting to the thought of taking my own life. I thought about it, but *never* considered it." Fatigue was often a real problem, and rest the solution. As Charles Hydeck put it: "I considered quitting many times, only to get a good night's rest and wake up smiling." In several cases distant wives, husbands, and parents kept the hikers going. They sometimes joined the hikers, met them along the way, and sent brownies, fudge, and long letters. There were a few cases where hikers had burned their bridges: Bill Gunderson wrote, "thinking about quitting— not really. Nothing to go back to."

If one compares those who finished with those who left the trail early, the numbers give no hint that hikers left the trail because it was too tough. Indeed, a small difference, not very significant, leans in the direction of hikers leaving the trail having rated it slightly *less* difficult than thru-hikers.

As discussed in Chapter 3, both men and women thru-hikers are more introverted than is general in the U.S. population; casual hikers are somewhat less introverted. This invites the generalization that the longer the distance hiked, the more introverted is the sample of those still on the trail. The person who is the life of the party may not be the best candidate for thru-hiking, but he or she may be just the right person to invite for a weekend hike.

"LOOKING AT THE TRAIL THROUGH MY TEARS . . ."

These were the words of Cindy Ross as she sat and cried alone deep in the woods trying to decide what to do about an injured foot. Cindy's stress fracture sent her home, but in two weeks she was back on the trail, healed and with renewed courage.

In my sample of 136 hikers, about half said they had cried, although, as in the outside world, it was a privilege more often indulged in by the women (82 percent) than the men (25 percent). Hikers recounted almost 50 instances where they had cried. Reading them gives a special insight into the attitudes, experiences, and fortitude of the long-distance hiker.

The following are some examples of trail frustrations that brought hikers to tears: "Two hundred miles from the end my knee locked up and I was in tremendous pain. But I hiked on—crying—knowing I may be doing irreparable damage, but I had to finish." "The entire first week, out in the cold, exhausted, lonely, being lost, being injured, afraid." "Missing the one I love." "While camping alone on my birthday." "When rain caught me two miles from a shelter for the third straight day."

As told in Chapter 2, some hikers seek the long trek as an opportunity for reflection, a time to work out past problems and renew themselves: "Yes, I cried, not about the trail, but about things that had happened over the last couple of years—a lot of the reason I went hiking was to be alone and get over such things."

But the tears were not always from pain, sadness, and frustration. At times, hikers of both sexes shed tears of pure joy. Greg Seay wrote: "Yes, I cried, not in fear, exhaustion, or pain, but in elation. For example, when I awoke with Tina in Hot Springs, North Carolina, at the Inn. It had stopped raining, the sun was rising, we could smell the breakfast cooking, and heard an old Simon and Garfunkel album playing. It just felt too good." "When I got to Katahdin—tears of joy."

Hopeful thru-hikers at the start

TRAIL PEOPLE

Hikers planning to do the whole AT seldom view their proposed travel plans from the standpoint of a people experience. Many try to arrange for partners before starting, but this often does not work out. As we have seen in Chapter 3, those who finish the whole trail are often introverts, a group whose personality inclines them to enjoy solitude rather than seek company.

But a people experience it is. Even those who eschew casual human contact end up rating trail interactions as an important and often wonderful part of the experience. Whether it be interactions with other long-distance backpackers, casual weekend hikers, or local inhabitants, the experience is a happy one.

> *Friendships made on the trail were like family.*
>
> —Buddy Newell

INTERACTIONS ALONG THE TRAIL

Other thru-hikers become part of your extended family, and there develops a strong kinship. Many commented on how other thru-hikers "were an incredibly varied bunch of people," "lots of characters with differing backgrounds."

But about nine out of every ten thru-hikers reflected a strong feeling of family.

Although it tended to be other thru-hikers who were regarded as kinfolk, the more casual day- or weekend hikers also were considered hospitable, warm people who often leaned over backwards to be helpful. This was particularly true in matters of food. Most of the long-distance crowd necessarily carried a Spartan, limited food supply, whereas weekenders brought (and sometimes shared) steaks, hamburgers, fresh fruit, wine, beer, and cookies.

The short-distance hikers were often fascinated by the stories they were told, curious, and openly envious of the thru-hikers. The latter were sometimes vaguely disparaging about weekenders, referring to them as "boot-campers in training" or "overequipped." But thru-hikers liked it when those out for only a few days held them in awe.

Although there have been occasional warnings about dealing with "locals," in fact the thru-hikers reported almost universally good relations with local people. Friendliness and helpfulness seemed especially common in the rural South. Joyce Vorbeau commented that her experiences with locals had "restored my faith in humanity with their goodness." And even when they did not comprehend the long hike, or had never heard of Maine, they would stop their pickup truck, saying, "Y'all climb right in back there and make yourself comfortable."

However, not every person along the trail was remembered so warmly. Over half the long-distance hikers were critical of the large hiking groups occasionally met on the AT. Faced with a large group organized by a church, children's camp, or the scouts, most long-distance hikers would check their maps and move on to quieter country (some teenagers have a penchant for running across shelter roofs after midnight). Of course, there were many well-behaved and friendly groups, generous with food and leaving space in the shelters. But this type of company runs contrary to the thru-hiker's fondness for an uncrowded and quiet place.

The AT is not always in the deep forest. In some areas, like Skyline Drive in Virginia and the White Mountains of New Hampshire, the thru-hiker must learn to deal with tourists. What happens is a love-hate relationship. The tourists are loved for their ego-building questions ("Did you really walk all the way from Georgia?") and their generosity with food. There is a mooching potential, and trekkers are variously gifted in the art of "Yogiing," as described in Chapter 14. But hikers were often somewhat condescending in their questionnaire responses, and there was sometimes a touch of arrogance in their attitude. The answers to the "100,000 questions" were not always polite. For example, this is the reported exchange between some "tourons" (a cross between a tourist and a moron) and thru-hiker Don in Shenandoah National Park:

Touron: So, how long have you been hiking?
Don: About two and a half months.
Touron (surprised): In the park?
Don: Yes. I lost my car.
Touron: How do you carry six months' worth of food?
Don: Three bouillon cubes a day.
Touron: Do you live off the land?
Don: Yes. We had earthworm stew last night.

Hiking over 2,000 miles is sufficiently unusual to fascinate the outside world, and questions rain down on the dirty, heavily loaded hikers as they enter an area filled with vacationing tourists. The most common questions (reported by 30 percent of the hikers) are about the trip length and destination: "Where did you start? Where are you going?" Tourists also want to know the details of miles

per day, pack weight, sleeping accommodations, and food. Some 15 percent reported questions about dangers: "Are you afraid?" "What about bears?" "See any snakes?"

Some of the hikers' favorite questions included: "Where do you go to the bathroom?" "Don't you miss taking a shower?" "The Appalachian what?" "Why are you all by yourself?" "Do you get tired?" "Why are you walking?" "Do your feet hurt?" "Don't you miss TV?" "Doesn't your mother worry?" "Are you crazy?"

Adam Ticknor has pointed out: "Tourists offer a receptive audience for the tales of seasoned thru-hikers. The interchange quickly alleviates any desire for return to the civilized world." So the consensus on tourists was that they were a cross between being friendly, inquisitive, and having all sorts of funny ways. On the other side, there was a certain disdain for them as examples of an obnoxious set driving around in gas-guzzling recreational vehicles and littering the parks. An interesting special observation by several hikers was that the tourists "smelled so nice."

Every once in a while it is possible to gain an insight between thru-hikers and some other, equally specialized group. Both glider pilots and thru-hikers are indulging themselves in a rather peculiar hobby. Beyond that they would not seem to have very much in common. Certainly the view of hikers from the sky is not the usual one. This exchange, reported by glider pilot Bob Cook and told by Gordon Glover in the newsletter of his club, is not likely to take place very often:

"As glider pilots, we regularly see many fantastic sights from the air, but for me the most unusual, even shocking, was the time that I saw five moons over the ridge.

"John Mucha and I were flying in the two-place Lark. We always enjoy flying together, and this day was no exception, since the ridge lift was working, making for super soaring conditions. We were able to fly at speeds of well over 100 MPH at treetop level. This type of flying is loads of fun but really gets the adrenaline flowing. . . .

"Several miles down the ridge we spotted a group of Appalachian Trail hikers resting on the open clearing at the very top of the mountain.

"'Do you see what I see?' I asked, leading him on.
"'Yep.'
"'You know what we must do then, don't you?'
"'Yes, we must,' John replied, knowing the routine.

"We dove down for a fast, low pass directly in front of the hikers. They waved at us as we went by. Little did they know that in our little game they were the enemy and we were making a strafing run. After a sharp pull-up and a tight turn, we dove on them again, our imaginary machine

TABLE 18-1.

INTERACTIONS ALONG THE TRAIL

Type of Persons Met	Favorable Relations	Negative Reactions
Thru-hikers	86%	2%
Weekenders	82%	7%
Locals	85%	4%
Large Groups	32%	62%
Tourists	45%	30%

Note: Responses and mixed reactions intermediate between favorable and negative are not listed.

gun blasting them to bits. We even tried a surprise attack, flying low below the ridge top and climbing up on them. We were having a blast! I flew past the people right at eye level while John yelled out at the top of this lungs. They probably could not hear him, but it was this time that the hikers probably had had their fill of our highjinks.

"'Let's give 'em one more,' I said as I made a diving turn, heading for the treetops directly in front of the clearing.

"As we approached, I noticed that the hikers had changed position on the rocky outcropping. They were up to something, but what? As we skimmed the treetops into the clearing, it was too late to turn back. They had it timed perfectly. As we flew closer, they all did an about-face in perfect unison. Just as we came the closest, they all bent over and dropped their drawers.

"What a sight! Five moons.

On the whole, the interactions between long-distance hikers and the peopled world were overwhelmingly satisfying and happy. By category, the hikers in the study rated their interactions as shown in Table 18-1.

WOMEN ON THE TRAIL

In 1901, the Sierra Club organized its first group hike in which female members were invited to join. It was unusual enough that the club issued specific advice on dress: "Skirts can be short but not more than half way from knee to ankle, and under them can be worn shorter dark colored bloomers." As happens so often in the male-dominated hiking world, there was amazement at how easily the women kept pace: "Their vigor and endurance was a revelation to us all."

It would be several decades before women gave up the full-length skirts and hiked in bloomers. Several more decades and World War II had to intervene before women

won their equality and climbed not only the mountaintops but into pants, long and short.

But the Victorian view of women as fragile, delicate ornamental objects, so much the mark of recent western history, was largely a vision of the aristocratic and upper classes. Those women who labored, tilled the soil, and worked in shops, homes, and factories were often competing with men. In 1897, during the Alaskan gold rush, the prospectors had to pack heavy loads over the vicious Chilkoot Pass—and the women were not just washing dishes, they were demonstrating unexpected competence in backpacking. According to Steve Howe in the February 1995 *Backpacker* magazine, Diarist William Haskell wrote that he ". . . could not fail to notice many instances . . . in which the women showed a fortitude superior to the men. It was a revelation, almost a mystery. But after a while, I began to account for it as the natural result of an escape from the multitude of social customs and restraints which in civilized society hedge about a woman's life. . . . Her nature suddenly becomes aware of a freedom, which is a way of exhilarating."

In earlier times when there were far fewer females on the AT, the men told each other sundry versions of the following tale: A couple, male and female, start at Springer to hike the whole trail. After a few difficult days and nights it just gets to be too much. The man escorts his girlfriend out and to the nearest city, puts her on the bus for home, and returns to finish the thru-hike. Although unquestionably apocryphal, the story illustrates what the "real man" believed to be typical outcome of trying to do a long-distance hike with the opposite sex. In the 1980s and 1990s, it was a rapidly disappearing belief.

Viewing the statistics of women on the Appalachian Trail reveals that among casual and day hikers, up to 50 percent are now women. Significantly fewer women are going long distances, but the fraction is steadily increasing. Harpers Ferry files indicate 5 to 10 percent before 1970, and 15 to 20 percent in the 1980s. More recent figures, taken from various registers along the AT and other sources, indicate 21 to 26 percent of long-distance hikers are women; in 1995, 28.6 percent of ALDHA members were women.

WOMEN AND MEN

Thru-hiking the AT is an unusual task for anyone—young or old, male or female, physically fit or handicapped. Above all, to complete the AT takes an overriding commitment; traversing the steep mountains, woods, swamps, and streams must be more important than anything else.

Hiking the AT is for all ages

For most it requires up to six months of daily challenges. With such a task at hand and with so many cultural and physical differences between the sexes, how do the records of males and females compare? Historically there have always been women who broke the cultural pattern and competed in the male arena. But even today it takes a special toughness and sense of independence for a woman to attempt the whole AT. In our society it is still more unusual for the female to turn her back on civilization for half a year and wander, often alone, from mountain to mountain.

In general on the trail, similarities between men and women vastly outnumber differences. In many categories where strength, size, and cultural expectations would lead one to believe men would outperform women, this is not the case. But there still seems to be a tendency to underestimate the female of the species. Why? A possible answer has been suggested by sociology professor Mary Jo Neitz of the University of Missouri. She has pointed out that given the cultural norm of women staying at home and men going out into the world to provide, it is a far greater step for a woman to take off on the AT for six months than for a man. Thus the women on the trail are a more selected group of the general population, than are the men. And the 35 women sampled were less representative of women in the general population than were the 101 men of men in the general population.

With a number of the couples in the sample, the man slowed up and took time off so that they could stay together. And in the questionnaire, sometimes the male made a point of this, wishing to make it clear that *he* could have gone faster. But there were also a number of examples in which the female proved to be more rugged. One male with knee injuries took on the role of car-support for his still-hiking wife. An athletically competitive woman easily out-hiked her male companion but carefully preserved his ego: "Sam has had a bout of GI troubles, so we are slowing down a bit."

In viewing the comparison statistics, therefore, the reader cannot assume that the results are necessarily indicative of the general population of men and women. But they do clearly indicate that there are few, if any, absolute areas of superiority, and that the trend toward more equal numbers of each sex on the trail reflects a condition where there is no intrinsic difference in the ability of women to thru-hike the AT.

To the extent that numbers tell us on-the-trail performance, the following are some of the interesting areas where the performance of men and women can be compared.

Miles per Day. As we have seen in Chapter 12, how far the long-distance hiker travels each day is the most widely discussed and reported indicator of backpacking power. Thus it is significant that the overall average for men and women is exactly the same, 14.5 miles per day. The most miles hiked in a day, a real test of endurance, averaged 27 miles for both sexes. The farthest hiked in a single day in this sample by either a male or female was (female) Tracy Hill's 43 miles, hiked in 18 straight hours and averaging 2.4 miles an hour. Days off the trail were the same for both sexes.

Pack Weight. The fairest way to measure pack weight is in terms of percent of body weight; for men it averaged about 25 percent, for women 27 percent. Measured mid-trip in pounds when loaded, packs averaged 48 pounds for men and 44 pounds for women. The heavyweight record among hikers I have encountered goes to René Cote. Although only a trim 5 feet 2 inches when checking in at Zealand Falls hut in the White Mountains in August 1996, she was carrying a pack estimated to be 60 pounds, or 65 percent of her body weight.

Reaction to Trail and Animals. Women reported greater difficulty surmounting certain trail conditions: loose rock, steep sections, finding the trail, getting lost. But mud and sloppy going affected men and women equally. In rating trail difficulty, many more women than men called the trip difficult, and while some men considered the hike easy, few women did. But mice, dogs, and snakes were rated more of a problem by men than women.

Personality. Measurements by psychologist O.W. Lacy indicate that women long-distance hikers tend to be more introverted and intuitive than non-hiking women in the U.S. population—even more of a difference than between hiking and non-hiking men.

Illness. Although the frequency of gastrointestinal illness was the same for both men and women hikers, the men had higher general susceptibility to sickness on the trail. But knee problems were more common among women, 46 percent versus 34 percent for men.

Physical Changes. Women lost less weight—5 to 6 percent of their body weight (6 to 9 pounds), whereas men lost 7 to 16 percent of body weight (11 to 31 pounds). Men often suffered some loss in muscular tissue; women did not. About 80 percent of the women experienced an increase in shoe size; for men it was 30 percent.

ON BEING A WOMAN ON THE TRAIL

An extra question put to some of the women returning questionnaires was, "Did you have any special problems being a woman on the trail?" Because about 15 of the women hiked alone most of the time, the question also implied considerations of personal safety. Many women answered simply "no," that is, no special problems. A number stressed the tried-and-true techniques for handling strangers: "You just have to be more aware. Never tell people you're alone. Look confident. Follow your instincts always." "You need to be more careful, especially along roads."

Kim Knuti was in a special situation because she hiked much of the trail accompanied by two men, both named Bill. She wrote: "I had some reservations about hiking as a lone woman on days when I was away from the Bills. I never had a problem of being a woman, but there were times when I found it comforting to tell a group of strange men that there were two men about five minutes behind me. One question we were always asked when someone talked to all three of us was, 'Can she keep up with you?' Sure I could!"

This kind of putting down of the women, even if not intentional, could be a real irritant. Kim Knuti commented: "My biggest problem was the attitude of many, mostly non-hikers, that a woman—I'm on the small side—is not capable of hiking the trail. I normally carried a heavier pack than my three-month hiking partner, who weighed 50 to 60 pounds more than me. We women had more to prove." Women were also irked by that favorite question, "What does your mother think?"

The female hikers proved just as resolute and competent as the males, but they also noted the value of bonding. Joyce Vorbeau wrote: "It's really good to talk to a woman, when you find one. And it's a lot harder being the minority who has to hike far away where there are no outhouses and no cover." A few other women noted the added burden of toilet privacy and the need for menstrual-cycle planning, but these problems were more at the level of annoyance than major obstacles to a good trip.

The age-old problem of an unwanted male approach, "machos," was reported by two women hikers. One woman successfully foiled an attempted rape but even so said that there were "fewer hassles than would be expected." She noted, on looking back, "I was pretty lucky and often careless." The second woman, followed by an ardent admirer through two states, eventually evaded him by hitchhiking ahead, leaving him bewildered and alone, complaining of his bad luck.

Basically, the question about any special problems evoked highly competent coping responses or little response at all. As noted by Professor Neitz, these women

could well be a selection of particularly able females. After all, any woman undertaking, of her own free will, a 2,000-mile hike over the mountains, is well equipped to tackle the problems of a woman on the trail. The most common response from these women thru-hikers, looking back on the experience, reflects a new self-confidence: "I said I would." "I can do anything I want to."

SEX ON THE TRAIL

Question 58 of the questionnaire asked the long-distance hikers: "The challenge to do the whole trail, the miles, being really tired, dirty, and lacking amenities or privacy prompted one couple to say 'There's no sex on the Trail.' Do you have any comments?"

There were many comments. And of course, there is sex on the trail—to expect anything else would imply some kind of monastic order controlling the activities of the hikers. Successful thru-hikers are unusually dedicated to the task at hand—walking. But just how all-encompassing is this challenge? In one sense, the question is unrealistic when you consider that the special population we are dealing with is made up of unusually healthy people, most of whom are younger than 35.

The question is really aimed at measuring the lowered priority of sex brought about by the demands of the long hike. One would certainly expect that there would be a greater interest in finding a partner for the night in a singles bar than on the AT. And certainly the problems of dirt, tiredness, comfort, and privacy cannot be ignored. Backpackers answered the question in many ways.

The prospect of combining the wonderful experience of hiking for months on end with the fun and pleasures of sexual intimacy is alluring. It conjures up the full-page color photograph of a tent perched on the edge of a canyon, a cozy fire, and a 50-mile view of distant mountains. The tent floor is covered by a 3-inch-thick foam mattress, and the two sleeping bags are zipped together. The accompanying text suggests that like beer and pizza, sex and backpacking go naturally together. Such a prospect has stimulated a recent small book by Robert Rose and Buck Tilton, *Sex in the Outdoors: A Humorous Approach to Recreation.*

In the literature covering over a hundred journal accounts of thru-hikers, very few even mention the subject of sex. An exception is from James Leitzell's 1971 thru-hike, which he describe in James Hare's *Hiking the Appalachian Trail:*

People sometimes asked how I could stand going so long without a woman. The answer was that I seldom felt the loss. This surprised me at first, because in the outside world one of my most insistent needs is to have a woman around. However, sex and female companionship are not such basic needs as food and shelter. Most of my time and energy was expended hiking, planning, and performing necessary camp chores.

The need to obtain adequate food and satisfactory shelter was a constant preoccupation, which left little time to dwell on sexual needs. The woods, the wild animals, the sky and my fellow hikers usually furnished as much companionship as I needed. Whenever I saw a pretty girl on the trail or an attractive woman in town, desire immediately welled up within me, but an hour after the stimulation the desire would subside. Sometimes I met someone with whom a tête-à-tête was a possibility, but more time would have been needed to seduce her than I was willing to spare. In these situations I would exert self-control and march on.

The closest I came to succumbing was the day I left the Long Trail in Vermont. The rain had stopped and the weather was clear and cold. After a 20-mile walk, during which I saw nary a soul on the trail, I approached Gulf lean-to in New Hampshire anticipating a night alone. To my great surprise a pretty blonde girl and a great black dog were in the lean-to. She was so petite and attractive that I assumed she must be camped with her boyfriend. She assured me that she was alone. Anne had hiked all the way from Baxter State Park alone, except for her dog. Looking more closely, I observed a worn pack and strong, tanned legs, confirming the veracity of her story. Her plan was to continue south on the AT and then up the Long Trail to the Canadian border and then call it quits for the season. She unnerved me. After three months in the woods without an iota of feminine companionship, here I was alone for the night with a charming young woman. My defenses and offenses were down, and I became frightfully bashful and tongue-tied. She too was a bit flustered, but soon we loosened up and became friends. I gathered wood and she built the fire. We shared our food and sat close together before the blaze in the frosty evening holding hands and talking. We went to bed intimately curled up against one another, but chastely separated by the goose down of the sleeping bags.

The poor dog, accustomed to sleeping beside his mistress but now relegated to the foot of the bunk, left the shelter and sulked alone in the forest all night.

The smell and feel of a warm, soft, female body curled up in my arms blew my mind. In the morning, the last thing I wanted to do was to get up and leave her. How delightful it would have been to stay at the shelter alone with her, strolling around in the crisp bright woods and reveling in

her company. However, my primary mission was to walk the trail, and if I stopped with her it seemed quite possible that I would say "to hell with the hike" and not finish it at all. It was important to me that I complete the trek, so we cooked our common meal and said a fond farewell. My head remained unglued for the next two days as I wandered along in an almost delirious trance. Then I came back to earth and was left with the memory of her clear smiling eyes as one of the finer recollections of the expedition.

More recently, David Brill, in his popular book *As Far as the Eye Can See: Reflections of an Appalachian Trail Hiker*, recounted an experience:

Just outside the tent, I met its occupant, a friendly, long-legged woman with brown hair topped by a blue wool watch cap. I eyed her ample shelter, and without presuming to ask if there was room inside for an extra boarder, I began complaining about my leaky digs for the night. Sensing my misery, she asked me to join her for a cup of hot tea inside the tent. A large gas stove had heated the tent to a comfortable seventy degrees, and a steaming kettle sat on the burner. From it she poured two cups of herbal tea, and, as we sipped our drinks, we talked about her frequent trips to the White Mountains and about my experiences along the trail. She was a bright, cheerful woman whose knowledge of the wilderness amazed me. At dusk I rose to leave, but she seem to sense my reluctance and asked if I'd like to stay the night in her tent. Without hesitating, I accepted her offer.

After we had finished our dinners, we sat close to a candle, and she showed me clippings from many of the edible plants that grew in the area: wood sorrel, a tart, tri-leaved plant that resembles clover and provides vitamin C; reindeer moss, a fungus of light green skeletal tines that boasts a musky, mushroom flavor; and Labrador tea leaves, taken from a low-growing evergreen heath, which she steeped in boiling water and served to me with honey.

As we sat close over the candle, I wanted to move closer, to smell her hair, to kiss her. I wanted to hold her, not necessarily make love to her, but just hold her. For all its gifts, the trail deprived us of that one thing—touch—which I believe we all craved. As we prepared to climb into our bags, I gently touched her back, and she drew away from me. I apologized and backed away, explaining how lonely for affection I had grown over the past few months and how much I enjoyed her company.

Moments later, with the candle out, I heard her slip from her clothes and enter her bag. I, too, lay naked in mine. Then I felt her hand reach for mine, and for an hour we lay silent, just stroking one another's hands. I reached over and kissed her, and she took me in her arms, kissing me back. Soon, we had rearranged our bags, laying one on the tent floor and covering ourselves with the other. We kissed and embraced through the night, sleeping and awakening in each other's arms, never making love but succumbing to blissful, innocent intimacy.

About half the individuals who returned questionnaires disagreed with the "no sex on the trail" comment. Their opinions reflected a range of observations, often emphasizing that, like the trail itself, sex under these conditions was not without its challenges.

Some hikers in the survey noted that there was, indeed, sex on the trail and recounted anecdotes and experiences. These people were most likely married or had been together for a fairly extended time. One couple wrote: "We had really great sex. Conditions make it all the more exciting—in a tent, motel, shelter, hostel, sometimes right on the trail."

A woman confided: "Yes, there is sex on the trail. Being tired and dirty is part of it—you are in the woods, for goodness sake! If you want privacy . . . don't schedule strictly . . . sleep away from shelters or tent sites." Another wrote: "When there's a will, there's a way. As one of my friends said to me in Monson, 'What do you think the blue-blazed trails are for?' The occasional hotel/motel saves a lot of trail couples' marriages and relationships, I am sure."

The two alternatives mentioned again and again were "Get a tent" and "Thank goodness for motels." Getting clean was given high priority by many: "Set up camp off the trail where you can swim and clean up. Or get a motel." One discriminating male wrote, "I'd be damned if I would get into the sack with any female who smelled as bad as I did." Another young man was less critical: "Don't worry, your partner smells, too."

Women responded more positively to the "sex on the trail" question than did men. Leaving out a few ambiguous answers, 76 percent of the women said there was sex on the trail; only 52 percent of the males were so sure. One woman explained, "There was such an uneven ratio of women to men. I will say all the women I knew except one had a romantic affair." Another recounted, "It's a great way to meet people . . . I made some good friends that could later grow into more."

Expectations were there. In one case, a man had optimistically equipped himself with condoms for the trip. However, the AT turned out to be very different than a single bar. He found, "I was a single male on the trail—there was no sex for me."

Lawrence Walsh, who thru-hiked the AT in 1976, made these comments on courtship in a November 14, 1976, *Boston Globe* article: "'Pssst! What about sex on the trail?' people inquire, hoping I might recount racy doings in the lean-tos, Petronian revels in glen and glade. However, I have to give them the bad word that the hike is G-rated, that the Appalachian Trail is not Club Mediterranée, and that there is little or no outdoor amour among the through-hiking population. Into-your-tent-I-will-creep stuff is strictly out of the question. . . . For one thing, people are just too tired for trysting come nightfall; for another everyone is usually far too grungy. . . . Over and above these considerations is the simple matter of numbers. The man-woman ratio does not favor amusing encounters."

The trail ratio of three or four males per female made it possible for women to be highly discriminating and led men to report, "The hardest part is finding the right person," or "Most women I encountered were attached." For most men, besides the problems of privacy, dirt, and whether they really felt like it, there was often simply no opportunity. One male reported that the only time he encountered any evidence of sex in his whole trip was one evening when the AT dipped down and he passed a couple parked by the roadside.

As for a woman's point of view, the situation is nicely summed up by Cindy Ross in her book *A Woman's Journey*: "There are many misconceptions about women on the trail. Their ratio to men is very unbalanced and some think we women have a regular field day. . . . The Appalachian Trail is not synonymous with a meat market. We don't travel the hills with nothing but lusty sex on our minds. The desire crops up, but it's far less frequent than in 'normal' life. Everything is put in its proper perspective. First, we try to survive. Ofttimes that takes all of our energy and concentration. Secondly, when we meet those of the opposite sex, we look on them as fellow human beings, not as sex partners. One very big thing is missing in this type of society. No one is inflicting any standards, rules of behavior, or perverted conditioning on us, so we're free to be ourselves. If this trail teaches us anything, it is how wonderfully rewarding relationships can be."

Although thru-hikers voted about equally on both sides of the question, it was three to one in favor of "sex on the trail" among those who dropped out before reaching their intended destination. Perhaps the priorities of thru-hikers resulted in their placing completing the trail higher than was common for long-distance hikers. There is some support for this amid the answers of those who responded "no sex": "I simply went for other reasons," "I lost all interest while hiking," "The trail brings out true personalities in people, and hikers realize there are things about a person that are more important than sex." Whether due to lack of opportunity or the rigors of the trail, several males noted a lowered sex drive during their thru-hike.

Despite the bleak prospects, the Appalachian Trail is not devoid of romance. Several hikers in our 1989 sample reported that they found true love, and four couples were later married. "I met my future wife on the AT, and that made the trip worth every step. I am the happiest man I could be. And, I know we share the same interests. Let's hear it for those Hot Springs!"

But most of the thru-hikers agreed that if you were looking for sex, this was not the place. Many commented on the incompatibility of the long, tough hike and trail dalliance. In *The Thru-Hiker's Handbook,* Dan Bruce elaborates on this in his guidebook on thru-hiking the AT: "Misconceptions about sexual activity among thru-hikers abound in some circles, especially in the fantasies of some younger male hikers and non-hiking types. Truth is, most thru-hikers exhibit and express virtually no desire for such activity during a thru-hike. The standing joke about sex on the Trail is that, at the end of a strenuous day of long-distance hiking, everyone is too tired and too dirty to be interested. That is not to say that romance does not blossom and liaisons never happen, but usually a good campsite, tasty meal, and relaxed fellowship with Trail friends are more important and satisfying goals to the people who thru-hike. In practice, the thru-hiking community operates as a big family, the men and women thinking of each other primarily as brothers and sisters rather than as potential sexual partners. Most thru-hikers value this sense of 'family' above all other aspects of the Trail experience."

So the answer to "Is there sex on the trail?" is both yes and no. Yes, if you have a partner (or have very good luck in finding one); no, for most of the unaccompanied serious thru-hikers.

The "Long Green Tunnel" in Virginia

LOOKING BACK

The journey along the Appalachian Trail—or any long-distance hike—is the ultimate celebration of self. There is no significant contribution to the outside world made by the traveler; no great service to family, friends, or state. Yet it is a unique purification of body and soul, intrinsically rewarding and deeply satisfying. And so it also is viewed by many outsiders, even those who never set foot beyond the city streets.

Sorting out the hikers' feelings after the thru hike, one finds they are not quite the same as the impulses that prompted the traveler initially to take to the trail, as described in Chapter 2—the challenge and adventure, love of the outdoors, and escape.

Looking back brings forth a myriad of experiences, many of which were not foreseen: the utterly simple life, nature and the wilderness environment,

> *Happiness is found along the way, not at the end of the trail.*
>
> —Noland Hisey, 1989 thru-hiker

loving companions and caring strangers, building of self-confidence, solitude and reconciliation of memories, and renewal of love of other humans. For some it was a time of peacefulness, for others an adventure into a new land among new people. And always there was a sense of freedom, to see, do, and feel for yourself, finally to end up physically strong and better "than I have ever felt in my whole life."

THE SIMPLE LIFE

Dominating the thoughts of most long-distance hikers are four problems: obtaining water; having enough food; finding shelter for the night; and planning the route ahead. Happiness is resolving these problems, yet taking each turn of the trail as it comes. Thoughts of the outside world get squeezed out and relegated to the back roads of the mind. Even fond memories of home and loved ones, the dangers of a crime-ridden nuclear world, the excitement of politics, and the violence so conspicuously paraded in the media fade. One feels these are things one *should* be worrying about . . . but they take on a distant, foggy hue. Many of our most cherished time-wasters and life goals—reading the newspapers, watching TV and movies, games, money, success, and power—become faded and distant memories of seemingly little importance. In contrast with hiking, the world seems unnecessarily cluttered and busy.

David Goode, one of the youngest thru-hikers in 1989, wrote: "For the first time in my short life I was actually living! I ate because I was hungry, drank because I was thirsty, slept because I was tired, and every day I had a goal to achieve." Others agreed: "I now tend to live more simply . . . unencumbered by things." "Forget the little things. Get the clutter out of your life." "The realization that life can be very simple, yet powerful, meaningful, and happy, at the same time." "Keep it simple—I've changed my whole philosophy of life work."

European philosophers and historians have for centuries admired the minimalist lifestyle of the American Indian. Living richly not by producing much but by desiring little, Indians went about their daily lives in harmony with nature and with an ease and sense of well-being the typical modern worker/consumer can only envy.

The seventeenth-century jesuit Pierre Biard noted the Indians' full but nonetheless leisurely existence, as quoted in William Cronon's *Changes in the Land.* "'They are never in a hurry. Quite different from us, who can never do anything without hurry and worry; worry, I say, because our desire tyrannizes over us and banishes peace from our actions.'"

A long-distance hike calls for at least temporarily discarding the inherited beliefs of our capitalistic society. It is a time for seeking happiness and desiring little. And like the Indians, the long-distance hikers perceive that they are living richly.

People

Two thousand miles of AT wilderness hardly appears the place to seek interpersonal experience. Nevertheless, the months on the trail often result in real and lasting relationships. Many of the hikers in the survey expressed renewed faith in humankind: "I met more sincerely nice anonymous strangers as a filthy, smelly, hiker—than ever in normal life." "A realization that people really do care for one another and will go to great lengths to be of help." And what kinder, more satisfying change could take place than that reported by Tena Merritt, who said she found ". . . a love for all people. . . . We are not all perfect, just a little different."

Nature and the Environment

It is not surprising that living in the mountains for six months vastly increases the sensitivity of many people to the environment. As described by Julie Elman-Roche, "I experienced a tremendous closeness with nature, the mountains, the earth, and my fellow hikers." For 18 of the hikers in the sample, this led to a job change to work in ecology and the environment, as described in Chapter 3.

When newly married Tina and Greg Seay thru-hiked the AT it was hardly a spur-of-the-moment idea; Greg notes that he had first heard of such "crazy people" as an 11-year-old. Tina says they discussed it on their first date. After thru-hiking, Greg described how their plans for the life ahead have changed: ". . . many changes have been made. I was vaguely aware of these changes as we hiked. In the time since we finished our hike they have become more and more clear. Tangible changes include joining the ATC and Earth First, actively recruiting people for the causes, and encouraging (almost to the point of being pushy) environmental consciousness. I give much more freely of myself and my time because I've grown to realize that my 'best' time is selfless."

Then and Now

Hikers have been backpacking the AT from end to end for about 50 years. During this time, equipment has improved, particularly in such areas as packs, tents, and boots. But what about the trail itself, what Garvey called the "adventure of a lifetime"? As described in Chapter 17, the AT now is longer and in some respects tougher. As the trail is relocated away from roads, private property, and towns it has steadily grown (despite fears to the contrary) and at this writing is approximately 2,160 miles.

In the 1950s, the trail followed about 400 miles of roads, mostly backcountry farm roads. There were small country stores and reports of delightful encounters and nights spent in barns, on front porches, and even in some farmhouse bedrooms. Today there are few farms along the way and only a few tens of miles of road walking. One pleasant aspect of road walking was that it was easy going. Hikers comparing their times on trails and roads, reported that they walked up to twice as fast on the roads.

On the other hand, the trail was often only sparsely blazed, and blowdowns in some cases were so severe that they required a day or more to get around them. And although hikers today on the AT still manage to get lost, it is usually only for a few miles. Earlier tales tell of being off the marked trail (if indeed it was marked at all) for 10 or 20 miles. A compass was mandatory, and only an occasional stranger knew where the trail really was.

Sad to relate, the years have also witnessed a decline and disappearance of dozens of staffed fire towers. There was not only a magnificent view, but an expert to explain it. The rangers knew the countryside, the trails, where water was, and what hikers were ahead. Some had brownies for their guests. Today, with fire detection now taken over by airplanes and helicopters, not only are almost all the towers closed but many have even been removed.

At the shelters today, long-distance hikers still build a fire, not for cooking but because exchanging stories around a fire, in good weather and bad, is one of the great pleasures of the trail. If anyone cooks over the fire, it is the weekend backpacker. The long-distance hiker lights up his or her stove.

Over the years the end-to-end challenge has become more popular, and there are probably a hundred times as many thru-hikers (or would-be thru-hikers) as in the 1950s and 1960s. For the backpacker who enjoys to-getherness, the time and place to leave is April at Springer Mountain. At this time as many as two dozen hopefuls may start there each day. In Georgia and North Carolina shelters will be filled to the brim. Looking backward to the mid-1960s, there were as many starters in the whole year as now sometimes take off in a single day. Even so, the hiker seeking solitude need not despair. The Appalachian Trail is long, and the ranks thin out. In 1989 the average thru-hiker still spent 24 of his trail nights alone. For those who go north to south, it is a different matter; one backpacker going from Katahdin to Springer in 1989 commented he had spent 91 nights alone on the trail.

So it is having company, at least at shelters and camp-grounds, that has changed so much since the 1970s. Today the hike also can be a wonderful social experience with friends made for a lifetime. Using the registers at each shel-ter and the ever-present grapevine, news is passed up and down the trail (for hikers do go in both directions). And if an interruption or problem slows the hiker down, he or she can always hitch a ride, catch up, and do that section later. By the time Maine is under the feet, old friends gather in groups, and the final climb up Mount Katahdin is sel-dom made alone.

The phenomenon of trail names has evolved since the 1970s, as has an unusual "consumer group," the Ap-palachian Long Distance Hiker Association (ALDHA). Both reflect the growth of a culture of long-distance hik-ers from a core of largely solitary adventurers. Although

the trek remains a highly individualistic experience still more readily survived by introverts than extroverts, thru-hikers are now seldom really alone. They sit around a common campfire in the evenings sharing a common ex-perience, still almost as exciting as when the first solo trav-elers went end-to-end.

THE EXPERIENCE AND SELF

A successful thru-hike gives a new sense of self-confidence. The wonderful physical conditioning was expected. But few realized it would end up being an exploration of self as well as wilderness. They report, "I didn't think I'd learn so much about myself," "I am more gentle now with my-self," and "I often think back to the lessons I learned while on the trail and find ways to work them into my present life." They write of an inner peace, of new insights into life, and even of "a reconciliation with a host of past aches and pains."

The most marked change is in self-confidence: "I get embarrassed a lot less easily now; I can criticize people and not worry about them knowing I was the one who said it." "I am willing to take more risks." "I know I can do anything I want to do." "I realize I am different from most people—accepting it and living with myself better. There is a Trail Goddess."

Cindy Ross says her life changed. She developed "per-sonal confidence and the belief that you can go after your dreams and have them come true—have real happiness in life."

For some, "once was enough" and they would not do it again. One hiker wrote, "The most important thing is my home life. I will take my adventures in the future in small doses." Many spoke of a new appreciation of the old life and what they had left behind. Buddy Newell discovered that he "enjoyed the comforts of home *more*." Bill Berthong wrote that the hike had given him a "sense of my place in the big scheme of things—what a wonderful world we have to live in."

For others, the siren call is overwhelming. They are the ones who live to hike, the career hikers. They will hold down a job, any job, and often competently—but it is sel-dom longer than six months before they get out into the woods again. My son Kim, the psychology professor, sug-gests: "Perhaps they are closer than normal backpackers in achieving the perfect balance of work and play."

Alex Kopista fits this mold. He is not a fussy man when it comes to work, though his skills are many and varied. Ask him what he does between hikes, and it could be dri-ving a truck, working the docks, or playing guitar in a

A long, rocky climb after crossing the Susquehanna River, Pennsylvania

blues band. Indeed, it is doubtful that filling out question-naires would seem worthwhile enough for him to take the time. However, a literate biographer (Catherine Eich) filled out the questionnaire while Alex jammed on the guitar an-swering questions. He put it to the rest of us: "I don't need the 9 to 5 rat race with two weeks off. . . . Taking a break in Vermont, soaking my feet in a stream, looking at the sunshine through the trees—I realize this is what I want to do the rest of my life."

Other long-distance hikers could readily sense, and indeed be tempted, by Alex and Catherine's lifestyle. They look longingly at the freedom of the career hiker, as they move back to normal life. And the readjustment to the outside world is sometimes painful. Bruce McLaren wrote: "I completely underestimated the reassimilation process after completing the hike. My perspective and philosophy has shifted considerably, and I often feel out of step with my highly urban and fast-paced family, friends, and colleagues. Even eight months later I am struggling with this. . . . Perhaps I should have listened to Thomas Wolfe—you can't go home again—and sim-ply stayed out on the trail."

Like many thru-hikers, Emilie Jeanneney, who fin-ished in 1990, found it tough going back in the world: "Life after the AT has been very difficult—much harder than before the hike. The world outside that 2,100-mile corridor seems cold and hostile—and life will never be as good or as challenging as it was on the AT." Ted Murry Jones wrote: "The white blazes are a lot harder to find for direction back in civilization. . . ." But Ted nevertheless dove in: "Having done the trail gave me the incentive to try and make it in a whole new songwriting career."

Bill Marcinkowski wrote: "It seems that once you get back to the real world, you just get in a grind. You go to work and go out but life isn't as exhilarating as it was on the trail. You never knew what to expect up around the next bend—the views, waterfalls, deer, people, what would you find in town. I guess the whole six months of the AT was an intense living experience. I learned you adopt a new set of standards when your basic needs for food and shelter are suddenly harder to fill."

Immediately after finishing the climb of Mount Katahdin on September 29, 1989, Bill wrote about the day's experience: "It sums up a lot about the way I felt then and still do about the Appalachian Trail. . . . No one slept a wink the eve of our finishing the trip—we were all so wound up. I don't know how many times I opened my eyes and wished I had a watch to tell if it was late enough to get up. Billy made it up before me, and I got up shortly afterwards. I can't even describe the feeling I felt then or when we got to the summit. There was joy that the trip was over; disbelief that we had actually done it; exhaustion, being mental and physical; sadness that it all was coming to an end. The Appalachian Trail will never be the same as it was during the summer of '89. It will always be there, but the trail names and faces will be unfamiliar. But I will al-ways be able to detect a thru-hiker: That face and body and clothes will never change, the well-worn gear and boots, the feet and mannerisms—I will always know the thru-hiker. . . ."

In looking back, the experiences were widely different but never bland, the memories varied but wonderful. The long months of hiking, the happiness and sorrow of fin-ishing, the adjustment and sometimes resistance to re-turning to civilization—everyone agreed that it was the adventure of a lifetime.

APPENDIX 1: THE QUESTIONNAIRE AND ITS STATISTICS

I put together the questionnaire on which this book was based shortly after I returned from my Georgia-to-Maine hike in October 1989. I spent five months designing the 11-page questionnaire, which encompassed 265 topics and questions. I mailed copies to 190 long-distance hikers during the period from April 1990 to April 1991, and I received 136 replies.

The survey took most respondents one to two hours to fill out. Respondents usually, but not always, answered most of the questions. Thus the total number of replies was sometimes 136, but more often anywhere from 70 to 136. Percentages are calculated on the basis of the total number of people answering that *specific* question. Occasionally the reader may note the sample size seems to vary even through the subject is the same. This comes from the fact that answers are sometimes equivocal—they can be counted to measure one thing but not another. In all cases I have tried to honestly reflect the mood of the respondents and to interpret the data in an unbiased manner.

By August 1990, hikers had returned almost 100 questionnaires. To encourage those who had not replied, I sent out a humorous reminder letter, and by May 1991, 136 completed questionnaires had drifted in. This amounted to a 72 percent return—not bad for a notoriously mobile population. The high return probably reflected my follow-up persistence, coupled with participants' lingering enthusiasm about the hiking experience.

The survey is an extended evaluation of experiences and equipment on the trail. It reflects the practices of a sizable sample of experienced long distance hikers. Practice sometimes contradicts conventional wisdom; sometimes it confirms it. Actual practice also may introduce some surprises, such as hiking in running shoes. Most important, practice by this considerable group reflects the true world, not just one individual's perception.

The sample data stemming from the answers runs to about 40,000 items (that is, answers to questions, numbers, and opinions on specific subjects) and permits testing an endless variety of hypotheses. I explored over 50 of these, such as sickness of men versus women (women were tougher) and the effect of pre-hike physical conditioning (limited to initial hiking period). Things that seemed to me to be logical assumptions turned out to be correct only about a third of the time when I looked at the numbers. I have noted negative findings as well as positive ones, but have confined the interpretation to simple statements that this was, or was not, evident from the statistics.

Statistical analysis is a fine art, as well as a science, but despite good sample sizes (in at least some areas) rigorous practices have not been followed in this book. Such valuable measures as confidence limits, correlation coefficients, and double blind experiments are far beyond this study. I have confined myself to averages, trends, and variability. I have always felt that no matter how mathematically neat is the "standard deviation," the statistic usually used to measure variability, it is obscure to the average person. Instead if it is useful to discuss population variability I have taken a clue from a modern trend and quoted 10th, 50th, and 90th percentiles.

What constitutes a reasonable sample size on which to base a conclusion? In this work I have considered that useful trends may be inferred if sample sizes are at least 30. If the sample is below 10, it clearly does *not* permit a significant conclusion. Nevertheless, I have allowed the mention a few times of a result which was intriguing but of no real consequence. An example was the fact that the four hikers who did the whole trail wearing running shoes were universally enthusiastic as to their choice of hiking footwear. Statistics are usually reported as opinion percentages. Thus, 81 percent of the hikers were satisfied with their Hi-Tec boots, or 10 percent of hikers carried tarps to sleep under. Where the number in the sample is not specified, its size is greater than 30.

The word *average* can stand for more than one thing. The most common average is usually referred to as the *mean*, or arithmetic average. Also widely used is the *median*, or 50-percent point, where half the sample is greater and half is less. (Another average, the *mode*, is not used here.) The averages all come out the same if the statistical distribution is "normal"—that is, not skewed. Normal distributions, when plotted on a curve, show a mountain where the two sides are equally steep and the high and low extremes are the same distance out. For such normal distributions an average is an average is an average. But in many cases the data are skewed and the mountain plot is steeper or longer on one side than the other. Picture as an example a plot of yearly income of people in the United States. The range would be from zero to hundreds of millions of dollars, and the plot peak would be much nearer the low end than the high end. The conventional arithmetic average is calculated by dividing the total dollars by the total number of people. But this would lead to an unrealistic figure that is much too high, because a few multimillionaires make so much more money than do most people. In this case a more reasonable average is the income of persons at the 50th percentile—that is, where exactly half the people make more and half make less.

In this book, most averages are means and are usually referred to simply as the *average*. In a few cases where the data are skewed, a truer picture of what is going on seems to be conferred by using a median average, the 50-percent point. These exceptions are always noted.

Readers should understand what the survey is and what it is not. Most importantly, it is not a faithful representation of *all* the hikers along the Appalachian Trail. Most of the people in the survey were fellow thru-hikers I had met along the way. I solicited some participants as early as the first days of April 1989, but most were contacts I made later, near the end. Since the intended central theme of the book was thru-hiking, I tried to sign up likely thru-hikers. However, to make comparisons, I also gathered information from other experienced long-distance backpackers, intending that, whether or not the participants were successful as thru-hikers, all should be experienced hikers. Thus, this survey is of *knowledgeable hikers out for extended periods*. Their answers, therefore, are not necessarily similar to those of hikers on the AT who are out for just the day or a long weekend. Of the 136 hikers who participated in the survey, I met 102 on the trail and contacted 34 through friends or the Appalachian Trail Conference. Most of the hikes depicted took place in 1989, but a few are from earlier or later years.

Because I contacted most of the participants enroute, neither they nor I knew how far they would go—that is, whether they would truly turn out to be thru-hikers. This ignorance was an advantage, because what I really wished to write about was how experienced long distance backpackers were fairing as AT thru-hikers.

The cut-off for the sample was that they were or had been backpacking the AT and that the trip was at least of several weeks' duration. Classified by the hike they eventually completed, the survey participants can be divided as follows:

TABLE A-1.
HIKER CLASSIFICATION BY THE TYPE OF HIKE

TYPE OF HIKE	NUMBER	PERCENT
THRU-HIKERS	87	64%
SECTION HIKERS	15	11%
INCOMPLETE (STOPPED EARLIER THAN INTENDED)	22	16%
LONG-DISTANCE HIKERS (ON THE AT SEVERAL WEEKS)	12	9%
TOTALS	136	100%

The survey included 101 men and 35 women. Because I wished to include a sufficient number of women to get a good sample, there is a higher proportion of women in our survey than there is on the trail. From other data, it appears that women make up about 20 percent of thru-hikers. Thus, our survey is not a "random selection" of hikers on the AT. Rather, it is a sizable sample of successful thru-hikers plus a sampling of other experienced long distance backpackers. In particular, this survey does not permit estimating what fraction of thru-hike starters were able to finish. Other guesses give the number of starters in recent years at 1,500 to 2,000. The number of persons finishing the full trail is better known from Appalachian Trail Conference records. It is now generally in the range of 180 to 200 each year. This indicates about a 10 percent probability of finishing the full trail.

In age, our respondents were young adults—not adolescents and not over 70.

TABLE A-2.
AGE OF LONG-DISTANCE AT HIKERS

Age	Percent
20–29	49%
30–39	25%
40–49	11%
50–59	7%
60–69	8%

Surveyed hikers' previous experience runs from none to over 10,000 miles. Surprisingly, a whopping 19 percent on the trail were more or less complete beginners and another 13 percent had hiked only one or two days. Some 6 percent reported that they took off literally at the spur of the moment. The success of some of these novice hikers proves to be one of the surprises of the survey. It underlines the observation that the experience required to do the trail can be acquired while hiking. But the average thru-hiker had been thinking about such a trip for 10 years. Some 8 percent had dreamed about it for 35 years or longer. One in five was less than 15 years old when he or she first considered the project.

Appendix 2 summarizes the major findings of the survey as determined from the questionnaire.

APPENDIX 2: QUESTIONNAIRE SUMMARIES

The initial survey covered the participants' total hike. Our 136 respondents answered over the period from April 1990 through April 1991. Although the basic sample size is 136, not all hikers answered all questions, so the sample size is often less. In some cases, where hikers used more than one product, as in footwear or packs, sample size is higher.

1989 LONG-DISTANCE HIKER QUESTIONNAIRE

(answer summaries given in italics)

Name _____

Age _____   *From 20 to 69*

F _____   *26%*   M _____   *74%*

Starting place _____   Finishing at _____

80% Springer Mountain   *85% Mount Katahdin*

5% Mount Katahdin   *15% Other*

15% Other

Starting date _____   Finished on _____

15% in March   *23% in May, June, July*

60% in April   *71% in September, October*

25% in May through August   *6% in November*

What were you doing before starting?

Professional, business, services   50%

University, military   22%

Temporary, odd jobs   18%

Retired   10%

How many miles of the AT had you hiked before starting this trip?

None   19%

Less than 100 miles   13%

100 to 300 miles   43%

Over 300 miles   25%

Background

1. When did you first think about hiking the whole Appalachian Trail?   *The typical hiker had been contemplating hiking the whole AT for about 10 years. Some had considered it for much longer, but others left purely on the spur of the moment.*

2. When did you actually pick a date for starting?
   Four hikers decided to go within 24 hours.
   Most hikers decided a few months before.
   The longest planning period was about 10 years in advance.

3. About how many days of hiking had you done in the preceding year?
   32% had done none.
   52% had done one to three weeks of hiking.
   20% had done one or two months.
   One hiker had been on the trail over six months.
   In the preceding five years?
   18% had done none.
   14% had done less than 10 days.
   37% had done a total of 11 to 50 days.
   30% had done 51 to 300 days.
   One hiker had been out backpacking a total of 450 days.

4. In what kind of physical condition were you?
   10% were "out of shape."
   30% were about average for the general population.
   25% were about the average for persons use to vigorous exercise.
   35% were athletes and highly experienced hikers.

5. Did you undertake any special training program or preparation? If yes, please describe:
   Carrying loaded packs, running, practice hikes   38%
   Walking, light exercise   22%
   None   40%

6. Did you plan to hike alone? If not, how many partners did you plan to hike with?
   66% planned to hike alone.
   30% had a single partner.
   4% traveled with two others.

7. Did you go as far on the trail as you had planned? If not, what factors made you decide not to continue? Check all that were important.   *75% went as far as they had planned. Those who did not go as far as planned:*

Ran out of time	16%
Persuaded by others	5%
Ran out of money	12%
Lost interest/enthusiasm	9%

Sickness/injury	16%
Other (describe)	42%

Friends and Nights

8. How often did you plan to meet hiking friends or partners for the night at a specific shelter or place?

Always	14%
Usually	30%
Half the time	8%
Occasionally	24%
Rarely	16%
Never	8%

9. For those periods when you were hiking with others (that is, getting together for stops or overnights) how much of the time on the trail were you together, that is, close enough to carry on a conversation?

Always	6%
Usually	22%
Sometimes	52%
Rarely	18%
Never	2%

10. If you planned to hike with another person, did you finish your hike together?   55% yes

   If not, how long did you spend together?   *Average three to four weeks*

11. How many nights on the trip were you alone?
   Average 24 nights

12. How many nights on the trip did you stay at

Shelters	57%
Tent	20%
Tarp	2%
In the open	3%
Hostels	8%
Motels	6%
Friends	2%
Home	2%

   Summary: In the "wilderness"   81%

   In "civilization"   19%

13. On the trail, what sleeping arrangement did you like best (for example, a tent on grass, a shelter in the rain)?

   Uncrowded shelters   53%

   Tenting in good weather on grass or pine needles   33%

   In clear weather in the open   10%

Dislike the most?

   Crowded shelters   31%

   Shelters when hot, with bugs, leaks, or snoring hikers   23%

   Tents in the rain   36%

Equipment

14. What kind of a pack did you carry?

Internal frame	42%
External frame	58%
Brand	*various*

   Did it hold up? Were you satisfied?

   Highest rated packs:

Gregory	*100% satisfied*
North Face	*92% satisfied*
Lowe	*83% satisfied*

15. What kind of a tent did you carry?

   Most common:

Sierra Designs	*29%*
North Face	*21%*
Eureka	*12%*

   Comments?   *In general, about 70% were satisfied.*

16. What kind of a stove did you carry?

MSR	*47% of all stoves carried*
Coleman	*21%*
Optimus	*15%*

   Were you satisfied?   *In general, about 80% were satisfied.*

17. What did you sleep in?

Fiber bag	57%
Down bag	35%
Other	8% (both)

   What did you do for a pillow?   *Mostly stuff sack, but five did without.*

18. How much of the time did you hike in shorts?
   Hikers wore shorts 95% of the time.

   Did you bother with underwear?   *About half the hikers did not wear underwear. They often selected lined swim wear or running shorts.*

19. How did you deal with the problem of rain while you were hiking?   *No completely satisfactory solution. If not too cold, the best approach is to hike in shorts and get wet.*

20. What kind of footwear did you use?

   Running shoes   3% of all hikers

   Light/Medium weight boots   63%

Heavy boots, all leather   34%

Were you satisfied?

Highest ratings:

Hi-Tec	*81%*
Merrell	*80%*

How long did your boots/shoes last?   *1,000 to 1,200 miles; 7 to 12 cents per mile*

Did you break in your boots before starting?

Heavy	*78%*
Medium	*71%*
Light	*32%*
Running shoes	*0%*

Did you waterproof them?

Heavy	*95%*
Light	*22%*

Did you wear gaiters?   *About 50% of hikers wore gaiters.*

Did you take along extra footwear?   *Three-quarters of hikers carried extra "in camp" shoes or slippers.*

21. How many socks did you wear and what kind?
    Most wore two, some one or three.

    How many pairs did you carry with you (total)?
    Most carried three to six pairs.

22. What items like maps, guides, and books did you carry along to help to plan the day-by-day hike?
    The Data Book *was considered invaluable and essential.*

    Did you cut out pages and take pieces?   *About half the hikers removed pages of guide books.*

23. What were the most valuable references you used along the trail and how satisfactory was each one?

Most valuable?	Data Book
How good?	*Accurate, very good*
Second	*Philosopher's Guide*
How good?	*"Inside" information*
Third	*Maps and trail guides*
How good?	*Helpful*

    Other comments?   *About 65% of hikers carried the* Data Book; *40% carried trail guides.*

24. Did you take along

Compass	*50%*
Radio	*40%*
Reading material	*60%*
Camera	*85%*
Snakebite kit	*30%*

Journal writing things   *80%*

Any other unusual or interesting items?   *Whistles, harmonicas, thermometers, altimeters, bibles, binoculars, mouse traps, portable computer*

25. Did you carry a staff?   *65%*

    If yes, what kind?

A ski pole	*10%*
A specially made walking stick	*20%*
Something picked up along the way	*35%*

Food and Water

26. Briefly, what did you usually eat on the trail for: (numbers = instances cited)

    Breakfast? *Oatmeal (91), cold cereal (44), pop tarts (27)*

    Lunch? *Peanut butter (77), cheese (54), candy (35), canned meat or fish (31)*

    Snack? *Candy (82), GORP and trail mixes (59), cookies (13)*

    Dinner? *Macaroni & cheese (44), rice (44), noodles (40), dehydrated dinners (32)*

27. For how many days would you typically plan to hike between buying or picking up your trail food?   *Hikers typically left the trail one day per week.*

28. What fraction (or %) of your trail food did you:

Buy along the way	*51%*
Get sent you	*45%*
Get from others	*3%*
Cache	*1%*

29. How often did you cook over an open fire?   *Very seldom*

    How often did you eat a cold breakfast?   *About one third of the hikers ate a cold breakfast, particularly in warm summer weather.*

    How often a cold dinner?   *Hikers ate cold dinners only rarely. Stove failure, rain when not at a shelter, and when it was hot weather were the primary reasons.*

30. What food or drink did you most crave and seek out when taking a break from the trail?   *Ice cream tops the list, followed by beer, pizza, milk, and shakes.*

31. Did you purify your water?

Always	*14%*
Usually	*27%*
Sometimes	*41%*
Never	*18%*

    How would you decide?   *Appearance, nature of source, proximity of farm animals*

32. If you purified your water, how did you do it?

Iodine   *43%*

Boiling   *11%*

Filter   *30%*

Comment   *3% used chlorine; 13% never purified*

33. Do you believe bad water ever caused you illness? *6% of all hikers contracted Giardia; 30% suffered some kind of gastrointestinal illness. There was no discernible trend indicating water treatment prevented infection.*

34. Did you carry any alcoholic beverage? (not counting beer after a stop) *15% of hikers carried an alcoholic beverage.*

    Did you smoke? *12% of hikers smoked.*

On the Trail

35. How much did your pack weigh the day you started? (Guess if you don't know.) *53 pounds (average)*

    Midtrip before getting provisions (going light)? *35 pounds (average)*

    Midtrip after getting provisions (fully loaded)? *45 pounds (average)*

    How many days did you carry a day pack? *2 days (average)*

36. From the start to the finish of your hike how many days did you *not* hike (a guess is okay)? *24 days off (average)*

    How many of these nonhiking days were spent resting? *(numbers are averages)*

Locally	*14 days*
At home	*4 days*
Special events like weddings, concerts, etc.	*3 days*
Sickness/injury	*3 days*
Other (describe)	*2 days*

37. Did you work along the way? *Half of the thru-hikers worked a few hours at AMC huts for room and board.*

    How often? *A few times*

    Whole days (how many)? *A very few hikers worked up to about two weeks for money to continue their hike.*

38. Did you have any trouble with:

	Initially	Later On	Comments
Blisters	*51%*	*21%*	
Sore ankles	*20%*	*16%*	
Knees	*35%*	*10%*	
Hips	*17%*	*11%*	
Back	*10%*	*5%*	
Other	*varied*	*varied*	

39. Were you ever sick or injured so you had to take time out?

    Sickness (describe): *About 40% suffered some, mostly gastrointestinal illnesses.*

    Injury (describe): *Four persons were forced off the trail by injury. Most hikers suffered a variety of minor injuries (see above) but continued hiking.*

    How long did it take you to reach peak hiking condition? *Half the hikers were fit within 25 days. About 90% felt fit by the time they were on the trail 72 days.*

40. How many miles per day did you average for the first two weeks? *11.5 miles per day (average)*

    Miles per day after a month or when fully conditioned? *16.2 miles per day (average)*

    What was your best day? *26.8 miles (average)*

    Your second-best day? *24.6 miles (average)*

    Note: These are hiker's own estimates. Cross checks indicate they may be 1 to 2 miles per day high.

41. What time in the morning would you typically start to hike? *7:30 A.M.*

    What was your earliest start? *6:00 A.M.*

    About what time would you typically finish for the day? *5:30 P.M.*

    What is the latest you ever made camp? *9:30 P.M.*

    Note: The above figures are averages. A few extreme cases were as much as six hours earlier or later.

    How many times did you hike in the dark? *Most hikers had one to four instances of backpacking in the dark, but 20% avoided it entirely.*

42. Did you ever unintentionally walk in the reverse direction along the trail? *37 did*

    If so, how come? *Confused blazing, missed turn, daydreaming*

    How far? *Usually 1 to 4 miles*

43. How did you feel about the following environmental difficulties when you encountered them along the trail?

	Serious Problem	Minor Problem	No Problem
Rain	20%	50%	30%
Snow & cold	30%	50%	20%
Heat	8%	60%	32%
Finding trail	7%	33%	60%
Finding water	8%	35%	57%
Mud	10%	37%	53%
Steep sections	11%	46%	43%

Rocks	10%	55%	35%
Bears	2%	5%	93%
Dogs	5%	37%	58%
Snakes	2%	19%	78%
Mice	10%	50%	40%
Dirt/litter	22%	48%	30%
Other	13%	8%	79%

44. Did you have any experiences with theft, drunkenness, hostile people, or the like? *Three-quarters of the hikers reported no troublesome experiences during their entire trip. Most common exception: drunkenness off the trail.*

45. As you know, much of the AT has been relocated in recent years away from roads and towns and back into the mountains. How do you feel about such relocations? *Half the hikers give unqualified approval to relocations, and 85% basically think it is a good idea. Some hikers, however, miss going through towns and following country roads and are not appreciative of miles added on and ever steeper and more hilly sections.*

46. How much difficulty did you experience with the following problems?

	Little or None	Some Problem	Very Much a Problem
Boredom	77%	17%	6%
Loneliness	74%	22%	4%
Fatigue	41%	55%	4%

47. How did you cope with the above difficulty (if applicable)?

    Boredom   *Radio headsets, journals, reading, talking with people*

    Loneliness   *Singing, talking to yourself, companions*

    Fatigue   *Rest periods, plenty of sleep, time off the trail*

    Which of your coping strategies were most effective? *Friends, resting, singing*

Personal (Strictly confidential, results compiled by group only)

48. Weight

    How much did you weigh at the start? *Men: 166 pounds; women: 140 pounds*

    After one month?   *Down moderately*

    At the finish?   *Men: 150; women: 130*

    Did you have any problems with losing too much weight? *About 10%*

49. How hungry were you the first few days? *A few were hungry, but most hikers report that they were not hungry at all.*

    After a month?   *Very and unendingly hungry*

    Later on?   *Even hungrier*

50. In planning for the trip, did you have any fears about snakes, animals, theft, getting hurt or sick, exposure, water, or other people? *A few fears, mostly with respect to dealing with strangers.*

    Looking back do you feel there are any dangers worth warning new hikers about? *Don't push too hard. Don't camp near roads. Watch out for strangers, dogs, mice, snakes, and impure water.*

51. Many people find the hike a fascinating "people experience." What were your reactions to folk you interacted with both on and off the trail?

    Other long distance hikers

    Weekenders, hikers out for a few days

    Locals (on the road, in town)

    Some 80 to 90% report favorable relations with the above three groups. Only about 5% report any bad experiences.

    Organized hiking groups   *62% negative*

    Tourists   *Mixed feelings*

52. What question were you asked most frequently by outsiders?   *Mostly about starting and finishing, technical questions about pack weight, food, shelter. They wanted to know about bears and snakes and "Does your mother miss you?"*

53. Hikers bringing along dogs are always enthusiastic about how it works out. What was your experience? *Very mixed returns. Hikers with dogs are enthusiastic. Others are polite but note that dogs create many problems.*

54. Initially, most thru-hikers plan to follow all of the blazed AT. But the long trip also gives rise to different ways in which people meet the challenge. Which of the following fit your own views and experiences? Check any applicable.

    I attempted to follow every bit of the AT, missing no significant portion, peak, road, relo, or anything else.   *32%*

    I walked every foot of the way but on a very few occasions I would not follow the latest relo, exact street etc. *18%*

    I walked the distance but often took a blue blaze, alternate route road, etc.   *7%*

    I tried to do it all but may have missed a few miles because of bad weather or in towns and when hitching back and forth to the trail.   *5%*

I walked the trail but skipped some paved roads and a short section here or there for practical reasons like taking a break, making money, catching up with friends etc. *5%*

I earned that 2,000-mile rocker (badge). *15%*

I walked major sections of the trail in all the states. *4%*

I walked because it was fun and did not concern myself with more than getting a real feeling of the whole trail— which I got. *14%*

On the basis of the above: 51% walked every bit of the trail; 17% allowed for some deviations; 32% were not mileage-oriented.

55. How do you feel about others who hiked fewer, or more, miles than you did? *Most long-distance backpackers subscribe to the "do your own thing" approach. About one-quarter are purist in evaluating the way others hike.*

56. Money problems are a real bind for many attempting the AT thru-hike. How much money did you spend *in advance* of your trip to prepare for it (equipment, food, maps, books, etc.)? *$1,000 (average)*

Including the amount spent in preparation, how much do you believe the whole trip cost? *$3,200 (average)*

Can you break it down, at least approximately? *(numbers are averages)*

Food on the trail:	$825
Hostels, campgrounds, showers, etc.:	$125
Motels, boarding houses:	$225
Restaurant meals:	$275
Travel, phone, mail:	$275
Equipment and clothing along the way:	$250
Beer and fun:	$225

Comments: *Younger and older hikers spent the same amount of money*

57. What do you consider the biggest bargain of the trip? *Walking the AT*

The biggest rip-off? *Very few. Occasionally motel prices, in parks and AMC hut arrangements.*

58. The challenge to do the whole trail, the miles, being really tired, dirty and lacking amenities or privacy prompted one couple to say, "There's no sex on the trail." Do you have any comments? *Of course there is sex. But, in general, hiking and finishing come first.*

59. While you were hiking did you ever seriously think about quitting early? *About half did, for a wide variety of reasons.*

Did you ever cry? *82% of the women and 25% of the men admit to crying some time from frustration, joy, or sadness.*

Did you have any special problems being a woman on the trail? (This question was included only in questionnaires sent to women.) *There were a few complaints, mainly about put-downs. Women in general responded, "I can do anything I want to do."*

60. What factor or factors were most important in keeping you going? *Highly varied. They ranged from challenge, pride, and commitment to curiosity and "having fun."*

61. All things considered, how difficult was it for you to hike the trail?

Very difficult	13%
Fairly difficult	20%
Somewhat difficult	28%
Not too difficult	29%
Not difficult	10%

Which factors made hiking the trail most difficult (check one answer)?

Physical fatigue (sickness, injury, discomfort) *41%*

Psychological (loss of interest, motivation, boredom, loneliness) *37%*

Other (family emergency, money, etc.) *22%*

62. How did you feel about hiking at the time you got off the trail (check all suitable)?

I felt like turning around and starting another hike. *16%*

Sad to leave. I would have liked to continue. *24%*

Both glad and sorry it was over. *39%*

Looking forward to a return to civilization. *13%*

Glad it was finished—enough is enough. *6%*

Barely made it. *1%*

Never again. *1%*

63. How was the end result different from what you expected at the beginning?

"I was a virgin hiker when I started. Now I am a vet."

"Bittersweet."

"It was better."

"It was the journey of a lifetime."

Now That It's Over

64. Looking back, why do you think you hiked the AT?

Challenge	60%
Love of the outdoors	20%
Escape	20%

65. Was there any specific event in the year before you started the hike that triggered your decision to go ahead?

Break in education or military service.

"My girlfriend walked out."

"My wife said, 'If you want to go, go.'"

"I was fired."

66. What is the happiest experience you can think of when looking back?   *Friends, the adventure, lounging around the campfire chatting and sharing, the hundreds of genuine good-hearted people. "Taking a break to soak my feet in a Vermont stream." "Fell in love."*

The worst?   *Cold rain, getting lost in the Smokies, hypothermia, getting sick, theft, fighting with my partner or partners, over-filled shelters. "Lost her."*

What section of the trail did you like the most?   *The trail in Maine*

The least?   *New Jersey, New York, and Pennsylvania. However, many hikers noted that each section had its own charm.*

67. What are you doing now that you are off the trail?   *The major occupational switch was to seek out new work and training in areas of ecology, environment, and the outdoors. Prior to their hike, few had jobs along this line. After the trip, 20 respondents said they would seek out this kind of work.*

68. Are you planning any long hikes (two weeks or more) for 1990–1991?   *More trips on the AT, PCT, John Muir Trail, Long Trail, Europe, Alaska. "No adventure is too unworthy."*

69. Have there been any changes in your philosophy or plans for your life since your experience on the trail?

"I long to simplify my life."

"I am more receptive, disciplined, and thoughtful of others."

"What a wonderful world we have to live in."

70. Looking back, what was the greatest thing you got out of your hike?

"For the first time in my life I was actually living! I ate because I was hungry, drank because I was thirsty, slept when I was tired, and every day I had a goal to achieve."

"It was a great adventure, and I made wonderful new friends."

71. Would you like to receive a summary of the questionnaire results?   *Yes*

72. General comments—if you have any, they would be appreciated. Use the back side of this page or extra sheets. Thank you very much!

Note: As I studied the original 136 questionnaires, certain new questions arose. To gain insight into such areas as hiking style, profanity on the trail, feelings of solitude versus sociability, changes in shoe sizes, post-hike work, and sanitation, I distributed several short followup questionnaires during the period of 1991–1995. Most of these 30 new questions probed more deeply into topics already discussed. Some followed up on questions about the source of gastrointestinal troubles; the answers implicated sanitary practices rather than impure water as the villain. The results of these followup surveys are discussed within the text of this book.

APPENDIX 3: SURVEY PARTICIPANTS

This book is written around the personal experiences of 136 long-distance hikers, 101 men and 35 women. Eighty percent of the backpack trips discussed took place in 1989, about 15 percent were more recent trips (1990 to 1995), and 5 percent were earlier hikes (1979 to 1988). Over half the respondents were thru-hikers, the other half being section hikers and a variety of long-distance backpackers on the AT. They are listed in this appendix in alphabetical order. In most respects the experiences and opinions of thru-hikers are not very different from those of other long-distance hikers, but individuals sometimes vary widely from the averages. The "Comments" column of the appendix reflects the variety of these hikers and the special flavor of their own experiences. In some cases the comments highlight some unusual aspect of the hiker or the trip.

Many of the survey participants were friends I met on the trail during my own hike in 1989. About 70 percent of those who were sent the long questionnaires filled them out and returned them. In doing so they provided the core material for this book. Practically all participants who returned questionnaires attempted to complete all questions. Their comments were detailed, insightful, amusing, and contained many surprises. Some of them sent long letters, published accounts, personal summaries, and even copies of their journals. (One of the surprises was that about two out of every three long-distance hikers kept at least some kind of a journal.)

This listing also serves as a "thank you" for the time (often many hours) and consideration given by these hikers in their replies. One of the nicest comments among these replies was that the respondent had enjoyed reliving the hiking experience. I hope this book will also be an enjoyable and interesting review of this great experience, and that it will whet the appetite of those who have not yet ventured into the world of the long-distance hiker.

LONG-DISTANCE APPALACHIAN TRAIL HIKERS

SURVEY PARTICIPANTS (IN ALPHABETICAL ORDER)

NAME	AGE	TRAIL NAME*	SEX	HOME**	START	START DATE	FINISH***	FINISH DATE
DEAN AHEARN	32	BLUE RIDGE RANGER	M	BURKE, VA	ROCKFISH GAP	6-8-89	MT. KATAHDIN	10-17-89
AN EXPERIENCED HIKER. HE NOTED THAT THE GREATEST THING WAS "FEELING FREE TO WALK ALL THE WAY ON MY OWN SCHEDULE"								
BOB ALCOTT, JR.	28	B'ARKILLER BOB	M	TOUNO, VA	SPRINGER MTN.	3-15-89	MT. KATAHDIN	10-2-90
"AIN'T NO MOUNTAIN TOO ROUGH / AIN'T NO TRAIL TOO TOUGH / AIN'T NO CLIMB STEEP ENOUGH / FOR 'B'ARKILLER BOB.'"								
DON ALLEN	28	CRACKER JACK	M	COLLEGE PARK, GA	MT. KATAHDIN	6-3-89	SPRINGER MTN.	11-22-89
". . . . IF I HAD NOT HIKED THE TRAIL I WOULD STILL BE SINGLE TODAY." HE MARRIED SUSANNE SEPTEMBER 1990.								
SHANE ANGUS	20	(N.A.)	M	LEVINGTON, SUFFOLK, UK	SPRINGER MTN.	4-13-89	MT. KATAHDIN	10-4-89
CAME FROM ENGLAND TO HIKE THE AT. MET AND HIKED WITH DENISE DANIEL.								
ANDREA AVANTAGGIO	25	(N.A.)	F	DURANGO, CO	SPRINGER MTN.	4-6-89	HANOVER, NH	10-22-89
ON LOOKING BACK: "A SENSE OF ACCOMPLISHMENT, OF STICKING WITH SOMETHING TO THE END. . . . THE BEST FEELING IN THE WORLD."								
NAMIE BACILE, II	29	LETITBE	M	RICHARDSON, TX	MT. KATAHDIN	7-8-89	SPRINGER MTN.	11-29-89
"SOUTHBOUNDERS HAVE MORE FUN. . . . I REALLY LOVED THE TRAIL."								
DON BACON	59	(N.A.)	M	SOMERSET, NJ	MT. KATAHDIN	1980	SPRINGER MTN.	5-90
"MORE FUN TO DO THE TRAIL IN SEGMENTS. . . . WE COULD LINGER AT POINTS OF INTEREST."								
DANIEL BADE	33	URBANA DAN	M	URBANA, IL	MT. KATAHDIN	7-16-90	US 60	11-15-90
HIKED LONG SEGMENTS. "IF I SAW A PLACE THAT WAS NICE I DIDN'T RUSH ON."								
BILL BAILEY	27	BUNGALOW BILL	M	NASHVILLE, TN	SPRINGER MTN.	5-3-89	MT. KATAHDIN	10-11-89
"IT WAS JUST LIKE I DREAMED IT WOULD BE."								
DAVE BALLY	20	DB	M	BRIDGEWATER, NJ	SPRINGER MTN.	4-1-89	MT. KATAHDIN	10-7-89
HIS CURE-ALL FOR ALL TRAIL PROBLEMS WAS TO SING. HIKED PART WAY WITH SHARON RISE.								

SURVEY PARTICIPANTS (IN ALPHABETICAL ORDER)

NAME	AGE	TRAIL NAME*	SEX	HOME**	START	START DATE	FINISH***	FINISH DATE
JACQUELINE BENET	24	(N.A.)	F	BOSTON, MA	SPRINGER MTN.	4-1-89	MT. KATAHDIN	7-31-89
HIKED WITH HUSBAND. FAST HIKE AVERAGING 20 MILES PER DAY.								
REED BENET	27	(N.A.)	M	BOSTON, MA	SPRINGER MTN.	4-1-89	MT. KATAHDIN	7-31-89
HIKED WITH WIFE. ATTENDED DOYLE'S APPALACHIAN TRAIL INSTITUTE FOR TRAINING AND PLANNING BEFORE STARTING.								
JEFFRY BENOWITZ	20	(N.A.)	M	NEW CITY, NY	SPRINGER MTN.	1-4-89	MT. KATAHDIN	6-13-89
FIRST THRU-HIKER OF 1989. SEVERE FOOT INFECTIONS. "I GOT TO KNOW MYSELF."								
ANDREA BERBERIAN	21	A & T '89	F	NATWICK, MA	SPRINGER MTN.	4-6-89	SHENANDOAH	7-10-89
MET ON TRAIL AND HIKED WITH TIM NOVAK.								
BILL BERTHONG	37	XO	M	VIRGINIA BEACH, VA	ROCKFISH GAP, VA	6-29-90	MT. KATAHDIN	10-7-90
FOUND A "SENSE OF MY PLACE IN THE BIG SCHEME OF THINGS. WHAT A WONDERFUL WORLD WE HAVE TO LIVE IN."								
JACK BETTLER	52	WEST VIRGINIA WINNEBAGO	M	BUCKHAVEN, WV	SECTION HIKER, COMPLETED TRAIL IN 15 YEARS			1992
THE GREATEST THING: "SOLITUDE, BUT AT THE SAME TIME, COMPANIONSHIP."								
GEORGE BIRD	66	THE CADILLAC HIKERS	M	ROCHESTER, NY	FOX GAP, PA	8-27-73	SPRINGER MTN.	5-28-89
SECTION-HIKED 16 YEARS IN A GROUP OF THREE. STARTED AS A CURIOSITY, CHANGED TO A CHALLENGE, BECAME A COMMITMENT.								
RAYMOND BRANDES	68	MR. BEE	M	GILLETTE, NJ	SPRINGER MTN.	4-30-90	MT. KATAHDIN	9-3-90
WARREN DOYLE SUPPORTED "CIRCLE EXPEDITION" CARRYING DAY PACKS. THE CIRCLE OF FRIENDS A VERY POSITIVE EXPERIENCE.								
BETSY CHALENDAR	30	NONE	F	DENVER, CO	SPRINGER MTN. APRIL 1989 (HIKED ABOUT 2 WEEKS)			
HIKING AND MEETING "WONDERFUL PEOPLE" HELPED HER ADJUST AFTER A PERSONAL TRAGEDY.								
JEAN COOLEY	34	THE BAG LADY	F	BETHESDA, MD	LEHIGH GAP	7-20-89	DEL. WATER GAP	7-24-89
FINISH OF SECTOR HIKE. HIKED ALONE. TRAIL FEARS: "EXAGGERATED. . . . IT WAS EVEN BETTER THAN EXPECTED."								
KEITH CORNELL	30	WHITE ROGUE	M	ARLINGTON, MA	SPRINGER MTN.	5-18-89	SPECK MT.	10-15-89
TOOK OFF 10 DAYS TO PAINT A HOUSE ALONG THE WAY. OFTEN HIKED WITH PICKUP FRIENDS ON THE TRAIL.								
DAVID CRAWFORD	22	CHOO CHOO	M	ATLANTA, GA	SPRINGER MTN.	4-2-89	MT. KATAHDIN	9-25-89
STARTED WITH A THREESOME. TWO FINISHED. THE THREESOME "CREATED GREAT CHEMISTRY."								
MATT CROSS	29	MAVERICK	M	SHARON, MA	SPRINGER MTN.	5-1-89	MT. KATAHDIN	10-3-89
"I ENJOYED IT SO MUCH THAT I CAN'T SEEM TO PUT IT BEHIND ME."								
DENISE DANIEL	27	CLOCKWORK KISSER	F	RIVERTON, NJ	KENT, CT	8-9-89	MT. KATAHDIN	10-4-89
HIKED WITH SHANE ANGUS. CLIMBED MT. KATAHDIN ON HER BIRTHDAY.								
NOEL DECAVALANTE	52	THE SINGING HORSEMAN	M	BELLEVILLE, IL	SPRINGER MTN.	4-2-89	MT. KATAHDIN	9-29-89
AN EXPERIENCED OUTDOORSMAN, "TOO MUCH GOING ON AROUND ME TO BE BORED OR LONELY."								
CATHERINE EICH	32	CATBIRD	F	CAPE MAY, NJ	SPRINGER MTN.	1987	MT. KATAHDIN	1987
A CAREER HIKER, CATBIRD HAS BEEN "STOMPING THRU RAVINES AND WOODS SINCE I WAS SIX YEARS OLD." OFTEN HIKES NOW WITH ALEX KOPISTA.								
JULIE ELMAN-ROCHE	30	THE PURPLE ROSE OF CAIRO	F	KNOXVILLE, TN	SPRINGER MTN.	4-13-89	MT. KATAHDIN	10-6-89
"WALKING THE AT IS FREE. . . . I'M GLAD I DIDN'T HAVE TO PAY TO WALK, CLIMB MOUNTAINS, BREATHE FRESH AIR, MAKE FRIENDS, SEE ANIMALS IN THE WILD, PICK BERRIES, AND SLEEP IN SHELTERS."								
CHUCK ENGLE	60	OLDE CHUCK ENGLE	M	TOBB, VA	KATAHDIN STREAM	7-31-89	ELK PARK, NC	10-12-89
HIKED VERY FAST CARRYING ONLY ABOUT 20 POUNDS. NO STOVE. HAD DONE ENDS OF THE TRAIL EARLIER.								
DIANE ENSMINGER	33	SWEEZEL	F	MICANOPY, FL	SPRINGER MTN.	5-1-90	MT. KATAHDIN	10-9-90
HIKED WITH FRANK SPIREK. PREPARED AN EXCELLENT JOURNAL OF THE TRIP. COOKED GOURMET MEALS ON THE TRAIL.								
JOAN FELTHOUSEN	46	THE FLORIDA PILGRIM	F	SEBASTIAN, FL	SPRINGER MTN.	6-89	CALADONIA, PA	7-89
SECTION HIKER AND RUNNER. HIKED ALONE. MISSED HER FAMILY AT HOME. "SEEING SOME OF THIS GREAT USA BEFORE IT'S GONE."								
BEV FINNIVAN	32	(N.A.)	F	BILLERICA, MA	SPRINGER MTN.	4-7-89	MT. GREYLOCK, MA	10-29-89
STARTED WITH HUSBAND; HE LEFT TRAIL; SHE CONTINUED DESPITE INJURIES. "LEARNED ABOUT MYSELF. I'VE GOT MORE GUTS THAN I THOUGHT I HAD."								
JOE FINNIVAN	32	(N.A.)	M	BILLERICA, MA	SPRINGER MTN.	4-7-89	HARPERS FERRY	6-22-89
FORCED OFF THE TRAIL BY INJURIES. "INCREDIBLY FULL AND RICH MEMORIES."								
MARK FLANAGAN	25	(N.A.)	M	OSSINING, NY	SPRINGER MTN.	4-9-89	HARPERS FERRY	8-89
HIKED WITH JENEFER WAABEN. "HIKING LONG DISTANCES IS LIKE LIVING IN ANOTHER WORLD."								

SURVEY PARTICIPANTS (IN ALPHABETICAL ORDER)

NAME	AGE	TRAIL NAME*	SEX	HOME**	START	START DATE	FINISH***	FINISH DATE
GLENN FLEAGLE	39	FIDDLEHEAD	M	SCHUYLKILL, PA	SPRINGER MTN.	4-15-89	MT. KATAHDIN	10-1-89

"ADVENTURE, MEET FRIENDS, BE OUTDOORS."

| SALLY FORD | 29 | THE CANYON KIDS | F | EAST LIVERPOOL, OH | SPRINGER MTN. | 4-15-89 | MT. KATAHDIN | 10-8-89 |

HIKED WITH WALLY STAE "TO BE WITH A LOVED ONE."

| DOUGLAS FRACKELTON | 58 | GEARCHANGER | M | CAYUGA, NY | SPRINGER MTN. | 4-4-89 | MT. KATAHDIN | 10-9-89 |

"I GET A KICK OUT OF SEEING THE APPALACHIAN MOUNTAIN RANGE ON A RELIEF MAP AND REALIZING THE EXTENT OF THE HIKE—A SENSE OF SATISFACTION."

| JUDY GALLANT | 29 | J WALKER | F | ROCHDALE, MA | SPRINGER MTN. | 4-6-89 | MT. KATAHDIN | 10-6-89 |

"FRIENDS WHO WILL BE FRIENDS FOREVER, AND A WONDERFUL MAN." MARRIED GREG ROOT (TRAIL NAME OXFORD) SEPTEMBER 1991.

| GORDON GAMBLE | 66 | OL' MAN GAMBLE | M | MORRISTOWN, NJ | SPRINGER MTN. | 3-27-80 | MT. KATAHDIN | 10-5-80 |

WROTE A VERY INTERESTING JOURNAL. HIKE RESULTS: "CONFIDENCE, PHYSICAL FITNESS, HEALTH."

| RANDALL GATES | 29 | RANGER RANDY | M | MANCHESTER, NH | SPRINGER MTN. | 3-27-89 | MT. KATAHDIN | 10-5-80 |

MET HIS FUTURE WIFE, LOU MCLAUREN, ON THE TRAIL. THE AT IS "THE ULTIMATE CHALLENGE FOR LONG-DISTANCE HIKERS."

| SARAH GLASS | 28 | NONE | F | ST. THOMAS, USVI | SPRINGER MTN. | 4-21-89 | MAINE | 10-3-89 |

"SO MANY EMOTIONS, HARD TO PUT INTO WORDS. IT WAS SUCH A UNIQUE EXPERIENCE—EVERYTHING ELSE PALES NEXT TO IT."

| DAVID GOODE | 20 | LONG LEGS | M | DUNWOODY, GA | MT. KATAHDIN | 6-24-89 | SPRINGER MTN. | 11-23-89 |

"THE JOURNEY WAS BOTH PHYSICAL AND SPIRITUAL. . . . I WAS ACTUALLY LIVING."

| JOYE GORDON | 24 | SWAMP BUNNIES | F | LAFAYETTE, LA | DAMASCAS, VA | 5-1-89 | WAYNESBORO, VA | 7-4-89 |

SECTION-HIKED WITH HUSBAND PETER PELLIGRIN. "ANYONE WHO HIKES THE TRAIL FOR MORE THAN TWO WEEKS DESERVES A MEDAL."

| BONNIE GOULARD | 34 | NONE | F | OCALA, FL | SPRINGER MTN. | 1989 | FRANKLIN, NC | (N.A.) |

SECTION HIKER GOING ALONE, SHE READ A DICTIONARY WHEN BORED, AND LIKE GARVEY SHE PICKED UP TRASH ALONG THE WAY.

| RANDALL GOWEN | 29 | RAND | M | CLEARWATER, FL | SPRINGER MTN. | 4-15-89 | DEL. WATER GAP | 7-31-89 |

"THE DREAM OF A LONG-DISTANCE HIKE KEPT ME GOING."

| BILL GRACE | 24 | BILL x 2 + KIM | M | BRECKENRIDGE, CO | SPRINGER MTN. | 4-9-89 | MT. KATAHDIN | 9-29-89 |

HIKED IN A THREESOME. "DREAMS ARE NOT ONLY MEANT TO BE DREAMED. THEY ARE MEANT TO BE LIVED."

| HELEN GRAY | 45 | SMILES IN OUR HEARTS | F | NEWAGEN, ME | SPRINGER MTN. | 3-12-89 | MT. KATAHDIN | 9-3-89 |

MET MICHAEL IN LATE APRIL, FINISHED THE HIKE TOGETHER, AND LATER GOT MARRIED.

| BILL GUNDERSON | 27 | STATS GODRIC | M | CAROL STREAM, IL | SPRINGER MTN. | 4-1-89 | MT. KATAHDIN | 9-28-89 |

PROVIDED VALUABLE STATISTICAL DATA. "I EXPECTED SOLITUDE AND CAME AWAY WITH A TON OF FRIENDS."

| LUCILE GUSSTAFSON | 67 | OLD HICKORY | F | NORRIS, TN | SPRINGER MTN. | 4-2-88 | MT. KATAHDIN | 8-21-90 |

HIKED THE TRAIL OVER A PERIOD OF THREE YEARS WITH HUSBAND PROVIDING CAR SUPPORT.

| BRUCE HARATY | 26 | RANGER RICK | M | LIBERTYVILLE, IL | SPRINGER MTN. | 4-1-89 | MT. KATAHDIN | 9-28-89 |

ON THINKING OF QUITTING EARLY: "YES, AND I ONLY MET ONE THRU-HIKER WHO DIDN'T ADMIT DOING THE SAME."

| NANCY HARRINGTON | 42 | DANNY | F | ELSWORTH, MA | SPRINGER MTN. | 4-10-89 | MT. KATAHDIN | 9-9-89 |

HIKED WITH HUSBAND. "WALKING THE TRAIL WAS AN INCREDIBLE EXPERIENCE."

| BILL HARRISON | 47 | WILD TURKEY | M | ROSWELL, GA | SPRINGER MTN. | 1984 | MT. KATAHDIN | ? |

IN 1995 WAS SECTION-HIKING AT A RATE OF 2–3 WEEKS PER YEAR AS ONE MEMBER OF THE THREE BLIND MICE.

| JOHN HENEGHAN | 32 | IRISH ROVER | M | OAK PARK, IL | SPRINGER MTN. | 4-1-89 | MT. KATAHDIN | 10-9-89 |

"I HAVE A MUCH BETTER IDEA OF WHO I AM NOW."

| ROBIE HENSLEY | 63 | JUMP START | M | CHUCKY, TN | SPRINGER MTN. | 3-9-89 | HARPERS FERRY | 10-27-89 |

PARACHUTED TO SPRINGER TO START HIS HIKE. FLIP-FLOPPED. "A MORE POSITIVE PERSPECTIVE; SPIRITUALLY, PHYSICALLY, AND MENTALLY."

| DENNIS HILL | 29 | HIKE-A-HOLIC | M | LAUREL, MD | SPRINGER MTN. | 3-25-89 | MT. KATAHDIN | 9-8-89 |

HAD 7000 MILES HIKING EXPERIENCE. ON COPING: "I KNOW I WILL MAKE IT. JUST TAKE YOUR TIME AND HIKE YOUR OWN HIKE."

| TRACY HILL | 29 | NONE | F | CONCORD, NH | SPRINGER MTN. | 3-29-89 | MT. KATAHDIN | 8-29-89 |

HIKED A RECORD 43 MILES IN ONE DAY. ALTHOUGH ALONE SHE WAS "NOT REALLY, BECAUSE I GENERALLY TRAVELED WITH GUYS AND FELT COMFORTABLY PROTECTED. . . . ALSO SHARED SOME 'FEMALE BONDING' WITH OTHER WOMEN."

| NOLAND HISSEY | 50 | RIP | M | CHARLEMONT, MA | SPRINGER MTN. | 4-13-89 | MT. KATAHDIN | 10-10-89 |

"BE FLEXIBLE AND NOT A SLAVE TO MAKING MILES—ENJOY. HAPPINESS IS FOUND ALONG THE WAY, NOT AT THE END OF THE TRAIL."

NAME	AGE	TRAIL NAME*	SEX	HOME**	START	START DATE	FINISH***	FINISH DATE
PAUL HOLABAUGH	47	LUCKY-LUCKY-LUCKY	M	MEADULLE, PA	MT. KATAHDIN	6-1-89	SPRINGER MTN.	9-29-89

TOOK OFF ONLY TWO DAYS DURING HIS WHOLE THRU-HIKE. ALONE 90 NIGHTS, AVERAGED 21 MPD. "WONDERFUL PEOPLE ON & OFF THE TRAIL."

| DAVID HORSFALL | 24 | MR. SKIDDAH | M | ALFRED, ME | SPRINGER MTN. | 4-15-89 | MT. KATAHDIN | 9-25-89 |

"A NEW PERSPECTIVE ON LIFE. GOT TO KNOW MYSELF MUCH BETTER."

| BILL HOSTERMAN | 25 | VAN GO | M | AARONSBURG, PA | SPRINGER MTN. | 4-7-90 | MT. KATAHDIN | 10-8-90 |

IT WAS "A CHALLENGE—TO SEE SOMETHING DIFFERENT, TO PUSH MYSELF, TO BE FREE."

| STEVE HOUGH | 31 | PONYBOY | M | TALLAHASSEE, FL | SPRINGER MTN. | 4-16-89 | MT. KATAHDIN | 10-7-89 |

HIKED WITH A PARTNER. "CHALLENGE, ACCOMPLISHMENT—BECAUSE I KNEW I COULD—BECAUSE I KNEW MOST PEOPLE COULDN'T."

| DICK HURD | 47 | THREE BLIND MICE | M | ALPHARETTA, GA | SPRINGER MTN. | 1980 | MT. KATAHDIN | 2000? |

AS OF 1995, SECTION-HIKING NEW ENGLAND. "THE WHOLE IS GREATER THAN ITS PARTS . . . THE MYTHICAL TRAIL . . . THE PEOPLE . . . THE EXPERIENCE . . . SPIRITUAL . . . THE SATISFYING SENSE OF ACCOMPLISHMENT."

| CHARLES HYDECK | 31 | THE HARE | M | CARIBOU, ME | SPRINGER MTN. | 5-8-89 | MT. KATAHDIN | 10-29-90 |

HIKED "TO DO IT—HAVE CONTROL FROM START TO FINISH . . . SELF-ACTUALIZATION."

| HUNTER IRVINE | 23 | HUNTER | M | ARLINGTON, VA | SPRINGER MTN. | 4-8-90 | MT. KATAHDIN | 9-18-90 |

TOOK OFF ONLY THREE DAYS. "I ENJOYED HIKING. I WANTED TO GET OUT AND 'LIVE,' AND I NEEDED TO TAKE TIME RATHER THAN BEING TAKEN BY TIME."

| EMILIE JEANNENEY | 24 | AIMLESSLY | F | CRAWFORDVILLE, FL | MT. KATAHDIN | 6-8-89 | SPRINGER MTN. | 6-24-90 |

HIKED TRAIL IN TWO SECTIONS. "NOTHING WILL EVER BE THE SAME—OR AS GOOD AS MY TRAIL EXPERIENCE."

| TED MURRY JONES | 30 | RAGGEDY MAN | M | NASHVILLE, TN | MT. KATAHDIN | 8-8-88 | SPRINGER MTN. | 11-12-90 |

"THE WHITE BLAZES ARE A LOT HARDER TO FIND FOR DIRECTION BACK IN CIVILIZATION."

| NANCY KETTLE | 55 | NONE | F | RANGELEY, ME | MT. KATAHDIN | 10-10-89 | MONSON, ME | ? |

HIKING SECTIONS. "KNOWING I LIKE TO BE ALONE FOR QUITE A LONG TIME."

| GREG KNOETTNER | 23 | POOH | M | HARVARD, MA | SPRINGER MTN. | 4-27-89 | MT. KATAHDIN | 10-8-89 |

"EVERYTHING IS CHANGED. THE AT WAS MY ENLIGHTENMENT. . . . RENEWAL. HOPE. A MORE CLEARLY DEFINED SENSE OF IDENTITY."

| KIM KNUTI | 23 | BILL x 2 + KIM | F | SEARSPORT, ME | SPRINGER MTN. | 4-9-89 | MT. KATAHDIN | 9-29-89 |

HIKED WITH TWO BILLS AS PARTNERS. "A RENEWED FAITH THAT HOMO SAPIENS IS INHERENTLY GOOD. . . . SINCERELY NICE ANONYMOUS STRANGERS. . . ."

| ALEX KOPISTA | 30 | CAPER | M | CAPE MAY, NJ | SPRINGER MTN. | 6-6-80 | MT. KATAHDIN | 10-27-80 |

"SOAKING FEET IN A STREAM, LOOKING AT SUNSHINE THRU TREES, I REALIZED THIS IS WHAT I WANT TO DO THE REST OF MY LIFE." HIKES WITH CATHERINE EICH.

| ED KOSTAK | 21 | (N.A.) | M | NEW HARTFORD, CT | SPRINGER MTN. | 4-6-89 | MT. KATAHDIN | 10-14-89 |

ON FINISHING: "I EXPECTED TO BE VERY JUBILANT. INSTEAD I WAS VERY QUIET AND SORRY IT WAS OVER AND WENT BY TOO QUICKLY."

| KARL KRAUS | 29 | PROFESSOR HORTENAUCKLE | M | FANWOOD, NJ | SPRINGER MTN. | 4-6-89 | MT. KATAHDIN | 10-14-89 |

"I HAD THE TIME, DESIRE, STRENGTH, AND MONEY."

| DENNIS LA FORCE | 43 | THE OLD GOAT OF MANCHAUG | M | MANCHAUG, MA | CRAWFORD NOTCH, NH 1973 | | SPRINGER MTN. | 5-31-90 |

HIKED SECTIONS FOR 17 YEARS. "THE FEELINGS AND EMOTIONS I CAME DOWN THE MOUNTAIN WITH THAT DAY HAVE NEVER BEEN SURPASSED."

| GREG LOHMUELLER | 21 | ROCK KICKER | M | READING, OH | SPRINGER MTN. | 4-15-89 | MT. KATAHDIN | 10-9-89 |

THE GREATEST THING: "THE FRIENDS I MADE ALONG THE WAY."

| CHRISTIAN LUGO | 25 | (N.A.) | M | RINGOLD, GA | MAINE | 8-25-88 | WOODSTOCK, VT | 8-25-89 |

HIKED THE TRAIL IN TWO PIECES. "I CHOSE THE ROAD LEAST TRAVELED, AND THAT HAS MADE ALL THE DIFFERENCE."

| LAURIE MACK | 33 | GIRL WILBURY | F | MT. DESERT, ME | SPRINGER MTN. | 4-4-89 | MT. KATAHDIN | 10-7-89 |

"I NEVER DREAMED I WOULD FEEL THE CONNECTEDNESS WITH THE OTHER HIKERS. I REALLY BELIEVED IT WOULD BE BASICALLY A SOLO JOURNEY."

| BILL MARCINKOWSKI | 24 | BILL x 2 + KIM | M | DURHAM, NH | SPRINGER MTN. | 4-9-89 | MT. KATAHDIN | 9-29-89 |

"IT WAS AN INTENSE EXPERIENCE. CONTINUOUSLY INTENSE. IT WAS A DIFFERENT WAY OF LIFE."

| CRAIG MAYER | 26 | BILL THE CAT | M | WESTFORD, MA | SPRINGER MTN. | 4-1-89 | MT. KATAHDIN | 9-9-89 |

CRAIG DID NOT LOSE WEIGHT ON HIS HIKE BUT "HAD TO EAT LIKE A COMPLETE PIG . . . NEW MEANING TO 'ALL YOU CAN EAT.'"

| MAURICE MCCASLIN | 31 | BIKER HIKER | M | SOMERS, CT | SPRINGER MTN. | 1-19-89 | GRAFTON NOTCH, ME | 10-7-89 |

KEPT A METICULOUS DAILY JOURNAL ALA GARVEY AND USED IN THIS STUDY. "TRYING TO ACHIEVE WHAT MOST PEOPLE FEEL IS UNACHIEVABLE."

SURVEY PARTICIPANTS (IN ALPHABETICAL ORDER)

NAME	AGE	TRAIL NAME*	SEX	HOME^^	START	START DATE	FINISH***	FINISH DATE
DOUGLAS McKAINE	44	STRIDER	M	BERLIN, CT	SPRINGER MTN.	4-10-89	LYME, NH	8-1-89

"A GREATER APPRECIATION FOR PEOPLE AS INDIVIDUALS. PEOPLE WHO DIDN'T BELIEVE . . . AS I DO, BOTHERED ME. NOW THEY DON'T."

NAME	AGE	TRAIL NAME*	SEX	HOME^^	START	START DATE	FINISH***	FINISH DATE
BRUCE McLAREN	30	THE HIGH-TECH HACKING HIKER (HHH)	M	McKEES ROCKS, PA	SPRINGER MTN.	3-30-89	MT. KATAHDIN	9-26-89

"THE REALIZATION THAT LIFE CAN BE VERY SIMPLE, YET POWERFUL, MEANINGFUL, AND HAPPY AT THE SAME TIME."

PAUL MELISKI	29	MR. WORCESTER	M	WORCESTER, MA	SPRINGER MTN.	4-10-89	MT. KATAHDIN	10-6-89

HE BECAME "MORE PATIENT AND TOLERANT, MUCH MORE CONFIDENT IN WHAT I DO."

TENA MERRITT	30	BEAVER	F	PORTLAND, ME	SPRINGER MTN.	4-15-89	MT. KATAHDIN	10-9-89

"BEING ABLE TO RELAX. SMILE AT EACH DAY KNOWING ALL WILL WORK OUT. AND LOVE FOR ALL PEOPLE BECAUSE WE ARE NOT ALL PERFECT."

DAVID MEYERSON	42	(N.A.)	M	CARMEL, NY	BEAR MTN., NY	1966	TO BE DETERMINED	?

IN 1989, SECTION-HIKING WITH FRIENDS. "RENEWED FRIENDSHIPS AND SHARED EXPERIENCES. . . . AN ANTIDOTE FOR CIVILIZATION."

KENNETH MILLER	32	SIX FEET	M	CONYERS, NY	SPRINGER MTN.	3-18-89	MT. KATAHDIN	9-2-89

"TO SEE AND EXPERIENCE THE TRAIL ALL THE WAY FROM END TO END."

CAROL MOORE	34	THE LAGUNATIC	F	LAGUNA BEACH, CA	SPRINGER MTN.	3-29-89	MT. KATAHDIN	10-9-89

"IT'S THE BEST THING I EVER DID FOR MYSELF—BESIDES BEING MORE PATIENT AND FLEXIBLE—IN A VERY POSITIVE WAY—ABOUT EVERYTHING."

ERIC MULLER	43	ERIC	M	CONYERS, GA	SPRINGER MTN.	4-11-89	SHENANDOAH	5-26-89

"I WAS VERY HAPPY ABOUT THE MILES I HAD DONE, BUT OVERJOYED ABOUT SEEING MY WIFE AND GOING HOME."

TARO NARAHASHI	28	TARO	M	CHICAGO, IL	VARIOUS	1988–1990	LONG SECTIONS	?

"FELL IN LOVE WITH HIKING."

BUDDY NEWELL	56	THREE Gs	M	WHITEFIELD, NH	SPRINGER MTN.	4-6-89	MAINE BORDER	9-1-89

"I WOULD NOT SELL THE EXPERIENCE FOR A MILLION DOLLARS. NOR WOULD I DO IT AGAIN FOR A MILLION."

TIM NOVAK	29	A & T 89	M	NATWICK, MA	SPRINGER MTN.	4-9-89	SHENANDOAH	7-10-89

HIKED WITH ANDREA BERBERIAN. HAD THRU-HIKED IN 1987. "FREEDOM AND SHARING EACH OTHER'S LOVE AND COMPANIONSHIP IN THE WOODS."

TOM PAPPAS	31	JACK BROTHERS	M	AYER, MA	SPRINGER MTN.	4-9-89	KATAHDIN	9-26-89

"TO KNOW WHAT IT WAS LIKE AND TO BE WITH NATURE. . . A SENSE OF ACCOMPLISHMENT."

PETER PELLIGRIN	29	SWAMP BUNNIES	M	LAFAYETTE, LA	DAMASCUS, VA	5-1-89	WAYNESBORO, VA	7-4-89

HIKED WITH WIFE JOYE GORDON. "GET THE HELL OUT. . . . CHEAP VACATION."

SIOBHAN PERRY	24	IRISH SETTER	F	WOODS HOLE, MA	FONTANA DAM, NC	4-29-89	WAYNESBORO, VA	7-4-89

HIKED 42 MILES IN A RECORD DAY. "FRIENDS AND A DEEPER APPRECIATION OF THE WILDNESS OF THIS COUNTRY."

CRAIG PHEGLEY	48	HYDRO	M	MELBURNE, FL	SPRINGER MTN.	4-7-89	MT. KATAHDIN	9-11-89

I HIKED "TO SET A GOAL AND ACHIEVE IT—TO SPEND FIVE MONTHS IN AN OUTDOORS ENVIRONMENT—FOR PHYSICAL CONDITIONING."

DAVID POULIN	64	THE BROTHER DAVE	M	ST. PETERSBURG, FL	SPRINGER MTN.	4-3-89	MT. KATAHDIN	8-31-89

"FANTASTIC BEAUTY. . . GREAT FRIENDSHIPS. . . . GET THE CLUTTER OUT OF YOUR LIFE."

JOE RAHANA	20	THE DUDE	M	VIRGINIA BEACH, VA	SPRINGER MTN.	4-15-89	MT. KATAHDIN	10-9-89

WHY? "TO DO IT! 'CAUSE NOT EVERYONE CAN, AND I LIKED THE IDEA."

SHARON RISE	22	APRIL FOOL	F	DOVER, NH	SPRINGER MTN.	4-1-89	MT. KATAHDIN	10-8-89

"THE TRAIL WENT TO MUCH GREATER EXTREMES—BOTH GOOD AND BAD. THE HIGHS WERE REALLY HIGH AND THE LOWS WERE WAY DOWN."

PEYTON ROBERTSON	62	LONE EAGLE	M	NORFOLK, VA	SPRINGER MTN.	3-29-89	MT. KATAHDIN	10-4-89

"EDIE, MY WIFE, SAID IF YOU WANT TO GO—GO." ON LOOKING BACK: "RECONCILIATION WITH A HOST OF PAST ACHES AND PAINS."

GREG ROOT	26	OXFORD	M	ROCHDALE, MA	SPRINGER MTN.	4-10-89	MT. KATAHDIN	10-6-89

ON ENDING: "I EXPECTED TO BE TRIUMPHANT. IT WAS TEMPERED WITH SADNESS."

CINDY ROSS	25	CINDY	F	RINGOLD, PA	GEORGIA	4-78	MAINE	9-79

PLANS FOR A FUTURE LIFE: "CHANGED MY WHOLE LIFE . . . ENABLED ME TO CREATE A LIVELIHOOD OUT OF WHAT I LOVE TO DO BEST."

BOB RZEWNICKI	31	RAINMAN	M	WORCESTER, MA	SPRINGER MTN.	3-20-89	MT. KATAHDIN	8-17-89

PROVIDED MANY DETAILS OF HIS INTERESTING TRIP. WROTE AT THE END: "IT IS THE HIGHEST YOU CAN GET ON LIFE."

NAME	AGE	TRAIL NAME*	SEX	HOME**	START	START DATE	FINISH***	FINISH DATE
GEORGE SCHINDLER	66	NONE	M	NEW PROVIDENCE, NJ	LEE, MA	1989	BENNINGTON, VT	1989

AS OF 1994 HAS COMPLETED 400+ MILES SECTION-HIKING. ON LOOKING BACK: "NEW FRIENDS PLUS THE FEELING (HOWEVER ILLUSORY) OF BEING FREE FROM THE DEMANDS OF MODERN CIVILIZATION."

BOB SCHROEDER	32	EGGMAN	M	VIRQUA, WV	SPRINGER MTN.	4-27-89	MT. KATAHDIN	10-5-89

PREPARED A DETAILED ACCOUNT. ON LOOKING BACK: "I DID SOMETHING SPECIAL. . . . AS THE LION WOULD SAY TO THE WIZARD OF OZ: 'I HAVE COURAGE.'"

GREGORY SEAY	26	THE HONEYMOONERS	M	CROZET, VA	SPRINGER MTN.	3-19-89	MT. KATAHDIN	10-8-89

MARRIED TO, AND HIKED WITH, TINA. ON CHANGES IN PHILOSOPHY: "I GIVE MUCH MORE FREELY OF MYSELF AND MY TIME BECAUSE I'VE GROWN TO REALIZE THAT MY 'BEST' TIME IS SELFLESS."

TINA SEAY	23	THE HONEYMOONERS	F	CROZET, VA	SPRINGER MTN.	3-19-89	MT. KATAHDIN	10-8-89

MARRIED TO, AND HIKED WITH, GREGORY. ON PHILOSOPHY: "TAKE THINGS ONE STEP AT A TIME AND ENJOY THINGS THAT ARE OCCURRING. . . ." ON SELF-CONFIDENCE: "I KNOW I CAN DO ANYTHING IF I WANT TO."

KURT SEITZ	26	THE SWALLOW	M	CHERRY VALLEY, NY	SPRINGER MTN.	4-6-80	MT. KATAHDIN	10-6-89

ONE FACTOR WHICH KEPT HIM GOING: "I NEVER GIVE UP. PATIENCE. OTHER THRU-HIKERS MAKE FOR ONE BIG FAMILY."

DAVID SHIMEK	28	GINGERBREAD MAN	M	HOUSTON, TX	SPRINGER MTN.	5-7-89	MT. KATAHDIN	9-11-89

ON PHILOSOPHY: "NO ADVENTURE IS UNWORTHY." LOOKING BACK: "SURVIVAL IN SOLITUDE . . . SERENE SPLENDOR."

ROBERT SILVERMAN	26	NICK ADAMS	M	JENKENTOWN, PA	SPRINGER MTN.	4-8-89	DEL. WATER GAP	11-19-89

ON LOOKING BACK: "A SENSE OF SELF AND A SENSE OF OTHERS."

ROBERT SPARKS	71	RERUN	M	HARPERS FERRY, WV	SPRINGER MTN.	3-31-89	HARPERS FERRY	10-22-89

SPARKS HAS BEEN ESTIMATED TO HAVE 10,000 MILES TRAIL EXPERIENCE. "THE GREATEST THING IS THE SUPPORT OF MY FRIENDS NEW AND OLD."

FRANK SPIREK	33	DWEEZEL	M	MICANOPY, FL	SPRINGER MTN.	5-1-90	MT. KATAHDIN	10-9-90

HIKED WITH DIANE ENSMINGER. MADE AVAILABLE HIS DETAILED TRIP ACCOUNT. THE GREATEST THING: "FREEDOM FROM THE DAY-TO-DAY WORRIES OF THE 'REAL WORLD.'"

WALLY STAE	32	CANYON KIDS/ CRASH DUMMIES	M	EAST LIVERPOOL, OH	SPRINGER MTN.	4-15-89	MT. KATAHDIN	10-8-89

HIKED WITH SALLY FORD. ON LOOKING BACK: "A HEIGHTENED SENSE OF OUR ABILITY TO ACHIEVE."

BRUCE STARBUCK	48	J.J. FLASH	M	LYNDONVILLE, VT	SPRINGER MTN.	4-1-89	MT. KATAHDIN	10-10-89

HIKED CARRYING A DAY PACK WITH WIFE PROVIDING CAR SUPPORT. "I COLLECT MOMENTS IN TIME AND STORE THEM IN THE RECESSES OF MEMORY."

JACK STEPPE	46	THE CAROLINA FLASH	M	ATLANTA, GA	SPRINGER MTN.	4-1-89	DAVENPORT GAP, TN	5-15-89

THE MOST LAID-BACK HIKER ON THE AT. THE MOST IMPORTANT THING: "PEACE OF MIND."

ALAN STRACKELJAHN	30	GONZO	M	HIGHLAND, IL	SPRINGER MTN.	4-14-89	ABOL BRIDGE, ME	9-30-89

HIKED WITH FREYDA AND DOG. VETERAN HIKER. ON LOOKING BACK: "THE ABILITY TO DO WITH WHAT YOU HAVE, TO MAKE IT WORK, AND THE KNOWLEDGE THAT YOU DON'T NEED MUCH IN LIFE AS THE MISC. GARBAGE COMMERCIALS TELL YOU NEED."

FREYDA STRACKELJAHN	39	I'M MIGHTY THOR	F	HIGHLAND, IL	SPRINGER MTN.	4-14-89	GRAFTON NOTCH, ME	9-30-89

HIKED WITH DOG CASI AND HUSBAND ALAN. ON WHY SHE HIKED: "TEST OF ENDURANCE AND THAT OUR RELATIONSHIP COULD SURVIVE. IF WE COULD SPEND 6 MONTHS TOGETHER DAY-IN DAY-OUT, WE CAN SURVIVE ANYTHING."

BRUCE SULLIVAN	25(?)	(N.A.)	M	STONE MTN., GA	SPRINGER MTN.	4-8-89	MT. KATAHDIN	8-8-89

HIKED CLOSELY WITH HIS BROTHER. ON WHY HE HIKED: "THE CHALLENGE, EXCITEMENT, ADVENTURE. . . . I LOVE TO HIKE. I LOVE THE OUTDOORS."

JOHN SWANSON	27	JOHN	M	E. BRUNSWICK, NJ	POCHUCK MTN., NJ	1978	MT. KATAHDIN	9-89

PROVIDED DETAILED ACCOUNTING OF HIS AT TRAVELS. "I ALWAYS RETURNED TO CONTINUE HIKING ON THE AT BECAUSE I ENJOY THE LIFESTYLE."

WALTER SZALVA	25	SOME DUDE NAMED WALT	M	DAVIE, FL	SPRINGER MTN.	4-24-89	MT. KATAHDIN	10-2-89

ON KEEPING GOING: "HAVING GOOD HIKING FRIENDS NEARBY." ON THE GREATEST THING: "SELF CONFIDENCE, ABILITY TO LOOK AT LIFE DIFFERENTLY."

ROBIN TANNER	25	ROBIN	F	SALEM, NC	SPRINGER MTN.	4-16-89	MT. KATAHDIN	10-7-89

HIKED WITH A PARTNER. ON WHAT IS BEST: "MEETING THE PEOPLE WHO I WOULD CALL 'THE SALT OF THE EARTH.'"

ROGER TARR	22	THE APPALACHIAN PEDESTRIAN	M	LAUREL, MD	SPRINGER MTN.	3-20-90	MT. KATAHDIN	10-21-90

ON CHANGE AS HE HIKED: "IN THE BEGINNING KATAHDIN WAS AN IMPOSSIBLE DREAM. AT THE END IT WAS ANOTHER ROCK."

Survey Participants (in Alphabetical Order)

Name	Age	Trail Name*	Sex	Home**	Start	Start Date	Finish***	Finish Date
Adam Ticknor	25	Egg	M	Otego, NY	Springer Mtn.	5-6-89	Mt. Holly Springs, PA	8-4-89

"I hiked to give myself time away from the confines of the society in which I found myself. Time to think about what I was doing, and where I was going in life."

Nancy Tremblay	32	Marshmallow	F	Jefferson, MA	Springer Mtn.	4-28-87	Mt. Katahdin	10-11-87

"I had a really good feeling about myself and was proud and confident."

Norman Tubbs	61	Wolverine	M	Kentwood, MI	Springer Mtn.	4-8-89	Shenandoah	7-18-89

"A realization that people really do care and will go to great lengths to be of help."

Robie Vance	32	(n.a.)	M	Mingo Junction, OH	Springer Mtn.	4-1-89	Mt. Katahdin	10-6-89

"I enjoyed the adventure and loved the Trail."

Joyce Vorbeau	23	Poor Nameless Hiker	F	Dover, NH	Springer Mtn.	4-15-89	Mt. Katahdin	10-16-89

"The simplicity of life, the closeness I feel with God, the spiritual and emotional growth, the intense people experience."

Jenefer Waaben	23	Mark and Jenefer	F	Princeton, NJ	Springer Mtn.	4-12-89	Harpers Ferry	7-2-89

Hiked with Mark Flanagan and felt "at ease with life."

David Walp	43	Sonny Dayz	M	Berwick, PA	Del. Water Gap	4-25-86	Springer Mtn.	7-20-86

"Feeling one with nature."

Troy Warren	63	Fritz	M	St. Pete Beach, FL	Springer Mtn.	3-30-89	Sam's Gap, TN	5-15-89

Trip cut short by an accident down a slippery muddy trail about 1 mile south of Sam's Gap resulting in a broken leg.

Christopher Whalen	27	Chris	M	Waitsfield, VT	Springer Mtn.	4-8-88	Mt. Katahdin	10-8-88

"Renewed physical and mental strength and the realization that there are still good people in the world."

Josh Wiesner	20	(n.a.)	M	Athens, GA	Mt. Katahdin	6-24-89	Erwin, TN	11-1-89

"The realization of how simple life can and should be."

Nick Williams	37	[cat logo]	M	Springfield, VA	Springer Mtn.	4-14-79	Mt. Katahdin	10-7-79

"The beginning and end of a dream coupled with everything in between."

Stuart Wilson	29	Swagman	M	Tasmania, Australia	Springer Mtn.	3-17-89	Mt. Katahdin	8-5-89

"A sense of completing a journey in a very satisfying way, and experiencing some of the diversity of the USA."

Bill Winnett	29	Rollin' Bill	M	San Francisco, CA	Springer Mtn.	5-15-89	Rangeley, ME	10-6-89

Why? ". . . to get away from civilization. . . . I felt great every day."

Paul Wittreich	58	Tenafly Tramper	M	Tenafly, NJ	Snickers Gap, VA	10-14-89	Harpers Ferry	10-14-89

Hiked sections for 44 years. "It is wonderful to look back and go mentally through each of the states, shelters, views, etc."

Anthony Young	23	No Matter	M	Raleigh, NC	Springer Mtn.	5-6-90	Mt. Katahdin	10-16-90

On a change in philosophy: "I don't want possessions any longer. I long to simplify life."

George Ziegenfuss	59	None	M	Woodstock, VA	Springer Mtn.	2-27-89	Mt. Katahdin	9-23-89

". . . it's all so much like a dream . . . the greatest experience of a lifetime. I am richer having done it."

* (n.a.) = not available

** Home towns and states are usually as of the time of the questionnaire. This population of mainly young adults is extremely mobile, and many have now changed addresses.

*** Start and finish locations have been standardized; thus, I have used "Mt. Katahdin" as the general northern terminus designation for "Baxter State Park" "Maine," "the Big K," and so forth.

BIBLIOGRAPHY

Anderson, J.R.L. *The Ulysses Factor: The Exploring Instinct in Man.* New York: Harcourt Brace Jovanovich, 1970.

Angier, Natalie. "Genetic Link Found to Personality Trait. Explanation for Impulsiveness." *San Francisco Chronicle* (Jan. 2, 1996).

Appalachian Long-Distance Hiker Association, Merrimack, NH. Membership directory (1995).

Appalachian Trail Conference staff. "Trail Security Measures: What are Your Ideas?" *Appalachian Trailway News* (Mar./Apr. 1993).

Barker, Harriet. *Supermarket Backpacker*, Chicago, IL: Contemporary Books, 1977.

Bird, Isabella. *A Lady's Life in the Rock Mountains.* Sausalito, CA: Comstock Editions, 1987.

Bolduc, Vincent. "Backpacking: A Pilot Study of Hikers." Regional Project NEM-35. Univ. of Conn, 1973.

Bouwman, Fred, et al. "Just Say 'no' to Untreated Water." *Backpacker* (June 1992).

Brill, David. *As Far as the Eye Can See: Reflections of an Appalachian Trail Hiker.* Nashville, TN: Rutledge Hill Press, 1990.

Brody, Jane E. "Knee Injuries: A Modern Plague for Women." *The New York Times* (Oct. 16, 1991).

Brody, Jane E. Personal Health section, *The New York Times* (Oct. 27, 1988).

Brown, Robert E. *Emergency/Survival Handbook.* 4th ed. Seattle, WA: The Mountaineers, 1987.

Bruce, Dan. *The Thru-Hiker's Handbook.* Hot Springs, NC: Center for Appalachian Trail Studies, 1994.

Bruce, Dan. *The Thru-Hiker's Planning Guide.* Conyers, GA: Center for Appalachian Trail Studies, 1994.

Bynum, Helen. Letters, *Appalachian Trailway News* (Sept./Oct. 1992).

Carr, Jess. *Murder on the Appalachian Trail.* Radford, VA: Commonwealth Press, 1984.

Chazin, Daniel D. *Appalachian Trail Data Book.* Harpers Ferry, WV: Appalachian Trail Conference, updated yearly.

Cook, Joe, and Monica Cook. *Appalachian Trail Companion.* Merrimack, NH: Appalachian Long-Distance Hiker Association, 1994.

Corriveau, David. "Old Man of the Trail." *(New Hampshire) Valley News* (Sept. 20, 1994).

Cowan, John P. "George F. Miller, Aged 72, Hikes 2,025 Miles on the AT." *The (Potomac Appalachian Trail Club) Bulletin* (1953).

Coyote, O.d. *Chained Dogs and Songbirds: The World's Slowest Traverse of the Appalachian Trail.* Government Camp, OR: Riggledeehopashelogee Press, 1994.

Crouse, Byron J., M.D., and David Josephs, M.D. "Health Care Needs of Appalachian Trail Hikers." *The Journal of Family Practice* (1993).

Danziger, Nick. *Danziger's Travels: Beyond Forbidden Frontiers.* New York: Vintage Books, 1987.

Doyle, Warren. "Helping Thru-Hikers Do the Long Haul." *Backpacker* (Feb. 1990).

Eaton, Walter P. "The Appalachian Trail." *Saturday Evening Post* (Aug. 7, 1928).

Farrow, Peter. *What Use Are Moose?* Thorndike, ME: Thorndike Press, 1983.

Fiennes, Ranulph. *Mind Over Matter: The Epic Crossing of the Antarctic Continent.* New York: Delacorte, 1994.

Fisher, Ron. *Mountain Adventure.* Washington, DC: National Geographic Society, 1988.

Flack, James, and Hertha Flack. *Ambling and Scrambling on the Appalachian Trail.* Harpers Ferry, WV: Appalachian Trail Conference, 1981.

Fletcher, Colin. *The Man Who Walked Through Time.* New York: Random House, 1967.

Franklin, David. "Playing it Safe: Backtalk." *Backpacker* (April 1994).

Garvey, Edward B. *Appalachian Hiker: Adventure of a Lifetime.* Oakton, VA: Appalachian Books, 1971.

Getchell, Annie. "Biting Back." *Appalachia Bulletin* (Jul./Aug. 1992).

Godshall, Karl. "The Scourge of Big Nose." *Appalachian Trailway News* (Jul./Aug. 1992).

Haire, Craig. *End to End on the AT: The Long Haul.* Self-published, 1986.

Hall, Phil. "Along the Appalachian Trail: One Hiker's Story." *American Hiker* (Spring 1989).

Hare, James R., ed. *Hiking the Appalachian Trail.* Emmaus, PA: Rodale Press, 1975.

Harkavy, Jerry (Associated Press). "Peak Performance." *Center Daily Times*, State College, PA (Oct. 3, 1993).

Harris, Wendy. "The Joys and 'Harsh Lessons' of Walking Alone." *Appalachian Trailway News* (Mar./Apr. 1993).

Hirsohn, Don. *The Appalachian Trail*. Canoga Park, CA: Canyon Pub. Co., 1986.

Hoffmann, Roald. "A Natural Born Fiber." *American Scientist* (Jan./Feb. 1997).

Holden, Harley P. "How Slow Can You Go?" *Appalachian Trailway News* (Nov./Dec. 1994).

Howe, Steve. "Hell Can't Be Worse Than This Trail." *Backpacker* (Feb. 1995).

Hoy, Suellen. *Chasing Dirt: The American Pursuit of Cleanliness*. London: Oxford University Press, 1995.

Hudson, Kathryn. "White Mountains High Brings Fine to Hiker." *Insight* (Nov. 14, 1988).

Johnson, Philip. "Waltzing with Bears." *AMC Outdoors* (Jul./Aug. 1994).

Kahn, F.H., and B.R. Visscher. "Water Disinfection in the Wilderness." *Western Journal of Medicine* (June 18, 1975).

Klauber, Laurence M. *Rattlesnakes: Their Habits, Life Histories, and Influence on Mankind*. Los Angeles: Univ. of Calif. Press, 1982.

Logue, Victoria. *Backpacking in the '90s: Tips, Techniques, and Secrets*. Birmingham, AL: Menasha Ridge Press, 1993.

Lutz, Karen L. "Dietary Adequacy and Changes in the Nutritional Status of Appalachian Trail Through Hikers." Masters thesis, Penn. State Univ. (1982)

Luxenberg, Larry. *Walking the Appalachian Trail*. Mechanicsburg, PA: Stackpole Books, 1994.

MacKay, Benton. "Outdoor Culture—The Philosophy of Through Trails." Paper presented at the New England Trail Conference, Jan. 27, 1927.

MacKay, Benton. "Progress Towards an Appalachian Trail." *Appalachia* (Dec. 1992).

Manning, Harvey. *Backpacking, One Step at a Time*. New York: Vintage Books, 1986.

Molenaar, Dee. *The Challenge of Rainier*. Seattle, WA: The Mountaineers, 1979.

Mueser, Roland. "For Whom the Mountain?" *T&T* (Nov./Dec. 1983).

Ongerth, J.E., et al. "Back Country Water Treatment to Prevent Giardiasis." *American Journal of Public Health* (Dec. 1989).

Ozmer, R.R. "Scouting the AT from Georgia to Maine." *Camping and Woodcraft* (1929).

Platt, Rutherford. *Adventure in the Wilderness*. New York: American Heritage, 1963.

Rose, Robert, and Buck Tilton. *Sex in the Outdoors*. Merrillville, IN: ICS Books, 1993.

Ross, Cindy. *A Woman's Journey*. Harpers Ferry, WV: Appalachian Trail Conference, 1991.

Ross, Cindy. *Hiking: A Celebration of the Sport and the World's Best Places to Enjoy It*. New York: Fodor's Travel Publications, 1992.

Ross, Cindy. "140,000 Miles Later." *Backpacker* (May 1990).

Ross, Cindy. "Shower Power: How to Stay Happy When the Sky Dumps on You." *Backpacker* (April 1993).

Ross, Cindy, and Todd Gladfelter. *A Hiker's Companion: 12,000 Miles of Trail-Tested Wisdom*. Seattle, WA: The Mountaineers, 1993.

Sands, Mary. *Appalachian Trail in Bits and Pieces*. Self-published, 1992.

Scheme, Diana Jean. "A Weapon in Waiting." *The New York Times* (Aug. 20, 1993).

Serra, Gary. Letters, *Appalachian Trailway News* (May/June 1992).

Shaffer, Earl V. *Walking with the Spring*. Harpers Ferry, WV: Appalachian Trail Conferene, 1983.

Sherman, Steve, and Julia Older. *Appalachian Odyssey*. Brattleboro, VT: Stephan Green Press, 1977.

Stephenson's Warm Light Equipment Catalog. Fall 1991. (22 Hook Road, Guilford, NH, 03246)

Suk, T.J., et al. "Water Contamination with Giardia: Back Country Areas." Paper presented at Proceedings of the National Wilderness Research Conference, Ft. Collins, CO (July 1985).

Sweetser, M.F. *White Mountains*. Boston: Houghton Mifflin, 1891.

Thomason, Hugh (Max). "Hiking Partners." *Appalachian Trailway News* (Mar./Apr. 1986).

Underhill, Miriam. *Give Me the Hills*. Greenwich, CT: Chatham Press, 1971.

Vernier, C. Vernon, M.D. "Walking Well." *Appalachian Trailway News* (May/June 1994).

Viehman, John. "Leave the Guns at Home." *Backpacker* (Feb. 1992).

Walsh, Lawrence. "Give the Trail a G Rating." *Boston Globe* (Nov. 14, 1976).

Waterman, Laura, and Guy Waterman. *Forest and Crag: A History of Hiking, Trailblazing, and Adventure in the Northeast Mountains*. Boston: Appalachian Mountain Club, 1989.

Whalen, Christopher. *The Appalachian Trail Workbook for Planning Thru Hikes*. Harpers Ferry, WV: Appalachian Trail Conference, 1992.

Whymper, Edward. *Scrambles Among the Alps*. Berkeley, CA: Ten Speed Press, 1981.

Wright, R.A., et al. "Giardiasis in Colorado: An Epidemiologic Study." *American Journal of Epidemiology* (1977).

Wright, P.H. "Why Mosquito Repellents Repel." *Scientific American* (July 1975).

INDEX